SHORTLIST

Marrakech

WHAT'S NEW | WHAT'S ON | WHAT'S BEST

www.timeout.com/marrakech

Contents

Marrakech by Area

Essentials

Published by Time Out Guides Ltd
Universal House
251 Tottenham Court Road
London W1T 7AB
Tel: + 44 (0)20 7813 3000
Fax: + 44 (0)20 7813 6001
Email: guides@timeout.com
www.timeout.com

Managing Director Peter Fiennes
Financial Director Gareth Garner
Editorial Director Ruth Jarvis
Deputy Series Editor Dominic Earle
Editorial Manager Holly Pick
Assistant Management Accountant Ija Krasnikova

Time Out Guides is a wholly owned subsidiary of Time Out Group Ltd.

© **Time Out Group Ltd**
Chairman Tony Elliott
Financial Director Richard Waterlow
Group General Manager/Director Nichola Coulthard
Time Out Magazine Ltd MD Richard Waterlow
Time Out Communications Ltd MD David Pepper
Time Out International MD Cathy Runciman
Production Director Mark Lamond
Group Marketing Director John Luck
Group Art Director John Oakey
Group IT Director Simon Chappell

Time Out and the Time Out logo are trademarks of Time Out Group Ltd.

This edition first published in Great Britain in 2008 by Ebury Publishing
A Random House Group Company
Company information can be found on www.randomhouse.co.uk
10 9 8 7 6 5 4 3 2 1

For further distribution details, see www.timeout.com

ISBN: 978-1-846700-76-7

A CIP catalogue record for this book is available from the British Library

Printed and bound in Germany by Appl

The Random House Group Limited makes every effort to ensure that the papers used
in our books are made from trees that have been legally sourced from well-managed
and credibly certified forests. Our paper procurement policy can be found on
www.rbooks.co.uk/environment.

Marrakech Shortlist

The **Time Out Marrakech Shortlist** is one of a new series of guides that draws on Time Out's background as a magazine publisher to keep you current with what's going on in town. As well as Marrakech's key sights and the best of its eating, drinking and leisure options, the guide picks out the most exciting venues to have recently opened and gives a full calendar of annual events. It also includes features on the important news and trends, all compiled by locally based editors and writers. Whether you're visiting for the first time, or you're a regular, you'll find the *Time Out Marrakech Shortlist* contains all you need to know, in a portable and easy-to-use format.

The guide divides Marrakech into five areas, each of which contains listings for Sights & Museums, Eating & Drinking, Shopping, Nightlife and Arts & Leisure, with maps pinpointing all their locations. At the front of the book are chapters rounding up these scenes city-wide, and giving a shortlist of our overall picks in a variety of categories. We include itineraries for days out, plus essentials such as transport information and hotels.

Phone numbers given include an area code (024), which must be dialled from within Marrakech. Some listed numbers (beginning 06, 07 or 01) are mobiles, indicated as such. The international code for Morocco is 212. To call Morocco from outside the country, follow with the number given, dropping the initial '0'.

We have noted price categories by using one to four $ signs ($-$$$$), representing budget, moderate, expensive and luxury. Major credit cards are accepted unless otherwise stated. We also indicated when a venue is NEW .

All our listings are double-checked, but places do sometimes close or change their hours or prices, so it's a good idea to call a venue before visiting. While every effort has been made to ensure accuracy, the publishers cannot accept responsibility for any errors that this guide may contain.

Venues are marked on the maps using symbols numbered according to their order within the chapter and colour-coded according to the type of venue they represent:

- ❶ Sights & museums
- ❶ Eating & drinking
- ❶ Shopping
- ❶ Nightlife
- ❶ Arts & leisure
- ❶ Hotels

Map key

Major sight or landmark	▢
Railway station	▢
Park or garden	▢
City wall	▬
Area name	GUÉLIZ
Mosque	☾
Church	✚
Post office	✉

Time Out Marrakech Shortlist

About Time Out

Founded in 1968, Time Out has expanded from humble London beginnings into the leading resource for those wanting to know what's happening in the world's greatest cities. As well as our influential what's-on weeklies in London, New York and Chicago, we publish more than a dozen other listings magazines in cities as varied as Beijing and Mumbai. The magazines established Time Out's trademark style: sharp writing, informed reviewing and bang up-to-date inside knowledge of every scene.

Time Out made the natural leap into travel guides in the 1980s with the City Guide series, which now extends to over 50 destinations around the world. Written and researched by expert local writers and generously illustrated with original photography, the full-size guides cover a larger area than our Shortlist guides and include many more venue reviews, along with additional background features and a full set of maps.

Throughout this rapid growth, the company has remained proudly independent, still owned by Tony Elliott nearly four decades after he started Time Out London as a single fold-out sheet of A5 paper. This independence extends to the editorial content of all our publications, this Shortlist included. No establishment has been featured because it has advertised, and no payment has influenced any of our reviews. And, for our critics, there's definitely no such thing as a free lunch: all restaurants and bars are visited and reviewed anonymously, and Time Out always picks up the bill. For more about the company, see www.timeout.com.

Don't Miss

Koutoubia Mosque p43

Sights & Museums

Marrakech can be a bewildering place for the first-time visitor, and one of the confusing things is the lack of conventional 'sights'. There are scarcely more than half a dozen must-see monuments and museums. Those palaces that can be visited have been left either ruined or bare by whoever came along to replace those who built them. Mosques and shrines can be seen from outside, but their interiors are off-limits to non-Muslims – a rule established by the French. There are no major museums or galleries. On a tight schedule, you can scamper around all the principal sights in a few hours and still have time to get fleeced in the souk before dinner.

There wasn't a single paved road in the country when European capitals were opening national museums and erecting triumphal arches. But various waves of rulers still managed to leave their marks. The original Almoravid city was entirely destroyed, leaving only the city walls and the Koubba El-Badiyn (p62) as testament to its 11th-century grandeur. The Almohads built the Koutoubia mosque (p43) and Bab Agnaou, and laid out the Agdal Gardens (p87). The Saadians added the Badii Palace (p87) and the Saadian Tombs (p89). The French built a whole new city alongside the Medina. And the main contribution of the current monarch will perhaps turn out to be the vast new *zone touristique* that is going up to the south of the city (see box p122).

The paucity of essential sightseeing does have an upside. It's kind of relaxing. As there's little you might later regret having missed, there's a delicious lack of obligation to 'do' everything. Instead you can feel extra free to lounge around on cushions at the riad, spend half the day people-watching from a café table, or wander aimlessly through the warrenous alleys of the Medina.

Wandering aimlessly is certainly the best way to get to know the place. It takes a while to get the hang of Marrakech, especially as the inward-looking orientation of the Arab world, where magnificence is typically concealed behind plain exteriors, means that much of what's interesting is not immediately obvious. But soon doors will start opening and interiors revealing themselves. You might not be able to peer around the religious monuments, but it's worth eating in some restaurants (Palais Soleiman, p78, for example, or Dar Yacout, see p77) as much for the showy surrounds as the expensive menus, and your boutique hotel, typically hidden behind an unmarked door in some dead-end alley, may turn out to be the architectural highlight of your trip. And meanwhile, every twist and turn of the Medina will reveal a new perspective, another mystery, one more doorway that could lead into anything from a poorhouse to a palace, sometimes in a fashion that is almost dreamlike.

The Medina

The Medina (it simply means 'city' in Arabic) is the area within the city walls, and this is where you'll spend most of your sightseeing time. The two principal landmarks of Marrakech stand at its heart. The

SHORTLIST

Best Islamic buildings
- Ben Youssef Medersa p61
- Koutoubia Minaret p43
- Saadian tombs p89

Dynastic remnants
- Badii Palace p87
- Saadian tombs p89
- Koubba El-Badiyin p62
- Medina walls p10
- Bahia Palace p93

Museums
- Dar Si Said Museum p94
- Maison Tiskiwin p94
- Museum of Islamic Art p100

Pungent pre-industrial processes
- The tanneries p68

Glorious gardens
- Agdal Gardens p87
- Marjorelle Gardens p100
- Menara Gardens p119

Essential experiences
- Jemaa El Fna by night p42-51
- Haggling in the souks
- Atlantic sunsets at Skala de la Ville p128
- Getting lost
- Coffee in place Moulay Hassan p128

minaret of the Koutoubia Mosque is the city's tallest structure, both an icon and point of orientation. Nearby is the vast open space that is the Jemaa El Fna (p42-51), host to a unique and ever-changing carnival of street entertainment, and, in the evenings, the world's largest open-air eatery. It's usually referred to simply as '*la place*' or, as Marrakech grows increasingly anglophone, 'the square'.

The South Medina contains most of the other main sights. The Saadian Tombs are in the Kasbah quarter – the walled precinct of the off-limits Royal

Palace. The Mellah, the old Jewish quarter, is over on the eastern side, with the Badii Palace in between.

To the immediate north of the Jemaa El Fna is the warren of the souks – a sight in themselves, even if you don't have the slightest intention of buying anything. To their north and west is a small cluster of monuments: the Musée de Marrakech, the Koubba El-Badiyn, and the Ben Youssef Medersa. The tannery quarter, where leather is still cured by medieval methods, lies a little further to the west, and shrines to Marrakech's seven favoured saints are scattered around to the north.

The street layout can confound anyone's sense of direction, but it gets easier once you learn a few of the main arteries and ignore, for route-finding purposes, the hundreds of dead-end alleys that snake off them in all directions. (If you're staying in one of the many riad hotels formed out of two or more houses, ask about back doors. Some places have ways out into several entirely different sections of the Medina.)

Small cars can get surprisingly far into this labyrinth, but most of the traffic is pedestrians and bicycles, scooters and donkey carts. The main through lanes bustle from early morning until around 11pm, and in the early- to mid-evening 'rush hour' some can get so busy there are people jams. The etiquette is to keep to the right, leaving passing room for two-wheelers and quadrupeds.

The ancient crenellated walls surrounding the Medina are another of Marrakech's landmark structures. Built of salmon-pink pisé, they make a ten-kilometre (six-mile) circuit, punctuated by 20 gates. Though they can look beautiful in the changing light,

especially against an Atlas mountain backdrop, there's no place to get up on top of them. The traditional thing is to circumnavigate them in a *calêche* – horse and carriage – ideally at sunset. You can pick up a *calêche* at Place Foucault, in between Koutoubia and the square (fixed prices are posted on the carriage). The circuit takes approximately an hour, but it's perhaps an overrated experience – lots of dust and traffic fumes, not actually that much to see.

The new city

In the first decades of the Protectorate, the French built new cities that left the old Moroccan medinas intact, but relegated them to the status of 'native quarters'. Guéliz and the Hivernage were built in the 1920s and 1930s for the colonial administration and European community, and Marrakech's booming tourist economy is now underpinning a new wave of development.

Avenue Mohammed V, named for the king (grandfather of the current one) who led Morocco to independence in 1956, is both the main commercial throughfare and the principal connection between the old and new cities. You'll want to take a stroll along its central section – from place Novembre 16 at the junction with Avenue Hassan II, to place Abdel Moumen at the junction with boulevard Mohammed Zerktouni – but this is really an area for shopping, eating and nightlife, such as it is, rather than sightseeing. No one should miss the Majorelle Gardens, however. Created in the 1930s by French painter Jacques Majorelle, and today maintained by Yves St Laurent, they are on the east side of Guéliz.

Over on the west side of the new city, avenue Mohammed VI (named after the current king) is the city's formal civic boulevard (see box p122), with landmarks such as Charles Boccara's still unfinished Theatre Royal, the Palais des Congrès, and a big new train station under construction to replace the charming old colonial-era terminus (see box p78).

Taxis are the easiest way to negotiate your way around the new city, and necessary for shuttling between it and the Medina (pay a maximum of 20dh in the daytime, 30dh at night, for a ride between central Guéliz and the Koutoubia). As you drive around the new city's 'European' streets, look out for some wonderful modernist villas and apartment blocks – all, just like the rest of the town, pretty in pink.

The *petit taxis* that run around town can't get out to the Palmeraie, however. To reach the ancient palm oasis that is these days full of swanky private villas and resort hotels, or anywhere else outside the city limits, you'll need a *grand taxi*.

Guides

You don't really need a guide (see box p95), but if you do feel one might be useful either for basic orientation or to explore a specialist interest, there are plenty of official guides, licensed by the local authorities. Your hotel will be able to arrange one for you, otherwise we've heard good things about the following guides, all of whom speak English: Ahmed Tija (024 30 20 50/mobile 061 08 45 57), Moulay Youssef (mobile 061 16 35 64), Mustapha Chouquir (mobile 062 10 40 99) and Mustapha Karroum (mobile 061 34 07 78).

Saadian Tombs p89

Jemaa El Fna p42

WHAT'S BEST
Eating & Drinking

The good news is that Morocco has its own distinct cuisine, quite different from the rest of North Africa and the Arab world. It can be sampled well at every price level – from the carnival of cheap eats in the Jemaa El Fna and the stalls in Essaouria grilling fish straight off the trawler, to upscale restaurants where dining becomes an extravagant oriental fantasia. And, Islamic country though this may be, you can often get a drink too.

The bad news is, well, couscous and tagine, tagine and couscous. Particularly in the middle price range, you're likely to find the same old dishes, prepared to an average standard and served in huge quantities, thanks to inflexible fixed-price menus.

But as Marrakech continues to boom, dining establishments are growing in both quantity and quality. There are some decent French restaurants (Grand Café de la Poste, p105; La Villa, p123; Le Guepard, p123; Pavillion, p79), as well as pretty good coffee and some fine pâtisseries (see box p90). Italian food is also reasonably well represented (Alizia, p119; Casanova, p104; Catanzaro, p104) and now there is a scattering of places offering non-European cuisines such as Thai (Narwama, p49), Japanese (Tatchibana, p91; Kosybar, p89), and Indian (Salam Bombay, p108). Even Essaouira has an Italian restaurant (Silvestro, p132) and a Mexican café (La Cantina, p131).

Such establishments are somewhat constrained by the availability of ingredients, but this can make for ingenious and interesting solutions. They are also a godsend for vegetarians, who will tire more quickly than most of the limited Moroccan dishes available.

Prix fixe

The Moroccan menu has absorbed influences from the Arab world, Andalucia and, most recently, France, but the overriding principle remains one of throwing everything into a pot and leaving it to cook very slowly.

The national dish is tagine, a stew named after the conically lidded pot it is prepared in. The most common ingredients are lamb or chicken with assorted vegetables and olives, and preserved lemons, prunes or almonds for flavouring. In Essaouira you'll find seafood tagines. Running a close second for ubiquity is couscous – coarse-ground semolina flour, steamed and topped with another rich meat or vegetable stew.

The fixed-price menu is a feature of most traditional restaurants of the pricier variety. Sit down and the food simply starts to arrive. The full monty begins with *salade marocaine*, a selection of small hot and cold dishes, each separately prepared and spiced. Along with carrots, peppers, aubergines and tomatoes, there are sometimes diced sheep brains or chopped liver.

Next come *briouettes*, deep-fried parcels of thin, flaky *ouarka* pastry filled with meat, vegetables or cheese. Then, the *pastilla*, which means more *ouarka* pastry, baked and layered with pigeon or chicken, almonds, boiled egg and spices, then dusted with cinnamon and powdered sugar. After that, a tagine, followed by couscous.

S H O R T L I S T

Best views
- Argana p46
- Pizzeria Venezia p50
- Taros p133

Grandest surroundings
- Narwama p49
- Palais Soleiman p78
- Tobsil p50

Modishly Moorish
- Dar Yacout p77
- Foundouk p63
- Kosybar p89
- Elizir p132

Fine Moroccan food
- Al Fassia p100
- Dar Moha p77
- Le Tanjia p94

French gastronomy
- Grand Café de la Poste p105
- La Villa p123
- Pavillion p79

Budget eating
- Chez Chegrouni p48
- Fish stalls in Essaouira p128
- Jemaa El Fna p42
- Toubkal p50

Garden tables
- Alizia p119
- Rôtisserie de la Paix p108
- Trattoria de Giancarlo p110

Souk shopping break
- Café des Epices p63

Leisurely lunching
- Café du Livre p103
- Jardins de la Koutoubia p141

Best pâtisserie
- Adamo p100
- Amandine p102
- Pâtisserie des Princes p49
- Table du Marché p123

Best cocktails
- Kechmara p105
- Le Lounge p107
- Narwama p49

DON'T MISS

DAR ENNASSIM
Fabrice Vulin

Gourmet restaurant managed by Fabrice Vulin, a member of the Académie Culinaire de France and Michelin two starred chef.

His cuisine is creative and elegant ; he knows how to delight his guests with copious light, aromatic dishes.

Dar Ennassim invites you to embark on a sensual voyage of discovery – ravishing French dishes with Oriental touches to engage epicures of all nationalities.

Dar Moha p77

Dessert will typically involve some combination of oranges, honey, pastry and almonds. Mint tea finishes it all off, usually served with yet more pastries.

All of the above comes in impossibly large portions. Any guilt at being able to finish only a fraction of what's put in front of you should be assuaged by the knowledge that the mountains of food inevitably returned to the kitchen will be distributed to the poor. And anyway, you've paid for it all.

The humungous quantities relate to a tradition of extravagant hospitality, and dinner is often accompanied by some kind of show. The entertainment varies from the shifting spectacle of the Jemaa El Fna to the *gnawa* or Arabo-Andalucian musicians that play in many restaurants. Costumed waiters and palatial surroundings add to the sense of theatre, taken to its extreme at Dar Yacout (p77). At Palais Soleiman

(p78) you can literally eat in a palace. Other restaurants in grand historic buildings include Ksar Es Saoussan (p77) and Tobsil (p50).

Only a few treasured establishments serve Moroccan dishes à la carte, such as Al Fassia (p100) in Guéliz, Marrakchi (p49) and Le Tanjia (p94) in the Medina. Even more rare are places that are trying to bring Moroccan food up to date, but you can occasionally find menus offering traditional-with-a-twist, notably at Dar Moha (p77) in Marrakech, or Elizir (p132) in Essaouira.

Meanwhile, most riads have cooks, and some of them are very good indeed. This is another way of sampling Moroccan specialities without having to order enough to feed a small army. You can discuss in advance what you want to eat and, usually, choose where you want to eat it – down in the courtyard, up on the roof terrace, wherever.

And to drink?

At the budget end of things you can eat very cheaply, but forget about having a drink with your meal. Most restaurants catering to tourists, however, will serve alcohol. In fixed-price places the wine will often be part of the deal. Otherwise, wine lists all include the same small selection of Moroccan vintages, sometimes augmented by a few imported bottles. The local wines are perfectly drinkable, while the imports are overpriced.

The Koran cautions against 'substances that cloud the mind', a ruling typically interpreted to mean 'lay off the booze'. Thus, the official fiction is that Moroccan wines – and three locally brewed brands of beer – are produced only for consumption by visitors. In reality, many Moroccans do like a drink. Most of them do it discreetly, however, usually with friends at home. Only the wealthiest and most westernised, who frequent the same bars and clubs as visitors, or the desperate and disreputable, the denizens of dodgy dives where many tourists fear to tread, go out and drink in public.

Outside of hotels and restaurants, bars are few and far between. Moroccan bars – as opposed to European-style bars – don't advertise their existence and huddle in obscure side streets. Kinked entrances and opaque windows shield the pious passerby from the disreputable business of beer-drinking. Inside you'll find basic fittings and lots of guys in *djellabas* quaffing straight from the bottle. In Marrakech these places mostly cluster around the northern end of rue Mohammed el Bekal in Guéliz, near the Cinema le Colisée. In the Medina, both tourists and locals can grab a cold one in the unpretentious foyer of the Grand Tazi hotel (p48).

Otherwise there is a sprinkling of more sophisticated places in Guéliz, such as Afric'n Chic (p119), Le Lounge (p107) and Le Comptoir (p123). See Itinerary p32.

Tea & coffee

The routine social lubricant is not alcohol, but mint tea. Served with great ceremony, sticky and sweet, it welcomes friends, facilitates discussion, cements deals, follows meals, or simply provides an excuse to sit in a café for a while. Moroccans credit mint tea with powers that, to the visitor, it simply does not seem to possess. 'Berber whisky', you sometimes hear it called. Nevertheless, it is refreshing enough, and goes wonderfully with Moroccan pastries.

French influence means coffee is also widely available and pretty decent quality. The main locus for cafés is around the Jemaa El Fna, where places like Argana (p46) or Café de France (p46) offer a vantage over the daily proceedings. In the souks, the excellent Café des Épices (p63) opened in 2006 but feels like it's been there for years. Another new arrival is the Café du Livre in Guéliz (p103), which offers light meals and secondhand books. Meanwhile, both Moroccan and French-style pâtisseries are scattered all over town (see box p90).

Prices & tipping

For anywhere but the cheapest places, a reservation makes good sense. Your hotel will be happy to take care of it. Prices vary from the unbelievably cheap – Restaurant Toubkal (p50) or Chez Chegrouni (p48) – to the not insanely expensive (700dh per head at Dar Yacout). Cash is always best, as hefty surcharges mean credit cards are unpopular. Tipping is expected. Round the bill up or leave about ten per cent.

Marché Couvert p18

WHAT'S BEST

Shopping

Founded on the confluence of ancient trade routes – last place to stock up before heading south to the desert, first port of call for caravans bringing goods from sub-Saharan Africa – Marrakech has always been, in some sense, about shopping. There may no longer be any trade in slaves or ostrich feathers, but Marrakech remains the main commercial centre of southern Morocco. And it's still home to a lively artisanal culture that, while sometimes sticking to ancient methods (see box p68), also does its best to produce items that might prise open the Western wallet.

The artisans of Marrakech will happily knock off whatever seems likely to sell and stay well tuned to trends in interior decor. Good buys include fashion accessories, fabrics, spices, natural oils and pottery. But there's also fun to be had in considering a few less conventional purchases. You'll find shops selling magic supplies, old teapots, hand-made chess pieces, obscure musical instruments, portraits of the king, and mummified baby alligators.

You might not be interested in the carpet shop that your guide is insisting you should visit. You may not fancy the ubiquitous yellow slippers sold at every other shop in the souk. Lanterns, traditional drums or camel-skin lampshades may not be your thing. But shopping remains way up on the Marrakech list of things to do. To avoid the hustle of the souk, or to peer at traditional handicrafts as if they were merely objects in a museum, is to miss out on the city's central activity and liveliest culture.

For more focused shopping, especially on a short visit, it might make sense to hire a personal shopper (see box p75). Remember also that Marrakech is an excellent place to have items made to your specifications (see Itinerary p28).

Souk shopping

Occupying a warren of lanes, alleys and small squares to the north of the Jemaa El Fna, the souks are commerce at its most colourful. What at first seems like one vast bazaar is actually a bunch of different markets, each specialising in one kind of item.

General handicraft shops are scattered everywhere, but particularly on the two main lanes: rue Moaussine and rue Semarine. There are other areas for leather goods, metalwork, carpets, spices and fabrics. Bric-a-brac and antique shops cluster around the Mouassine Fountain and along rue Sidi Ishak on the east side of the souk. Mustapha Blaoui (p80) is a handy one-stop for every kind of Moroccan homeware item. Miloud Art Gallery (p73) does the same job for every aspect of modern Moroccan design. Selections of Moroccan-made items chosen with a non-Moroccan sensibility can be found in quirky shops such as Atelier Moro (p65), Kifkif (p79) and Michi (p71).

Basic clothes, such as slippers and *djellabas*, are everywhere. Beautiful vintage kaftans can be found at Costumes 1001 Nuits (p70) while a huge and more modern selection is offered at La Maison du Kaftan Maroc (p71). Other fine fashion shops include Akbar Delights (p51), Au Fil d'Or (p71), Kulchi (p80), Marrakech Maille Sarl (p112) and Beldi (p66).

More on markets

Basic markets offering local produce are scattered all over town, such as the Bab es Salam market in the Mellah and the nearby Marché Couvert. Guéliz has the Marché Central, recently relocated from a prime location on avenue Mohammed V to a somewhat obscure spot behind place Novembre 16. This is where to find booze and European grocery products.

Guéliz

Haggling may be de rigueur in the souks, but shops in Guéliz work like European ones. Most of the new city's interesting retail opportunities cluster on and around avenue Mohammed V. Rue de la Liberté is the closest thing to Bond Street, with upmarket shops in all genres, such as the chocolaterie Jeff

de Bruges (p112), the Pâtisserie Al Jawda (p114) and Atika (p111) which offers copies of the latest European styles for a fraction of what they'd cost back home. Mysha & Nito (p112) has an interesting selection of eveningwear from local designers, stylish leather goods can be found at Place Vendôme (p114), and for unique interior design items look in Yahya Creation (p116) or African Lodge (p111).

Money matters

Haggling is expected in many places in the souks. There are no hard and fast rules about how to do it, but once you've spotted something you're interested in it's wise to scout around and get a few quotes on similar items. Don't feel you need to go through the charade of offer and counter-offer. Simply expressing interest and then walking away when being told the price is often enough to induce a fairly radical discount. To avoid having to haggle at all, try shopping at either the Centre Artisanal (p91) or the Ensemble Artisanal (p79), both of which offer common items at fixed prices.

Payment is usually in dirhams only, although a few places are authorised to take US dollars, euros or pounds sterling. The only way to find out which are accepted is by asking. Many places purport to take credit cards but would really rather not – so much so that if you're short of cash, shops are often prepared to deliver to your hotel and accept payment on receipt.

Many places offer shipping services, but tales of goods disappearing in transit are legion. It's usually best to bite the bullet and fork out for excess baggage fees (about 100dh per kilogram on British Airways), or else pay a visit to the main post office at place du 16 Novembre in Guéliz.

SHORTLIST

Moroccan-inspired fashion
- Akbar Delights p51
- Au Fil d'Or p71
- Beldi p66
- Miloud El Jouli p73
- Mysha & Nito p112

Traditional clothing
- Costumes 1001 Nuits p70
- El Yed Gallery p70
- La Maison du Kaftan Maroc p71

Jewellery
- Bazaar Atlas p111
- Bellawi p66
- Boutique Bel Hadj
- Kifkif p79

Carpets
- L'Art de Goulimine p65
- Bazaar du Sud p66
- Bazaar les Palmiers p66
- Tapis Akhnif p74

Leather goods
- Chez Said p69
- Galerie Birkemeyer p112
- Place Vendôme p114

Moorish homewear
- Atelier Moro p65
- Cherkaoui p66
- Founoun Marrakech p71
- Lun'art Gallery
- Mustapha Blaoui p80

Modern Moroccan design
- African Lodge p111
- Dinanderie p94
- Miloud Art Gallery p73
- Yahya Creation p116

Ceramics
- Caverne d'Ali Baba p66
- Création Chez Abdel p70
- Chez Aloui p66

Palais Jad Mahal p124

WHAT'S BEST
Nightlife

The phenomenon of Marrakech as uber-fashionable destination has not so far resulted in very much worth bothering about in terms of nightlife. Clubs are mostly located in chain hotels in the new city or out in the Palmeraie, and these remain the preserve of foreigners and the wealthy Moroccan middle class. There has never been anything resembling a clubbing tradition, and even if the locals suddenly acquired an interest in alcohol and dancing to house music, most of them would have to hoard their dirhams to manage the 100dh-150dh entrance fee common in most places.

In 2005 a Pacha franchise opened in its own walled compound, south of town in the new *zone touristique*. To some extent, this has put Marrakech on the international clubbing map, with name DJs and Pacha devotees from Europe flying in for the weekend. But there's a degree to which it has also had a deleterious effect. Some clubs have closed down. Others are now emptier than ever, as Pacha's half-decent soundsystem, crowded dancefloor, chill-out room and pair of raucous restaurants sucks in those who want to party.

The gaudy ambience of most places reflects their role as the stomping-ground of the nouveaux riches. Good sound and creative music policies take second place to cigar bars and pricey restaurants, while many of their denizens seem to have copied their looks from the cheesiest styles on Fashion TV. In places such as Paradise Club (p124) or Actor'S (p124), expect to hear a bit of last year's house music, mixed in with some jazzy Latino sounds, Arab pop and Euro cheese.

The best

Théâtro (p125) is the most forward-looking club in town, and it's here that you'll encounter the hippest local crowd and hear the best Moroccan DJs. Look out for nights featuring the Sound of Marrakech crew, when DJ Zitroz spins his own brand of minimal techno. Other DJs such as Leo Veil, Miko, Mednes and DJ-Unes come down here from Rabat, certainly Morocco's best club.

And the rest

Once you've abandoned any idea of fabulousness, there is a different kind of fun to be had at some of the city's cheesier establishments. Diamant Noir (p124) has a mixed crowd and is something of a refuge for Moroccan gays, with Arabesque and electrobeats spun by reasonably good DJs. The VIP Room (p125), once laughably touted as Marrakech's answer to Studio 54, features couples dancing to an Arabic orchestra that churns out Egyptian and Lebanese classics.

Entertainment

Jad Mahal (p124) in the Hivernage is one of a few places offering 'oriental cabaret'. A Moroccan favourite, these shows involve balladeers, belly dancers and a Middle Eastern ambience unusual for the Maghreb. The longest-running of these can be found in the Hotel Es Saadi.

Bars usually stay open until 1am or 2am. Montecristo (p107) has no dancefloor but usually features some kind of entertainment to accompany its expensive drinks. People crowd into Afric'n Chic (p100) as much for the draught

beer as the occasional live act but the place has a buzz about it. And Comptoir (p123), with its well-heeled crowd and nightly belly dancers, is probably the most reliable party venue in town.

Information

Such clubbing information as there is can be found on local what's-on websites www.made-in-marrakech.com and www.maroceve.com. The former only contains paid-for listings. The latter is more objective, but you have to sift out Marrakech information from listings that cover the whole of the country. Both are in French only. While bars get going earlier, there's little point in hitting the clubs before midnight or you'll find staff outnumbering customers – and what customers there are will mostly be 'working'. Pacha and Théâtro are the only places that attract a crowd outside weekends.

SHORTLIST

Local DJs
- Théâtro p125

Best for cheesy fun
- Actor'S p124
- Diamant Noir p124
- VIP Room p125

Best for belly-dancing
- Comptoir p123
- Palais Jad Mahal p124

Best bars with music
- Afric'n Chic p100
- Monte Cristo p107
- Palais Jad Mahal p124

Walk on the wild side
- Musica Bar p108
- Samovar p108
- La Strada p108

Best for 'oriental cabaret'
- Palais Jad Mahal p124

Cinéma le Colisée p116

WHAT'S BEST
Arts & Leisure

Nobody in their right mind would come to Marrakech expecting a wealth of western-style cultural activity, but even so it's surprising to discover just how little there is actually going on. Cinemas are few and far between, dedicated live music venues are non-existent, and the performers in the Jemaa El Fna are the closest you'll get to live theatre.

Morocco is a poor country that lacks government arts subsidy and a paying audience. Only in the field of fine art is Marrakech beginning to acquire a kind of rude health, with several galleries opening recently. Meanwhile, homegrown music, arts and entertainment can be sampled every July during the National Festival of Popular Arts (p24).

Film

Morocco is a favourite for filmmakers on account of its wide variety of locations and ability to stand in for everywhere from Tibet to the Middle East. Moroccan filmgoers, on the other hand, have to content themselves with a few Hollywood blockbusters, Bollywood films, martial arts pictures and mainstream French releases.

The Cinéma le Colisée in Guéliz is the nicest picture house in town. In the new *zone touristique*, there is now also the ten-screen Megarama. Movies are usually dubbed into French and shown with Arabic subtitles.

Only at the annual Marrakech Film Festival, which takes place in December, is there ever very much to see. Its raison d'etre is mostly to encourage filmmakers to shoot here, but screenings around town are open to all.

Music

A variety of traditional music can be found in Morocco. Arabo-Andalucian music is sedate. *Grika* is Berber music – raucous and usually performed at harvest and religious festivals. The gnawa, descendents of slaves from sub-Saharan Africa, perform a kind of trance music with iron castanets, *gimbri* and chanting. But there's really nowhere to hear any of this stuff outside the few restaurants that employ musicians and the buskers in the Jemaa El Fna.

Hypnotic gnawa is the most accessible, but this is most authentically performed in all-night trance and possession rituals. You can, however, see gnawa masters jamming with musicians from other parts of the world at the Festival d'Essaouira, which takes over the town for a week every June.

Galleries

Moroccan fine art is alive and well and mostly abstract. You can see work from the best painters and sculptors at Galerie Ré (p117) and Matisse Art Gallery (p117) in Guéliz. The nearby Galerie 127 (p116) recently opened to showcase international photographers, while the Light Gallery (p92) in the Kasbah has a programme of international contemporary art. It's also worth looking in Dar Cherifa (p74), a beautiful exhibition space in a restored 16th-century Medina house. In Essaouira, the Galerie Damgaard (p136) represents the town's stable of gnawa painters.

Sport

There are plenty of opportunities for climbing, horse-riding and adventure sports in the nearby mountains and

DON'T MISS

SHORTLIST

Best festivals
- Marrakech Film Festival p25
- Festival d'Essaouira p24
- National Festival of Popular Arts p24
- Printemps Musical des Alizes, Essaouira p24

Best cinema
- Cinéma le Colisée p116

Best galleries
- Dar Cherifa p74
- Galerie Damgaard p136
- Galerie Ré p117
- Light Gallery p92
- Matisse Art Gallery p117
- Ministerio del Gusto p73

Best photography
- Galerie 127 p116

Wonderful windsurfing
- Essaouria p127

Top tennis
- Royal Tennis Club of Marrakech p125

Hottest hammams
- Hammam El Bacha p80
- Maison Arabe p80

Sumptuous spas
- Bains de Marrakech p90
- Hotel Hivernage & Spa p125
- L'Oriental Spa p125
- Secrets de Marrakech p117
- Sofitel Marrakech p125
- Sultana p92

desert, but otherwise golf is the only game in town, with several courses in the Palmeraie. Spa culture has proved well suited to Marrakech. There are stunning spas at the Hotel Es Saadi (p125) and the Sultana (p92), and Secrets de Marrakech (p117) is a rare stand-alone facility in Guéliz. Most riads have small hammams and massage rooms.

Calendar

As with so many things in Morocco, the exact dates and locations for some of these events may vary from year to year. The major festivals have websites in English and French that should be able to provide the relevant information for trip-planning, but for some of the smaller events your best bet is to ask at the ONMT tourist office (p179).

January

1 **New Year's Day**

Late Jan **Marrakech Marathon**
Start and finish in the Medina.
www.marathon-marrakech.com
The gruelling Marrakech marathon draws several thousand athletes from around the world to race through the city's streets. The course snakes through the Palmeraie and Guéliz before finishing back in the Medina

February

Feb **Dakka Marrakchia Festival**
Various locations.
An annual festival of traditional Marrakechi music.

March

Mid March **International Magic Festival**
Various locations.
Four days of prestidigitation at several locations including the Théâtre Royal, the Jnane El Harti park and (where else?) Jemaa El Fna.

April

Mid April **Festival of Garden Art**
Various locations.
www.jardinsdumaroc.com/festival
The Festival de L'Art du Jardin, or Jardin'Art for short, was founded to connect modern landscaping and design to the centuries-old Moroccan garden and park tradition. Events, art installations, concerts and conferences take place in the city's green spaces over four days.

Late April **Printemps Musical des Alizés**
Essaouira
Essaouira's 'other' music event, the Printemps Musical des Alizés covers genres that don't get a look in at the more famous Festival d'Essaouira (below). The emphasis here is on classical music, as respected orchestras perform works by major composers. There is also some operatic singing and even a touch of jazz.

June

Late June **Festival d'Essaouira**
Essaouira
www.festival-gnaoua.net
The Festival d'Essaouira Gnaoua et Musiques du Monde draws around 200,000 revellers to Essaouira for four days and night of gnawa, world music and jazz. Performers from Africa, the Americas and Europe join the musicians of Morocco's gnawa brotherhood on several stages, and the town turns into one big, heaving party. Once regarded with suspicion, the festival has led to the gnawa – descendants of slaves from sub-Saharan Africa, who now constitute an itinerant brotherhood of healers and mystics – being valued as a cultural treasure and given the nod from on high. The king's closest advisor is a regular festival attender.

July

Mid July **National Festival of Popular Arts**
Various locations
www.marrakechfestival.com
Centred on the ruins of the Badii Palace, but taking in venues around the city, the

Islamic holidays

Of all the Islamic holidays, **Ramadan** is the most significant and the one that has the greatest impact on the visitor. This is the Muslim month of fasting. Many Moroccans abstain from food, drink and cigarettes between sunrise and sunset. Many cafés and restaurants will close during the day. It's bad form to flaunt your non-participation by smoking or eating in the street. Ramadan nights are some of the busiest of the year as, come sundown, eateries are packed with large groups communally breaking their fast, a meal known as *iftar*. Jemaa El Fna gets particularly wild.

The end of Ramadan is marked by the two-day feast of **Eid El Fitr** ('the small feast'). People buy new clothes and visit relatives. A few months later the feast of **Eid El Adha** ('the festival of the sacrifice') commemorates Abraham's sacrifice of a ram instead of his son.

Three weeks after Eid al-Adha is **Moharram**, the Muslim New Year. The other big Muslim holiday is **Mouloud**, a local celebration of the birthday of the Prophet Mohammed.

Islamic religious holidays are based on a lunar calendar, approximately 11 days shorter than the Gregorian (Western) calendar. This means that Islamic holidays shift forward by 11 days each year.

	2007	**2008**	**2009**
Ramadan	13 Sept	2 Sept	22 Aug
Eid El Fitr	13 Oct	2 Oct	21 Sept
Eid El Adha	20 Dec	9 Dec	28 Nov
Moharram	20 Jan	10 Jan	29 Dec
Mouloud	31 Mar	20 Mar	9 Mar

Note that these dates are approximate as the exact start of the celebration depends on the observation of the moon.

Festival National des Arts Populaires is a five-day celebration of Morocco's arts, music and entertainment. Receiving the patronage of the King himself, the festival features everything from acrobats and Berber dancers to trance-like gnawa rhythms and guitar recitals of the Andalucian music that returned to the Kingdom with the expulsion of the Moors from Spain.

December

Early Dec
Marrakech international Film Festival
Various locations
www.festival-marrakech.com

The FIFM (Festival International du Film de Marrakech) has managed to attract a decent selection of Hollywood A-listers and the media attention that comes with them. Francis Ford Coppola, Martin Sorsese, Oliver Stone and Catherine Deneuve have all made the trip, and the 2006 jury was headed by Roman Polanski. The main *raison d'être* of the event is to encourage international filmmakers to shoot in Morocco – and this is does very well, with screenings taking second place to exclusive dinners and events. However, the films are for all. Tickets are available from cinema box offices, and the public screenings in the Palace Badii and the Jemaa El Fna draw huge crowds.

le **BIS** jardin des arts restaurant

Itineraries

Boutique Bel Hadj p31

Souks Made to Measure

It's easy to get lost in the souks. In fact, it's almost unavoidable. Wandering randomly, enjoying their maze-like quality, and pausing at whatever catches your eye is both edifying and fun. But the souks also reward a more determined and proactive approach. There's more going on than meets the eye, and what's on display is only the tip of an artisanal iceberg.

We have put together a walk that takes you to some of the souks' less obvious corners. Taking about an hour (depending on how long you stop to shop), it concentrates mainly on clothing and accessories, and links shops that not only offer interesting stock of their own, but will also – cheaply, quickly and to a

high standard – knock up your designs, modify their own, or copy styles that you supply. Start the walk at any time of day; the souks are particularly quiet in the early afternoon, but it's best to avoid them between 5pm and 7pm as they can get very busy.

We begin outside the gate of the **Dar El Bacha** – there's a Moroccan pâtisserie over the road where you can sit with a freshly pressed fruit juice if you need a place to rendezvous. Back to the gate, turn right along the pedestrianised section of rue Dar El Bacha. It's a few minutes' stroll to our first port of call. After the lane begins to narrow, sandal-maker Sabir Abeljalil is on the left at No.94 (no phone). He has a great choice of good quality women's footwear in both local and European style, and will copy whatever you give him in 24 hours.

Carry on down rue Dar El Bacha, crossing **rue Mouassine**, and you'll pass a row of guys with barrows, always waiting outside a big public hammam on the right. Take the third turning on the left (check there's a sign on the wall to the left just beyond it, reading '**Souk Bradiaq**'). Immediately, there's a fork. Bear left again. This lane presently leads over a crossroads marked with old bedsteads and other bits of wrought iron, then passes a few metalworkers' dens, sparks shooting in their gloomy interiors.

The lane ends at a busy confluence of several alleys. Take the second one on the right, at two o'clock as you emerge into the junction. This is **Souk Cherratine** (not to be confused with the adjacent lane signed Souk Attarine). From here on, the alleys we follow are mostly covered and tunnel-like. This one is lined with shops selling woollen and leather goods. Walk down, past the right-hand turning which leads to the slipper souk, and on the right at No.9 (opposite No.8, whose number is more visible) is beltmaker Mohammed Charrat (062 56 37 83). A friendly chap who has manufactured for Topshop, he has an excellent selection of styles and will lengthen, shorten, narrow or widen as you wish, or knock up the belt of your dreams. Don't be afraid to bargain hard.

Continue down Souk Cherratine take the first right on to **Souk El Kebir**. Shortly, on the right at No.161, is bookbinder Hassan Makchad (070 72 52 84). He has a small but nice selection of leather- and suede-bound agendas, notebooks and picture frames, in a variety of colours. These can also be made to order, or embossed with the text or design of your choice.

Proceed further along Souk El Kebir. Presently you will pass under a square arch (look back at it and you'll see a sign above reading 'Souk des Sacochiers'). You are now entering the **Kissariat**, heart of the souks, and there are several turnings through arches into parallel lanes on the right. Take the fifth turning on the right. It's called **Kissariat Eloussia**, though marked only by an Arabic sign above the arch (ask at any shop if you're not sure it's the right one).

At No. 97, down at the far end on the right among shops selling clothing and jewellery, is Boutlane Brahim (066 64 83 90). His leather bags evidence lots of good ideas – hardly surprising as they're often straight from the world's best bag designers. He'll also make a top-quality copy of any bag you bring him – as long as you don't mind your bag later appearing all over the place – and stocks a range of materials and skins for the purpose. This will be done in 24 hours, or even as you wait and watch.

Further on, Kissariat Eloussia joins the **Souk des Babouches**. Turn left and left again when Souk des Babouches emerges into another lane opposite the door of a mosque. This is **Souk Attarine**, one of the area's main thoroughfares, and you are now strolling south. You'll pass the Artisanat Berbère (see p65) on the right and arrive at the junction with another main lane. This one is **Souk Semmarine**, and you should bear right to continue in the same southerly direction.

If you feel like a sit-down and a beverage, take the next turning on the left, following a sign pointing to the Café des Épices (p63). This excellent establishment is on the

left, just after you emerge into open air on the **Rahba Kedima**. Ground-floor tables are good for people-watching – this square is full of spice merchants, magic supply shops and hat sellers. Upstairs, the first floor is for lounging and the terrace at the top for looking over untidy rooftops.

Back on Souk Semmarine, opposite the turning to the Café des Épices, is a sign pointing right to '**Petit Souk**' and '**Kissariat Bennis**'. The turning leads into a small, circular arcade of clothiers. Straight ahead at Nos.7-8 is the boutique of Mohammed El Bouaoudi (024 42 60 56). It has a big selection of traditional cotton and linen kaftans and tunics. Choose from the stock, or suggest a modification – this linen tunic, say, in the colour of that kaftan. The small crew that runs the shop

are devout folk, and, even if your haggling skills are rudimentary, they never hike the price up too much. At No.4, a few shops around and next to a normal-looking tailor, is the tiny cubicle of Baddou Ali (067 49 27 88). He stocks some traditional clothes but the main story here is that he's great at copying whatever shirts you might want to bring him.

Turn right out of this small arcade and continue down Souk Semmarine. At No.12, on the left side of the clothes and slipper shops that line the next stretch, is the store of Youssef Lazrak (no phone). His shop is good for traditional cotton men's shirts and *gandouras* (the plainer male equivalent of the kaftan, useful as luxurious nightshirts) but be prepared for some fairly determined haggling or else pay over the odds.

Café des Epices p29

Continuing further down Souk Semmarine, you'll see an arch on the left marked with a number 40. Through this there is a whole small area of textile merchants. If you're thinking of getting a shirt copied at Baddou Ali back up the road, this is the place to find some fabric to have it copied in. You can choose from all varieties of simple cotton and linen to luxurious silks and specialist hybrids.

Souk Semmarine ends as it passes under an arch. A left turn here will lead you into bustling **Place Bab Fteuh**. On the north side you'll see the Pharmacie Place Bab Fteuh. Just after it on the right is a narrow passage. Follow this and head up the stairs to the left. These lead to a mezzanine and, round on the other side from where you emerge, you'll see the Boutique Bel Hadj (see p51).

Owner Mohammed Bari is a sweet guy whose shop brims with a huge assortment of bits and pieces of jewellery, including an enormous and fascinating selection of beads in every size, shape, colour and material. Pick the beads that you like (we liked the black coral beads studded with tiny pieces of silver) and he'll quickly thread them into a bracelet or necklace while you wait.

Jemaa El Fna is just around the corner, but before you leave the souks you may wish to pop into Akbar Delights (p51), opposite the pharmacy in **Place Bab Fteuh**. This is not the place to get things made up and prices are among the highest in the souks, but it's home to a small but exquisite collection of Kashmir-manufactured slippers and accessories; maybe you'll even get ideas for something you can have made somewhere else.

Piano Bar p49

Bar Crawl

Marrakech is not the most obvious city for bar-crawling. Bars are few in number and rarely advertise their existence. Cocktails are sipped behind closed doors, beers poured only with the utmost discretion. There is good news here. Islam's aversion to alcohol means that this is one budget airline destination where you're unlikely to run into a stag party. And for those who enjoy a challenge, pine for something stronger than mint tea, or simply can't stand another night of forking through a five-course Moroccan set meal, rest assured that a bar crawl can be done.

Yes, available venues are limited in both quantity and quality. But the upside is that finding enough places to fill up a dedicated evening's crawling will not only involve navigating through an amusing assortment of venues, but also visiting some places quite unlike anywhere you've ever drunk before.

We begin in the heart of the Medina, sometime in early evening, at the **Piano Bar** (p49) of the Hotel les Jardins de la Koutoubia. A sophisticated joint by Marrakech standards, it's perfect for a rendezvous. The piano-playing is bland but rarely intrusive, meaning plans can be made in an atmosphere of peace and contemplation. There's also a good chance you'll be able to get a stool at the bar and watch the expert staff mix up some classic cocktails.

Fortified by a martini or manhattan, turn right out of the hotel exit and then right again down the last alley before the junction.

You'll see a sign pointing to **Nawarma** (p49) and, after a few twists and turns of the alley, this is where you'll end up. A funky, pastel-coloured palace, this place is mostly dedicated to the serving of Thai cuisine. But the midnight-blue bar operates as a separate entity, and you don't need to order pad thai when all you really want is a long drink. Here the cocktails are more fruity than classical, and served to a loungey soundtrack.

Go back down the alley, right to the main road, which happens to be avenue Mohammed V. You'll have little problem hailing one of the taxis which pass here all night long. Tell them you want the Hotel Nassim, and in five minutes or so you'll pull up at an unpromising-looking entrance further down the same long street. Up on the first floor there is the **Chesterfield Pub** (p105), a small, old-school

kind of place with nice prices and an unpretentious atmosphere that's a relief in modern Marrakech. If you don't like the cosy, low-ceilinged bar, you can also drink out on the poolside patio, a rare opportunity to mix alcohol and fresh air.

Turn left out of the hotel, left again down boulevard Mohammed Zerktouni, and then right after the Cinema le Colisée into rue Mohammed El-Bekal. This is the area for bars frequented by ordinary Moroccans. Some are quiet, some are less to do with the disreputable business of beer-drinking than the equally disreputable goings-on in private rooms upstairs. **Samovar** (p108) at No.133 is the place to head for.

Beyond the doorman and the usual kinked entrance, you'll find a rowdy crowd of guys in *djellebas* drowning their sorrows with bottles of Stork. The atmosphere is incredible. There's a whole lot of tension being released, absolute drunkenness rules, and the place seems to teeter on the brink of violence. But there's also a we're-all-in-this-together kind of mood, which will include you once you're settled. Sit back and enjoy the show.

Most women will feel uncomfortable here, however, so if you're crawling in mixed company miss out that place and aim straight for the **Kechmara** (p105). From the Chesterfield Pub, it's right and right again into rue de la Liberté; from Samovar, it's left, then straight down the road across Boulevard Mohammed Zerktouni, right on Boulevard El Mansour Eddahbi and then left into rue de la Liberté. Either way, ignore the bar in the downstairs restaurant and take a genteel drink up on the first-floor terrace.

From here it's a short cab ride to rue Oum Errabia – back up avenue Mohammed V almost to the place de la Liberté and a turn to the north. At No.6 you'll find **Afric'n Chic** (p100), a place usually heaving as much on account of its draught Flag beer as the occasional live music. Sink some of those, cast your eye over the well-heeled young crowd and faux 'African' decor, and then head back out in search of a taxi.

Moving a little further upmarket – and into the Hivernage – our next destination is **Comptoir** (p123). Any cab driver will know this place, long established as one of the chicest spots in town. If you arrive before 10.30pm, you'll catch the hilarious floorshow. If you don't, never mind. The drinks might be expensive but the crowd is easy on the eye.

Comptoir, like most Marrakech bars, closes at 1am. If you still feel like drinking after that, turn left at the entrance and follow rue Echouada as it curves around past the Sofitel and ends up at the Medina walls by Bab Jedid. The big building on the corner is **Jad Mahal** (p124), which has two different entrances along rue Haroun Errachid. The first of them leads into a beautiful ground-floor bar which would be a wonderful place to chill if it wasn't for the second-rate French rock band usually found banging out ancient hits from the tiny stage. No matter, there are few other options when it's late, late, late.

When this place closes at 3am, or if the cover versions pall before then, there is still the option of walking a little further along the street, forking out 100dh, and descending to the Jad Mahal club in the basement. A big space that used to be a dance club, today it houses an 'oriental cabaret'. Meryem Hilmi ('*la diva de chanson Arabe*') joins the small Middle Eastern style orchestra nightly at 2.15am. Rachid Anouar ('*le star de la chanson orientale*') follows at 3am. The whole place shuts up shop at 4am. After that, you're on your own.

Nawarma p49

Into the Valley

On a clear day, the peaks of the Atlas Mountains beckon visitors from Marrakech. It's an especially welcome invitation in the summer dust and heat. A drive up the Ourika Valley to the village of Setti Fatma, 63 kilometres (39 miles) from Marrakech, is a popular day trip for both locals and tourists, taking in some beautiful scenery and culminating in what's known as the Walk of the Seven Waterfalls.

Buses and shared grand taxis depart from outside Marrakech's Bab Er Rob. Fares for these are minimal, but the downside is that you won't be able to stop wherever you feel like it. A better option is to hire your own grand taxi or a private car and driver for a day. This should cost around 800dh and your hotel will be able to arrange it all. If you have your own rental car, be reassured that it's an easy road. The journey takes about two hours.

The **route d'Ourika** begins at the fountain roundabout outside Bab Jedid, by the Mamounia Hotel. Arrowing south, it runs between the long walls enclosing the Agdal Gardens to the east, and the vacant lots and half-built hotel complexes of the new '*zone touristique*' to the right, before crossing 34 kilometres (21 miles) of agricultural flatland to the foot of the valley.

The small village of **Aghmat** (Rhmate on some maps), set among olive groves just east of the road 29 kilometres (18 miles) south of Marrakech, was the first Almoravid capital of the region. It has a 1960s mausoleum dedicated to Youssef Ibn Tachfine, founder of Marrakech.

Tnine de l'Ourika, just short of the valley, is named after its Monday souk. Take the lane east from the centre of the village, and on the outskirts there is **Nectarome** (024 48 24 47, www.nectarome.com, open 9am-5pm daily), a walled

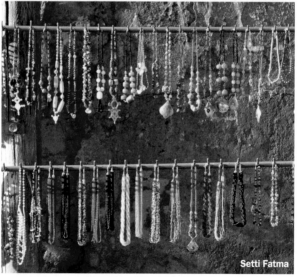

Setti Fatma

organic garden full of aromatic plants and medicinal herbs, plus a small shop selling products made from them. First you get a tour of the peaceful gardens, where the properties of plants are explained. Afterwards browse soaps and shampoos, aromatherapy and massage oils.

The first of many potteries appears as you enter the valley. The red earth their wares are made from forms a brilliant contrast to the deep luminous greens of the valley floor and cultivated terraces. Berber villages hug the steep valley sides, built from the same ruddy clay.

The road is decent, with few hair-raising turns. At the time of writing, work was just beginning on a giant billion-dollar 'golf and ski' development near the existing mountain resort of Oukaimeden. A complex of 2,000 hotel rooms, 300 retail units and 25,000 square metres of business and conference facilities, this will eventually bring more vehicles, but the traffic at the time of writing is usually light.

The turn-off to **Oukaimeden** is at Arhbalou. It's the valley's only significant settlement, but there's not much to see there. On the stretch beyond it, as the valley grows increasingly steep sides, there are a couple of good options for lunch: the French-owned **Auberge le Maquis** (024 48 45 31, www.le-maquis.com), just before the roadside settlement of Oulmès, and **Ramuntcho** (024 48 45 21, www.ramuntcho.ma). The latter is our favourite, with a wonderful outside terrace and a cosy *salon de thé*.

Beyond this point, the valley becomes increasingly gorge-like. The road runs to the west of the river, which here occupies a deep cut. Houses and cafés, many accessible only via perilous-looking rope bridges, cling to the opposite bank while serious mountains begin

to loom up ahead. Then, after a final turn, the valley opens up as the road peters out in **Setti Fatma**.

The village is nothing special – lots of simple cafés, souvenir shops and breeze-block houses – but the setting is wonderful, ringed by mountains with lots of burbling streams, ancient almond trees and grassy terraces. If you arrive in mid August, you may encounter the village's annual *moussem* – a religious festival and sociable fair.

On the other side of the river from the bulk of the village – reached by whatever ramshackle bridges have been constructed since the most recent flood washed the last lot away – are a number of brochette and tagine joints. Concealed behind these is a steep-sided valley, and a short climb up it brings you to the first of the **seven waterfalls**. It's quite a strenuous scramble over boulders and up a small cliff or two. Anyone will point the way or, for a small fee (20 or 30dh) lead you up it. (Official guides are available at the bureau de guides near the Hotel Asgaour.) There's a rudimentary café near the foot of the first waterfall where you can pause with a cold drink. After that, only six more to go. Otherwise, if you don't fancy the walk, there are plenty of cafés in which to sit and admire the scenery, or watch local life unfurl.

On the way back to town, just 3.5 kilometres (two miles) short of Marrakech on the west side of the road, the restaurant **Bô-Zin** (024 38 80 12, www.bo-zin.com, open 8am-1pm daily) is a good stop for dinner. It's a stylish and dressy place, with a menu that takes in Moroccan, Thai and a miscellany of other cuisines. There are several sprawling rooms, but the tables to go for are those in the splendid rear garden. And from here, it's just a 15-minute drive back into Marrakech.

Colonial Canter

Our Essaouira itinerary lasts around two hours and takes us to some of the few remaining landmarks left behind by former – and nearly forgotten – residents of Mogador, as Essaouira used to be known. A century ago, the town was a very different place. A free port in the 19th century, and one of the hubs of trade between Morocco and London or Manchester, Lisbon or Amsterdam, Essaouira was characterised by two kinds of presence that have long since vanished. The first was a 9,000-strong community of Jews, which at its height outnumbered other locals and whose menfolk wore black coats and bowler hats. The second was a community of Europeans who, although the British by far outnumbered the rest, were represented by consulates and trade missions from all the

seafaring powers. Lyautey's decision to develop Casablanca as Morocco's principal port meant that the international trading community soon faded away. The Jewish community took longer to vanish, but by the 1960s most of its members had emigrated to Israel.

We begin at the clock tower on **avenue de l'Istiqlal**, set into the walls of the old Kasbah district. The buildings on the other side of the road, in the direction of Bab Sbaâ, were built during the Protectorate and once housed the local French colonial administration. It's still the home of officialdom: both the police station and the tourist office are on **avenue du Caire**.

Cut through the arch under the clock tower, ignore the square beyond it, and turn immediately right along the alley between the walls and the houses. The narrow

Essaouira

and sometimes gloomy streets in this quarter were mostly built in the 19th century, and it is around here that most of the foreign legations were located.

Turn first left under the arch and first right under another arch. Along on the right, opposite the first turning to the left, is an unmarked door to what was once the Danish consulate. Take that left turning and, next to Chez Françoise on the right just before the junction with avenue Sidi Mohammed Ben Abdellah, is the former consulate of the Netherlands. This one is marked by a sign – fading blue script notes its former function in Arabic, French and English – and such signs mark most of the former consulates in the Medina.

Turning left on **avenue Sidi Mohammed Ben Abdellah**, the long, pedestrian-only lane that parallels avenue de l'Istiqlal, brings you, after a right turn at the end, into **place Moulay Hassan**. If you already feel like a coffee or a sit

down, here are cafés aplenty. On the right, just after the Café de France, a tunnel-like alley angles away into another corner of the Kasbah. It looks older than its early 20th-century origin. It also looks a bit creepy, but have no fear.

Continue along here past the Salle d'Exposition of the Cooperative Artisanale (you can watch guys working with wood in the workshops at the rear) and you emerge near the southern gates to the ramparts. A hard right brings us down a dead-end alley. Looking up you can see a Gothic window at the end: this building was once a Portuguese church, and the door to its right, signed as such, was the Portuguese consulate. The latter was a Jewish restaurant until the 1970s, but both buildings are now unoccupied and in poor condition.

Turn right down the road that runs below the ramparts. There are woodworkers in the arches on the left, the now-closed Protectorate-era Scala cinema is on the right. Turn right again down **rue Lallouj**. On the corner of the first turning to the right is the former French consulate, now the local office of the Alliance Française. Further down rue Lallouj, look down the last turning to the right before the junction with avenue Sidi Mohammed Ben Abdellah. Here is one of a handful of still-functioning synagogues (once there were 32) founded by merchants from Manchester and modelled after a synagogue there.

Double back to rue Lallouj, and turn right. The building on the right-hand corner at the junction was once the British consulate, and when we last passed was being renovated as a private home. Turn left on to **avenue Sidi Mohammed Ben Abdellah**. Stroll to its southern end and, after it narrows, emerge on to a small square. If you need refreshment, a more recent European outpost is La Cantina (see p131), a British-owned 'vaguely Mexican' café. Otherwise, carrying on down

the lane opposite, on the north-east corner of the square, brings you into the **rue de Mellah**.

Once the heart of the Jewish community, this quarter is now the most delapidated in the Medina. The family of Leslie Hore-Belisha, inventor of the belisha beacon, once lived at No.56. Like many buildings around here, this house has recently fallen down. There are no houses left at all on the left-hand side, where there's now nothing but waste ground before the sea wall. There is, however, a functioning synagogue in the house at No.3 (call 076 04 83 52 if you want to arrange a visit).

At the far end turn right down **rue Taflilelt** and then left through **Bab Doukkala**. A little beyond the gate on the left is the Consul's cemetery, filled with the graves of former British residents. It's rarely open, but you can peer through the second gate along. Past the row of waiting horse-drawn calèches, the 'old' Jewish cemetery is behind walls to the left, the 'new' one behind walls to the right. If you want to look inside, knock at the blue door of the lone house on the right, just before the right turn and the beginning of the industrial district.

Finally, take one of the calèches to **Bab Marrakech**. It should cost no more than 3dh per person; 20dh is a generous price for the whole carriage. In a few minutes you alight at the Medina's western gate. Walk through it and turn left into the Centre Artisanale opposite the L'Heure Bleue hotel (p169). At the far end, beyond various small workshops, a small passage to the right leads to a courtyard containing nothing but the oddest remnant of Essaouira's colonial past: an enormous Phytolacca Dioca tree, a native species of Argentina and Brazil, planted here centuries ago by Portuguese traders.

Marrakech by Area

Jemaa El Fna

Jemaa El Fna & Koutoubia Mosque

MARRAKECH BY AREA

The square, towering minaret of the **Koutoubia Mosque** is Marrakech's most recognisable icon and pre-eminent landmark. At over 800 years old, it's also one of the city's oldest structures. While the mosque and its minaret are unquestionably the heart of Marrakech, the soul lies 200 metres to the west in the amorphous form of **Jemaa El Fna**, the city's thronging market square and forum almost since its foundation.

The best way to experience the buzz of Jemaa El Fna, at any time of the day, is to be in among it all (watch your wallet and bags), but several of the peripheral cafés and restaurants have upper terraces with fine ringside seating, among them the **Café de France**, **Argana**, and **Terrasses de**

l'**Alhambra**. At any one of these, the purchase of one soft drink ('*obligatoire*') allows you access to the cafés' balconies, each with sweeping panoramas.

Day or night, whether you choose stealthy observation from the terraces or a headlong plunge into the mêlée, the Jemaa El Fna always remains somewhat elusive. 'All the guidebooks lie', writes Juan Goytisolo, 'there's no way of getting a firm grasp on it'.

Sights & museums

Jemaa El Fna
Map p45 C/D3 ❶
It's the main open space in Marrakech but to call Jemaa El Fna a public square is misleading. Uncontained, disorderly, untainted by grandeur or pomp, untamable by council or committee,

Jemaa El Fna is nothing less than bedlam. It's an urban clearing, as irregular in shape as an accident of nature, and thronged day and night with a carnival of local life – from dentists to snake-charmers, and totally at odds with its name, which roughly translates as 'Assembly of the Dead'.

Also known simply as 'La Place', Jemaa El Fna is as old as Marrakech itself. It was laid out as a parade ground by the Almoravids in front of their royal fortress (the Dar El Hajar). When the succeeding Almohads built a new palace to the south, the open ground passed to the public and became what it remains today – a place for gathering, trading, entertainment and even the occasional riot. The name (pronounced with its consonants tumbling into each other to come out something like 'jemaf'na') refers to its former role as a venue for executions, with the decapitated heads put up on spikes for public display. The French put a stop to that.

During the 1970s, the municipality attempted to impose order with a scheme to tarmac the square and turn it into a car park. This was opposed and defeated. Since then, thanks in part to the lobbying efforts of Spanish writer Juan Goytisolo (who has lived just off the square since the late 1970s), Jemaa El Fna has been recognised by UNESCO as part of mankind's cultural heritage and its preservation is secured. There's still some tidying-up impulse at work, however. The design of the orange-juice carts has recently been regularised in a faux traditional style and the whole square has been paved over – a blessing in wet weather.

Koutoubia Mosque

Off avenue Mohammed V in the Koutoubia Gardens. **Map** p44 A4 ❷

The minaret of the Koutoubia Mosque – Marrakech's most famous symbol – is visible from near and far. It is not actually very high (77 metres, 252 feet), but thanks to local topography and a local ordinance that forbids any other building in the Medina to rise above the

height of a palm tree, it towers majestically over its surroundings. Two previous mosques have stood on the same ground: the first, constructed by the Almoravid dynasty, was demolished by the Almohads, who built their own on the site in 1147. This building, torn down because it was not correctly aligned with Mecca (don't you just hate it when that happens?), was rebuilt as the present mosque, and its minaret was finally completed more than half a century later under the patronage of the Almohad Caliph Yacoub El-Mansour.

The name Koutoubia is derived from *el-koutoubiyyin* – Arabic for booksellers – since a booksellers' market once filled the surrounding streets. The mosque's exterior is of red stone, but it's thought to have originally been covered with plaster. The tower is 13 metres (43 feet) wide. Six rooms, one above the other, constitute the interior; leading around them is a ramp by way of which the muezzin could reach the balcony – it was supposed to be wide enough for him to ride a horse to the top.

The Koutoubia was built in a traditional Almohad style and the minaret is topped with four copper globes; according to legend, these were originally made of pure gold. There were also supposed to have been only three of them: it is said that the fourth was donated by the wife of Yacoub El-Mansour as compensation for failing to keep the fast by eating four grapes during Ramadan. As penance, she had her gold jewellery melted down to fashion the fourth globe. Hardly more credible is the claim that in times past only blind muezzins were employed because a sighted person would have been able to gaze into the royal harem from the minaret. Modern life does seem to be imitating legend, though: the Moroccan authorities have blocked the internet application Google Earth to avoid Moroccans being able to see into the grounds of the king's many palaces.

Glassed-over, sunken areas on the plaza outside the mosque are the remains of reservoirs that belonged to the Dar El Hajar (House of Stone), a fortress built by city founder Youssef Ben Tachfine towards the end of the 11th century, and the first permanent structure in the encampment that was to become Marrakech. The fortress was short-lived, destroyed by the conquering Almohads who replaced it with the site's first mosque.

The small white-domed structure on the plaza is the Koubba of Lalla Zohra, a shrine that used to be open to the public until the inebriated son of a former city mayor ploughed his car into the structure and, as part of the repairs, the door was sealed up.

The Koutoubia Mosque is still an active place of worship and as such non-Muslims are not permitted to enter. But it's possible to get a good view of the exterior by walking around either side of the Koutoubia, clockwise between the main entrance and the wall that encloses the grounds of the French Consulate, or anti-clockwise along the top of the Almohad ruins. Either route leads into the rose-filled Koutoubia Gardens, which spread south and west of the mosque.

Across avenue Houman El-Fetouaki, south of the gardens, a high wall cuts from sight a modest crenellated building; this is the humble Tomb of Youssef Ben Tachfine, founder of Marrakech. A padlocked gate ensures that the great desert warrior rests in peace, his mausoleum off limits to the public.

Mamounia Gardens

Mamounia Hotel, avenue Bab Jedid (024 38 86 00/www.mamounia.com).
Open hotel and gardens closed at time of writing.
The world-famous Mamounia Hotel, south-west of Jemaa El Fna, takes its name from its gardens, the Arset El-Mamoun, which predate the hotel by more than a century. They were established in the 18th century by Crown Prince Moulay Mamoun on land gifted to him by his father the sultan on the occasion of his wedding. A central pavilion served as a princely residence, occasionally lent out to visiting

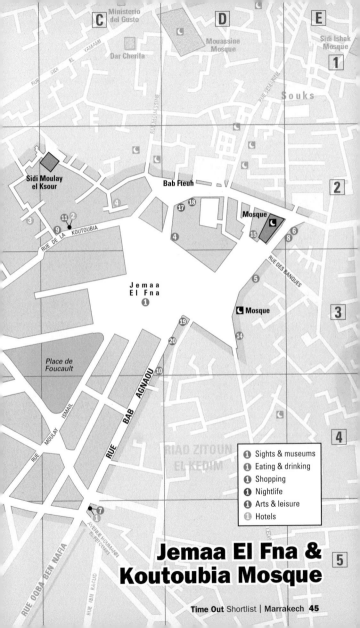

Sidi Moulay
el Ksour

Bab Fteuh

Mosque

Jemaa
El Fna

Place de
Foucault

Mosque

Ministerio
del Gusto

Mouassine
Mosque

Dar Cherifa

Sidi Ishak
Mosque

Souks

RIAD ZITOUN
EL KEDIM

❶ Sights & museums
❶ Eating & drinking
❶ Shopping
❶ Nightlife
❶ Arts & leisure
❶ Hotels

Jemaa El Fna &
Koutoubia Mosque

diplomats. Ten years after the imposition of French colonial rule in Morocco, the gardens were annexed and a 100-room hotel built on the site. Happily, the gardens remain. They're designed in a traditional style, on an axis, with walkways, flowerbeds, orange groves and olive trees and attended by 40 gardeners who, twice a year, plant 60,000 new annuals.

Non-guests can visit – in the context of a buffet lunch at the poolside Trois Palmiers restaurant or afternoon tea at one of the terrace cafés. Dress smartly (no jeans or shorts) or you risk being sent packing. The Mamounia was closed for major renovations at the time of writing, due to reopen by 2008.

Eating & drinking

The early evening in Jemaa El Fna sees the arrival of massed butane gas canisters, trestle tables and tilly lamps to form an array of food stalls. Most specialise in one particular dish, and between them they offer a great survey of Moroccan soul food.

Several places do good business in ladled bowls of *harira* (a thick soup of lamb, lentils and chickpeas flavoured with herbs and vegetables). Similarly popular are standbys of grilled *brochettes* (kebab), *kefta* (minced, spiced lamb) and *merguez* (spicy sausage; stall No.31 apparently sells the best in all Morocco). Families perch on benches around stalls selling boiled sheeps' heads, scooping out the jellyish gloop inside with small plastic forks. Elsewhere are deep-fried fish and eels, bowls of chickpeas drizzled with oil, and mashed potato sandwiches, while a row of stalls along the south side have great mounds of snails, cooked in a broth flavoured with thyme, pepper and lemon. Humblest of the lot is the stallholder selling nothing more than hard-boiled eggs.

Menus and prices hang above some of the stalls, but not everywhere. It's easy enough to just point, and prices are so low that they're hardly worth worrying about. Etiquette is basic: walk around, see something you like, squeeze in between fellow diners. Discs of bread serve instead of cutlery. For the thirsty, orange juice is fetched from one of the many juice stalls that ring the perimeter of the square.

The food is fresh and prepared in front of the waiting diners, so you can actually see the cooking process. Few germs will survive the charcoal grilling or boiling oil; but plates and dishes are a different matter. The single same bucket of water is used to wash up all night, so play safe with your stomach and ask for the food to be served on paper.

Argana
Jemaa El Fna (024 44 53 50). **Open** 5am-11pm daily. **$$**. No credit cards. **Moroccan**. Map p45 D2 ❹
A no-frills (plastic tablecloths, garden furniture) eaterie on the edge of Marrakech's mayhemic main square, Argana's formula of pack-'em-in seating, canteen catering and ringside views makes it a big hit with tour groups. Stairs at the back of the ground-floor café (good ice-cream) lead up to two floors of restaurant terrace. Choose from a trio of three-course set menus (90dh, 100dh or 140dh), or order à la carte from a basic menu (in English) of salads, ten kinds of tagine, or meat from the grill. The quality is so-so, but portions are large. It makes for a good lunch spot, but the views are best at dusk.

Café de France
Jemaa El Fna (no phone). **Open** 6am-11pm daily. **$$**. No credit cards. **Café**. Map p45 D3 ❺
The most famous of Marrakech cafés is these days distinctly grotty, but it boasts a prime location and terrace fronting right on the main square. No one knows exactly how old the place is

A day in the life

During the early part of the day Jemaa El Fna is relatively quiet. The orange-laden carts of the juice-sellers line the perimeter, wagon-train fashion, but otherwise there's only a scattering of figures, seated on boxes or rugs, shaded under large shabby umbrellas.

The snake-charmers are early starters with their black, rubbery reptiles laid out in front or sheltered under large drums. For a few dirhams visitors can have a photograph taken with a large snake draped over their shoulders; for a few more dirhams they can have it removed. Gaudily clad water-sellers wander around offering to pose for dirhams. Other figures may be dentists (teeth pulled on the spot), scribes (letters written to order), herbalists (good for whatever ails you) or beggars (to whom Moroccans give generously). Overlooking all, the prime morning spot for unhurried businessmen and traders is the patio of the landmark Café de France (p46). The action tends to wilt beneath the heat of the afternoon sun and it's not until dusk that things really kick off.

As the light fades, ranks of makeshift kitchens set up with tables, benches and hissing flames, to make one great open-air restaurant serving everything from snails to sheep's heads.

Beside the avenues of food stalls, the rest of the square takes on the air of a circus. Performers typically include troupes acrobats, musicians and their prowling transvestite dancers, storytellers and magicians, and boxing bouts between underage boys who can hardly lift their hands in the heavy leather gloves. The tourists and visitors who provided the raison d'être for the daytime entertainers are now negligible in this far more surreal evening scene.

Approaching midnight, the food stalls begin to pack up, the performers wind down, and the crowds thin. Only the musicians remain, attended by wild-eyed devotees giddy on repetitive rhythms, helped along by hash. At the same time, the place becomes one great gay cruising ground, busy with tight-shirted, tight-trousered teens, sharp and cynical beyond their years.

s hassle

...orocco used to be notorious for its hassle. Bothered by beggars, harassed by 'guides', molested by scam artists – tourists in a place like Marrakech were never left alone.

It's not nearly so bad these days. Mindful of the importance of the tourist economy, one of Mohammed VI's first moves as king was to form the '*brigade touristique*' – the tourist police. Agents in plain clothes prowl the souks and alleys, loiter near sights and hotels. Their mission: to apprehend any miscreant who badgers or bedevils the visitor. It's draconian, but effective.

They're not everywhere, though. Around tourist sights far from the Jemaa El Fna – near the Musée de Marrakech, for example, or around the tanneries – fake guides still pester and panhandle.

Remember that you needn't respond to everyone who says hello. Playing deaf is often the best policy; once someone has managed to engage you, it can be surprisingly difficult to escape. Be polite but firm and don't lose your cool. The Arabic for 'no' is '*la*' (short 'a', as in apple). Say it clearly and wag your finger, and the guy attempting to buttonhole you will often simply fade away.

But remember, too, that while many Moroccans will approach you with money on their mind, once they realise they're not getting any, they still want to talk. The coin's other side is that you can chat with just about anyone, if you like.

but it crops up in Peter Mayne's *A Year in Marrakesh*, written in the early 1950s. It remains a prime meeting place for travellers and locals with business in the Medina: assorted Morocco guidebooks and copies of the day's Arabic-language press are present in about equal numbers. Neither category is favoured and prices are posted ensuring fair trade for all.

Chez Chegrouni

Jemaa El Fna (065 47 46 15). **Open** 6am-11pm daily. **$**. No credit cards. **Moroccan**. Map p45 E2 ⑥

Everybody's favourite cheap restaurant in the Medina, Chegrouni has a first-floor dining-room and a rooftop terrace with a partial view of the Jemaa El Fna, as well as the ground-floor terrace – a great vantage point for watching locals sweep in and out of the square by foot or on mopeds. Chegrouni is clean, well run and deservedly popular with both Marrakchis and tourists. All the usual dishes (salads, grills, cous-cous and tagines) are served briskly, accompanied by big baskets of fresh bread. Note to vegetarians: there is no meat stock in the vegetable couscous, while the vegetable soup is excellent. The menus are in English and glasses on the tables contain paper napkins on which you scribble your order and then hand it to a waiter; it returns at the end as your bill.

Grand Tazi

Hotel Grand Tazi, corner of avenue El-Mouahidine and rue Bab Agnaou (024 44 27 87). **Open** 7-11pm daily. **$$**. No credit cards. **Bar**. Map p45 C5 ⑦

The Tazi's a godsend – the only place in the central Medina where the weary and footsore can kick back with a cheap beer. There's no real bar as such, just a sofa space off to one side of the lobby (and a large empty room beyond that) where accommodating waiters will fetch a cold one for anybody who succeeds in snaring their attention. You don't have to be a resident, just not too fussy about the company you keep or addicted to quality furnishings.

Fellow drinkers tend to be young locals in leather jackets and budget travellers swapping stories of loose bowels amid the dunes of Merzouga.

Marrakchi

52 rue des Banques, Jemaa El Fna (024 44 33 77/www.lemarrakchi.com). **Open** 11.30am-11pm daily. Alcohol served. **$$**. **Moroccan**. **Map** p45 E2 ❽
There are two pluses to this place: one is the location, on the edge of Jemaa El Fna, which is laid out panoramically beyond the wrap-around windows. The second is that it serves Moroccan food à la carte – although there are also set menus. Skip the claustrophobic first-floor salon with its heavy Fes tiling and continue up to the top-floor, made luscious with dusky-pink tablecloths, maroon tableware and a billowing ceiling of swagged black material. The lighting is dim and the black-clad staff charming. The menu holds no surprises (tagines and couscous) but the food is good, and there's a list of local wines.

Narwama

30 rue de la Koutoubia (024 44 08 44). **Open** 8pm-12.30am daily. Alcohol served. **$$$**. **Bar/Thai**. **Map** p45 C2 ❾
Opened in early 2005, Narwama was the city's first proper Thai restaurant, and has a bar on the premises too. It's a fun place. The setting is the central courtyard of a palatial 19th-century residence tucked down an alley behind the Jardins de la Koutoubia hotel. It's an enormous space that, with its potted palms, pastel hues and global lounge music, feels like a Buddha Bar night in some orientalist conservatory. Some intimacy is offered in a smaller rear room with fantastic old painted ceilings and a couple of curtained diwans.

The kitchen doesn't have the courage of its convictions and the Thai dishes (prepared by a team from Bangkok and mostly pretty good) are supplemented by a miscellany of Moroccan and international standards.

Proprietor and all-round nice guy Ali Bousfiha has developed Narwama's front-of-house bar as a stand-a[...] entity. Painted a midnight blue, [...] comfortable seating, a long co[...] menu and a bearable lounge-core soundtrack, all of which you can enjoy with no obligation to eat. Plans for further expansion – a 'long bar' is envisaged – now seem to be afoot. If it's not in operation, ask a waitress to turn on the fire-shooting, water-spewing feature at the centre of the room. It reflects the restaurant's name, which means 'fire and water'.

Pâtisserie des Princes

32 rue Bab Agnaou (024 44 30 33). **Open** 5am-11.30pm daily. **$$**. No credit cards. **Café**. **Map** p45 C3 ❿
A weak-kneed wobble from Jemaa El Fna, this offers gloriously icy air-conditioning in a dim coldstore of a back room. It may sound gloomy but, the hotel pool aside, there's no better retreat on a sweltering afternoon. The front of house is taken up by glass cabinets filled with fine cakes and pastries, to be accompanied by cappuccino, English tea, orange juice or shakes. There's a large salon upstairs.

Piano Bar

Hotel les Jardins de la Koutoubia, 26 rue de la Koutoubia (024 38 88 00). **Open** 5pm-midnight daily. **$$$**. **Bar**. **Map** p45 C2 ⓫
A modest space in red and gold, the piano bar is just off the lobby of this conveniently located hotel – a mere stumble from the Jemaa El Fna. From 7pm to 11pm there is music, and the quality of your drinking experience will partly depend on how well you take to whoever is at the actual piano. Otherwise, the bar is well stocked, the experienced staff know how to mix a cocktail and the counter is a fine place for perching. Drinks aren't cheap (50dh-100dh) but there's no dress code, and if the current pianist insists on singing with tons of echo and a cheesy percussion track, you can always take your drink out to the poolside terrace and contemplate the sky instead of the cigar selection.

Pizzeria Venezia

279 avenue Mohammed V (024 44 00 81). **Open** noon-3pm, 6pm-midnight daily. **$$$**. **Italian**. Map p44 A3 **12**

It's worth eating at the Venezia at least once, if only for the view: it occupies a rooftop terrace opposite the Koutoubia minaret and overlooking Mohammed V with its shoals of darting mopeds. Although it's only a pizzeria, freshness and quality of ingredients is the priority here, so the wood-oven cooked pizzas are good. The menu also stretches to salads and meat dishes, including a good fillet steak in a green peppercorn sauce. On Friday and Saturday there's a self-service buffet with an enormous choice including vegetable dishes and puddings. Although no alcohol is served you are allowed to BYO.

Portofino

NEW *279 avenue Mohammed V (024 39 16 65/www.portofinomarrakech.com)*. **Open** noon-11pm daily. **$$$**. **Italian**. Map p44 A3 **13**

At street level below the Pizzeria Venezia, this big, modern rival to its upstairs neighbour is increasingly favoured by Marrakchis who like a good pizza but don't need a view of the Koutoubia to go with it. The menu also includes a range of pasta dishes and steaks, and a very good selection of fish. There's almost too much space here, so there's rarely any trouble finding a table – actually the place can get a bit draughty when empty. We wish staff would change the boring pop music.

Restaurant Toubkal

48 Jemaa El Fna (024 44 22 62). **Open** 7am-11pm daily. **$**. No credit cards. Map p45 D3 **14**

Big with backpackers from the budget hostels off nearby Riad Zitoun El-Kedim, but also popular with Marrakchis, Toubkal is the next to last stop on the restaurant chain, just above eating al fresco at the food stalls on Jemaa El Fna. The prices are the main draw. The Toubkal does some of the cheapest tagines around (25dh); couscous dishes cost between 18dh and

30dh, and brochettes, chicken and lamb served with fries are all around 25dh. The premises are as basic as it gets, with plastic furniture and plastic tablecloths, but the wildlife is real. Chiller cabinets at the rear sell basic grocery-style provisions including yoghurt, packets of biscuits, cheese, chocolate and juice to take away.

Terrasses de l'Alhambra

Jemaa El Fna (no phone). **Open** 8am-11pm daily. **Main courses** 50dh-100dh. **$$**. No credit cards. **European**. Map p45 D2 **15**

A smart, French-run café-restaurant on the east side of the main square (across from the landmark Café de France). The ground floor and patio is a café for drinks and ice-cream; the first floor with terrace is for diners; the top-floor terrace is for drinks (non-alcoholic). The menu is brief – salads, pizzas and pasta, plus a few desserts, ice-cream and milkshakes – but the food is good. If you're new to Marrakech, it's somewhere you can eat and feel confident that your stomach will hold up. Settle in air-con comfort indoors or slow roast in the open air overlooking the madness of Jemaa El Fna.

Tobsil

22 Derb Abdellah Ben Hessaien, Bab Ksour (024 44 40 52). **Open** 7.30-11pm Mon, Wed-Sun. Alcohol served. **$$$$**. **Moroccan**. Map p44 B2 **16**

Considered by some to be Marrakech's premier Moroccan restaurant, Tobsil offers a lesson in local gastronomy. There is no menu. On being led by a uniformed flunkey to the door (the place is otherwise impossible to find), diners are greeted by owner Christine Rio, then seated either downstairs in the courtyard or upstairs in the galleries. And then the endurance test begins. Aperitifs (included in the price of the meal, as is the wine) are rapidly followed by a swarm of small vegetarian meze dishes. Then comes a pigeon pastilla, followed by a tagine, then a couscous dish, and finally fruit and tea or coffee accompanied by an array of

Café de France p46

cakes or pastries. Everything is delicious but you need a very good appetite to manage it all. Reservations (and a doggy bag) are recommended.

Shopping

Akbar Delights
45 place Bab Fteuh (071 66 13 07). **Open** 10am-1pm, 3-7.30pm Tue-Sun. **Map** p45 D2 ⑰
This extremely upmarket French-owned boutique specialises in luxury clothing and textiles from Kashmir, with some items made to their own designs. The tiny space is crammed with embroidered tops and dresses, cotton robes, silk shawls and scarves, and shimmery, golden shoulder bags. The only made-in-Morocco items are extraordinary brocaded babouches. The most recent innovation is bags made from mink. A new showroom recently opened on the rue de la Liberté in Guéliz, as some of the extremely well-heeled customers (including members of the royal family) may baulk at an excursion to the Medina. The new space stocks more home linens and a wider selection of clothing than you'll find in the Medina, and is open by appointment; call the owner to arrange a visit (071 66 13 07, rue de la Liberté, Imm 42C, apartment 47, just past Atika Shoes).

Boutique Bel Hadj
22-33 Fundouk Ourzazi, place Bab Fteuh (024 44 12 58). **Open** 9am-8pm daily. **Map** p45 D2 ⑱
Take the passage to the left of the pharmacy on place Bab Fteuh, then head up the staircase on the left. Mohammed Bari's shop is around the other side of the mezzanine, visible from the top of the stairs. Inside there's a huge collection of beads, and other peices of jewellery, old and new. Choose your beads, and the charming Mohammed will make them up into a necklace or bracelet, as per your specifications.

Pharmacie du Progrès
Jemaa El Fna (024 44 25 63). **Open** 8.15am-12.30pm, 2.15-6.30pm daily. No credit cards. **Map** p45 D3 ⑲
Knowledgeable, qualified staff will advise on minor ailments and suggest medication. English is spoken.

Arts & leisure

L'Univers de la Femme
22 rue Bab Agnaou (024 44 12 96). **Open** 9am-1pm, 3-8pm Tue-Sun. **Map** p45 F2 ⑳
All manner of beauty treatments are available here. The pleasant surroundings are perfect for pampering at affordable prices.

Mustapha Blaoui p80

North Medina & Souks

The area of the Medina north of the Jeaa El Fna is commercial, with a fibrous network of souks (bazaars), plus three of the city's moderately interesting monuments: the **Musée de Marrakech**, **Koubba El-Badiyin** and **Ben Youssef Medersa**.

Souks

North of the Jemaa El Fna are the souks (markets), with alleyway upon alleyway of tiny retail cubicles. In the most heavily touristed areas, the overwhelming number of shops is offset by the fact that most seem compelled to offer exactly the same non-essential goods: slippers (*babouches*),

embroidered robes and brass platters. It is hard to believe that so many people sell so many of the same thing to such ambivalent customers. These areas are where you are most likely to hear entreaties such as: 'Look for free, no charge just to look' (as if any shop charges you to look). It's all a lot quieter than it used to be, though. The Moroccan authorities twigged that foreigners dislike full-on hassle and souk shopkeepers are models of good behaviour compared to what they were some years ago (*see p48* **Less hassle**).

The further into the souks you venture the more interesting they become. The two main routes into their heart are **rue Semarine** and

place'. The way between Semarine and the Rahba Kedima is a perpetual crush because it also leads to a small court, the **Souk Laghzel**, formerly the wool market but now a car-boot sale of a souk where women – and only women – come to sell meagre possessions such as a single knitted shawl or a bag of vegetables. The Rahba Kedima used to be the city's open-air corn market but it's now given over to an intriguing mix of raffia bags and baskets, woollen hats and sellers of cooked snails. Around the edges are spice and 'magic' stalls.

The upper storeys of the shops on the northern side of the Rahba Kedima are usually hung with carpets and textiles, an invitation to search for the partially obscured passageway that leads through to the **Criée Berbère** (Berber Auction). These days this partially roofed, slightly gloomy section of the souk is the lair of the rug merchants, but until well into the 20th century it was used for the sale of slaves, auctioned here three times weekly. According to North African historian Barnaby Rogerson, the going rate was two slaves for a camel, ten for a horse and 40 for a civet cat.

Back on rue Semarine, just north of the turning for the Rahba Kedima, the street forks: branching to the left is the **Souk El-Attarin**, straight on is the **Souk El-Kebir** (Great Souk). Between the two is a ladder of narrow, arrow-straight passages, little more than shoulder-width across and collectively known as the **Kissaria**. This is the beating heart of the souk. Stallholders here specialise in cotton, clothing, kaftans and blankets.

Further along the Souk El-Kebir are the courtyards of carpenters and wood turners, before a T-junction forces a choice: left or right. Go left and then immediately

rue **Mouassine**; the former offers the more full-on blast of bazaar, the latter is a more sedate path leading to choice boutiques.

Semarine & the Great Souk

Entrance to the rue Semarine (aka Souk Semarine) is via an elaborate arch one block north of Jemaa El Fna – reached via either the spice market or the egg market, both pungent experiences, one pleasant, the other not. Semarine is a relatively orderly street, broad and straight with overhead trellising dappling the paving with light and shadow. Every section of the souk has its own speciality and here it has traditionally been textiles, although these days cloth merchants have been largely supplanted by souvenir shops.

About 150 metres along, the first alley off to the east leads to a wedge-shaped open area known as the **Rahba Kedima**, or the 'old

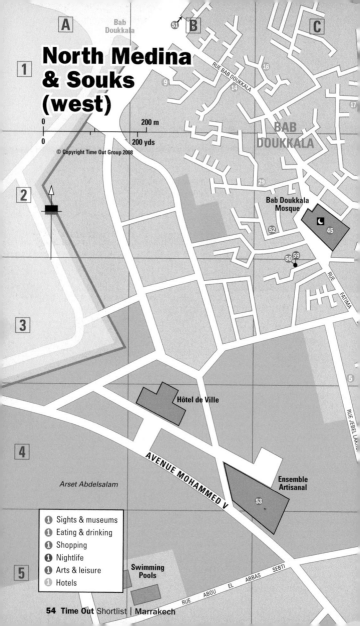

North Medina & Souks (west)

A **B** **C**

1

Bab Doukkala

RUE BAB DOUKKALA

51

16

9

14

17

200 m

200 yds

© Copyright Time Out Group 2008

BAB DOUKKALA

2

29

Bab Doukkala Mosque

52

45

50 59

RUE FATIMA

3

5

RUE JEBEL LAKhdar

Hôtel de Ville

4

AVENUE MOHAMMED V

Arset Abdelsalam

Ensemble Artisanal

53

❶ Sights & museums
❶ Eating & drinking
❶ Shopping
❶ Nightlife
❶ Arts & leisure
❶ Hotels

5

Swimming Pools

RUE ABOU EL ABBAS SEBTI

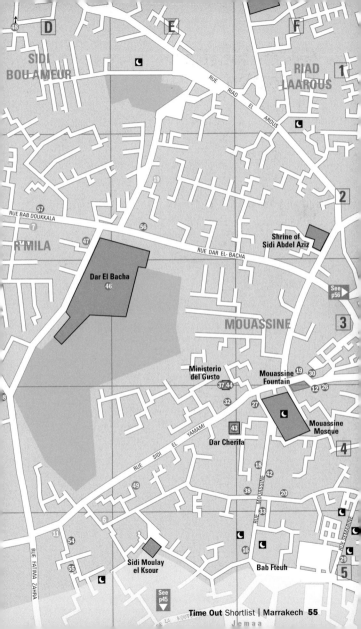

SIDI
BOU AMEUR

RIAD
LAAROUS

RUE RIAD EL AROUS

19

RUE BAB DOUKKALA

57

7

R'MILA

47

56

Shrine of
Sidi Abdel Aziz

RUE DAR EL- BACHA

See
p56

Dar El Bacha
46

MOUASSINE

Ministerio
del Gusto

Mouassine
Fountain

19   30

37 44

12   26

32

27

Mouassine
Mosque

43

Dar Cherifa

18

42

RUE SIDI EL YAMAMI

49

38

20

33

RUE MOUASSINE

RUE SEMARINE

6

11

54

16

29

55

Sidi Moulay
el Ksour

Bab Fteuh

See
p45

Jemaa

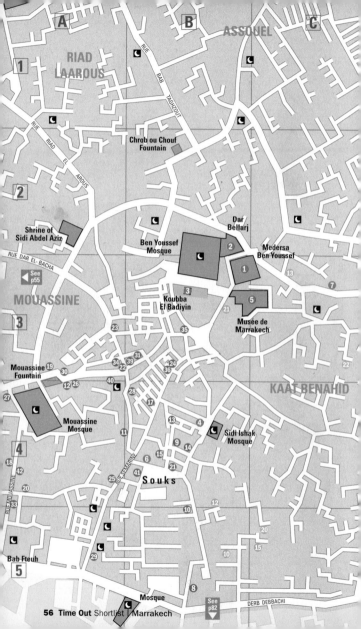

A
B
C

ASSOUEL

RIAD LAAROUS

RUE

BAB

TAGHZOUT

**Chrob ou Chouf
Fountain**

RUE

RIAD

EL-

AROUS

**Dar
Bellarj**

**Shrine of
Sidi Abdel Aziz**

2

**Medersa
Ben Youssef**

**Ben Youssef
Mosque**

RUE DAR EL-BACHA

▶ See
p55

13

1

MOUASSINE

3

**Koubba
El Badiyin**

7

5

**Musée de
Marrakech**

23

21

35

22

31

**Mouassine
Fountain**

19

34 39

22

36

KAAT BENAHID

30

24

12 26

40

27

28

**Mouassine
Mosque**

17

11

13

4

**Sidi Ishak
Mosque**

9 14

RUE

MOUASSINE

6

15

18

42

21

20

25

RUE SEMARINE

41

Souks

33

10

12

29

20

15

10

Bab Fteuh

5

10

Mosque

8

See
p82
▼

DERB DEBBACHI

North Medina & Souks (east)

ROUTE DES REMPARTS

D · E · F

1

2 · Bab Debbagh

MOQF

PLACE DU MOQF

RUE DE BAB DEBBAGH

DAR DEBBAGH

3

ESSEBTIYNE

RUE ESSEBTIYNE

4

200 m
200 yds
© Copyright Time Out Group 2008

Shrine of i Ben Salah

ARSET SIDI YOUSSEF

5

See p83

RUE SIDI BOULABADA

- ❶ Sights & museums
- ❶ Eating & drinking
- ❶ Shopping
- ❶ Nightlife
- ❶ Arts & leisure
- ❶ Hotels

bô ೞ zin

drinking and fooding

Tél : 212 (0) 24 388 012 bo-zin.com
Marrakech Royaume du Maroc

right at the Meditel shop to emerge once again into streets that are wide enough for the passage of cars.

Just north is the dusty open plaza of the place Ben Youssef, dominated by the **Ben Youssef Mosque**, which is easily identifiable by its bright green pyramidal roofs. The original mosque went up in the 12th century and was the grandest of the age, but what stands now is a third and lesser incarnation, dating from the early 19th century. Non-Muslims may not enter. However, in the immediate vicinity of the mosque is a cluster of tourist-friendly sights, including the decidedly average **Musée de Marrakech,** the enchanting **Ben Youssef Medersa** and the venerable **Koubba El Badiyin**.

Mouassine

Although it's far from immediately apparent, **Mouassine** is rapidly becoming the most chic of Medina quarters. West of the main souk area and north of Jemaa El Fna, it's home to a growing number of smart boutiques, interesting galleries and hip *maisons d'hôtes*.

Immediately on entering rue Mouassine from place Bab Fteuh is **Beldi**, a must-stop shop for the likes of Jean Paul Gaultier and sundry international fashion types. West of the junction with rue Ksour three elaborate brass lanterns above the alleyway mark the doorway of **Ksour Agafay**, Marrakech's own private members' club. If you ring the bell it's possible that staff will allow you in to look around – it's a well-restored 19th-century house with, unusually, the courtyard up on the first floor.

At the point where the street widens to embrace the walls of the **Mouassine Mosque** (which lends its name to the quarter and was erected in e 1560s by Saadian sultan Abdellah El Ghalib), a side

street off to the west winds left then first right to reach a large wooden doorway with a signplate reading **Dar Cherifa**. Inside is a stunning late 16th-century riad with filigree stucco and beautiful carved cedar detailing. It operates as a gallery and performance space, doubling as a café during the day.

Where rue Mouassine hits rue Sidi El-Yamami, a dim little archway under a sign reading '*A la Fibule*' jogs left and right to the fantastical façade of the **Ministerio del Gusto**, an extraordinary gallery-cum-sales space executed in an architectural style that co-creator Alessandra Lippini describes as 'delirium'.

Following rue Sidi El-Yamami west leads to the city gate **Bab Laksour**, in the vicinity of which are the boutiques Kulchi and Kifkif and the Moroccan restaurants Ksar Es Saoussan and Tobsil. In the opposite direction, a few paces east along Sidi El-Yamami is the **Mouassine fountain** with quadruple drinking bays, three for animals and one – the most ornate – for people. It's here that the character Louis Bernard is fatally stabbed in Hitchcock's 1955 version of *The Man Who Knew Too Much* – although not so fatally that he can't stagger half a mile to Jemaa El Fna to expire in the arms of Jimmy Stewart.

Beside the fountain is an arched gateway beyond which is the **Souk des Teinturiers** (p61). A couple of rooms within the gateway, above the arch, are now part of a boutique called Atelier Moro (114 place de Mouassine) run by Viviana Gonzalez of Riad El Fenn. It's a good place for buying funky decorative items, clothes, glass and bead work.

Further up the street are a couple of good examples of *fundouks*. A *fundouk* – in Marrakech – is the

Ben Youssef Medersa

distant forerunner of the modern hotel. It was a merchant hostel, built to provide accommodation and warehousing for the caravan traders who had crossed the desert and mountains to the south to bring their wares into the marketplaces of Marrakech. A *fundouk* offered stabling and storage rooms on the ground floor, bedrooms off the upper galleries, and a single gated entrance to the street that was locked at night for security. Most of the city's surviving *fundouks* now operate as ramshackle artisans' workshops, such as the one at No.192 rue Mouassine. This *fundouk* also featured in the film *Hideous Kinky* as the hotel where Kate Winslet and daughters lodged. Up on the first floor, the 'room' numbers painted by the film production crew remain – Winslet's was No.38, the only one with a bright new door. Another grand *fundouk* across the street is thought to be the oldest surviving example of this building type in Marrakech.

Dyers' Quarter

Between rue Mouassine and rue Semarine are some of the most fragrant and colourful souks, among them the **Souk El Attarin**, or Spice Souk. Contrary to the name, this part of the souk no longer deals in spices. Instead its traders largely traffic in tourist tat, from painted wooden thingamajigs to leather whatjamacallits. Almost opposite the subdued entrance to a workaday mosque is the **Souk des Babouches**, an alley devoted to leather slippers – and their almost identical synthetic counterparts.

Ringing hammer blows announce the **Souk Haddadin**, accessible from the Souk El Attarin, the ironworkers' quarter. One of the most medieval parts of the souk, it's full of dark, cavern-like workshops in which firework bursts of orange sparks illuminate tableaux of grime-streaked craftsmen, like some scene by Doré.

West of Attarin three alleys run downhill into the **Souk des Teinturiers**, which is the area of the dyers' workshops. Labourers rub dyes into cured hides (to be cut and fashioned into *babouches*) and dunk wool into vats of dark-hued liquids. This results in brightly coloured sheaves of wool that are then hung over the alleyways in a manner irresistible to passing photographers. It also results in the labourers having arms coloured to their elbows. You know you're nearing this part of the souk when you start seeing people with blue or purple arms.

Sights & museums

Ben Youssef Medersa

Place Ben Youssef (024 39 09 11).
Open 9am-6.30pm daily. **Admission** 30dh. **Map** p56 B3 ❶
A *medersa* is a Koranic school, dedicated to the teaching of Islamic scripture and law. This one was founded in the 14th century, then enlarged in 1564-5 by the Saadian sultan Abdellah El-Ghalib. It was given a further polishing up in the 1990s courtesy of the Ministry of Culture. Entrance is via a long, cool passageway leading to the great courtyard, a serene place centred on a water-filled basin. The surrounding façades are decorated with zelije tiling, stucco and carved cedar, all executed with restraint. At the far side is the domed prayer hall with the richest of decoration, notably around the mihrab, the arched niche that indicates the direction of Mecca. Back in the entrance vestibule, passageways and two flights of stairs lead to more than 100 tiny windowless students' chambers, clustered about small internal lightwells. Medieval as it seems, the medersa was still in use until as recently as 1962. The building stood in for an Algerian Sufic retreat in Gillies Mackinnon's 1998 film *Hideous Kinky*.

Dar Bellarj

9 rue Toulat Zaouiat Lahdar (024 44 45 55). **Open** 9am-6pm daily. **Admission** 15dh. **Map** p56 B2 ❷

North of the entrance to the Ben Youssef Medersa is a large wooden door in the crook of the alley emblazoned with a bird's head: this is Dar Bellarj, the 'Stork's House', so called because it was formerly a hospital for the big white birds. The stork is holy to Marrakech. There are countless tales to explain its exalted status, and the impression it gives of prayer-like prostration when at rest. The most commonly repeated is of a local imam, dressed in traditional Moroccan garb of white djellaba and black robe, drunk on wine, who then compounds the sin by climbing the minaret and blaspheming. Shazam! Man suffers wrath of God and is transformed into a stork. Even before the arrival of Islam, an old Berber belief held that storks are actually transformed humans. To this day the offence of disturbing a stork carries a three-month prison sentence.

Restored in the 1990s, Dar Bellarj now serves as a local cultural centre hosting exhibitions, workshops and performances. Unless you're lucky enough to drop in on a happening there's little to see; the courtyard is attractive with seating and caged songbirds, and sweet tea is offered to visitors, but you may wonder exactly what it was you paid admission for. And despite the posted opening hours, the big door is sometimes firmly locked.

Koubba El-Badiyin

Place Ben Youssef (024 39 09 11). **Open** Apr-Sept 9am-7pm daily. Oct-Mar 9am-6pm daily. **Admission** 10dh. **Map** p56 B3 ❸

Across from the Ben Youssef Mosque, set in its own fenced enclosure and sunk several metres below the current street level, is the Koubba El-Badiyin (it's also known as the 'Koubba Almoravide'). It looks unprepossessing but its unearthing in 1948 prompted one French art historian to exclaim that 'the art of Islam has never exceeded the splendour of this extraordinary dome'. It's the only surviving structure from the era of the Almoravids, the founders of Marrakech, and as such it represents a wormhole back to the origins of Moorish building history, presenting for the first time many of the shapes and forms that remain the basis of the North African architectural vocabulary. It dates to the reign of Ali Ben Youssef (1107-43) and was probably part of the ablutions complex of the original Ben Youssef Mosque. It's worth paying the slight admission fee to descend the brickwork steps and view the underside of the dome, which is a kaleidoscopic arrangement of a floral motif within an octagon within an eight-pointed star.

Musée Lucien Viola

NEW *17 rue Sidi Ishak.* **Map** p56 B4 ❹

North of Place Rahba Kedima near the leather and carpets sections of the souks, this new museum is supposed to open at the end of 2007. Lucien Viola promises to have a big collection of ancient Moroccan art, Berber textiles and even large carved wooden doors from Berber palaces of the Atlas. The museum will be on three floors, have one permanent exhibition and some temporary ones. There will also be a coffee shop and gift shop. Sounds promising.

Musée de Marrakech

Place Ben Youssef (024 39 09 11/www.museede marrakech.ma). **Open** 9am-6.30pm daily. **Admission** 40dh (60 dh for museum, Koubba and Ben Youssef Medersa). **Map** p56 B/C3 ❺

Inaugurated in 1997, the Musée de Marrakech is a conversion of an opulent early 20th-century house formerly belonging to a Marrakchi grandee. Entering the outer courtyard, there's a pleasant café off to one side and a mediocre bookshop opposite. Within the museum exhibits rotate. We were impressed by the collection of old sepia photographs of the city from the early 1900s (Jemaa El Fna looked almost as manic as it is today) and the ethnographic records of Morocco's different peoples. But the star attraction is the building itself, particularly the tartishly tiled great central court, roofed over and hung with an enormous chandelier like the mothership from *Close Encounters of the Third Kind*. The former hammam is lovely and makes a fine exhibition space for the prints and photos on show. If nothing else, the museum is a cool refuge from the blazing heat. Even the toilets are pleasant and clean. The three-monument ticket for 60dh is good value but it normally specifies (rather pedantically) the order in which you must visit the sights, and it's valid for one day only.

Eating & drinking

Café des Epices

NEW *75 Rahba Kedima (024 39 17 70).* **Open** 8am-8pm daily. **$$**. No credit cards. **Café**. Map p56 B4 ❻

Marrakech was crying out for a place like this: a spot in the souks to sit down in pleasant surroundings and refresh with a soft drink or light snack. In a small building overlooking the spice souk, there's a ground-floor terrace, a first-floor salon for lounging and tables on the roof. The decor is simple, the staff young and friendly, there's Wi-Fi and good music. A basic menu comprises tea and coffee, salads and sandwiches, juices and sodas. The only problem is its popularity.

Foundouk

55 rue du Souk des Fassi, Kat Bennahid (024 37 81 90/www.found ouk.com). **Open** noon-midnight Tue-Sun. Alcohol served. **$$$. French/ Moroccan.** Map p56 C3 ❼

The rutted trench of a street that leads to this restaurant appears so unpromising that many probably turn back. Those who locate the two lanterns marking the door enter into a gorgeous courtyard space with creamy leather seating around a flower-filled sunken water tray. A massive spindly chandelier hangs above, looking like something from one of Tim Burton's skewed fantasies. Softly glowing side rooms are filled with plush sofas and armchairs; one holds a tiny bar. There is more dining space upstairs at candlelit tables ranged around a gallery open to the sky most of the year. French-Moroccan food (couscous and

Bazaar les Palmiers p66

MARRAKECH BY AREA

uovo

Riad Due, Riad 72, Riad 12
www.uovo.com
Phone +212 (0) 24 38 76 29
Fax +212 (0) 24 38 47 18

tagines are on the menu alongside modern French dishes) is served by nattily dressed waiting staff, but the menu is doggedly inflexible. It's generally good, though not everything lives up to the surroundings. Highlight of our recent meal was the puddings, particularly a luscious pistachio crême brulée. Stick to the simple stuff and leave experimentation to the expert bar staff. Drinks are ideally sipped on the roof terrace beneath the stars.

Shopping

L'Art de la Couture

42-44 rue Rahba El Biadyne (024 44 04 87/061 34 40 26). **Open** 9am-1pm, 3.30-7.30pm daily. **Map** p56 B5 **8**

It looks nothing from the outside – nor within, for that matter – but this tiny shop sells wonderful classic coats and jackets for men and women, and has made to order for the queen. Cuts are simple, with embroidered details in subtle colours. The best garments are made from B'zou wools, the speciality of a small mountain town. Prices start at 1,000dh and custom orders take two weeks (shipping overseas is available). Coming from Derb Dabbachi, look for a modest light-pine frontage on the right with an AmEx sticker on the glass.

L'Art de Goulimine

25 Souk des Tapis (024 44 02 22). **Open** 9am-6.30pm daily. **Map** p56 B4 **9**

For something a little different, Rabia and Ahmed are two young dealers specialising in Rhamana carpets from the plains north of Marrakech. A small showroom displays choice pieces downstairs from the main sales space, where you'll find plenty of the more usual carpet types at competitive prices.

Art Ouarzazate

15 rue Rahba Kedima (067 35 21 24). **Open** 10am-6.30pm daily. **Map** p56 B5 **10**

A small sparsely stocked shop, but with an interesting stock, including beautiful throws hand-woven from agave fibres. Colours are jewel-like

and prices pretty reasonable. There are also old kaftans and *djellabas*, and *babouches* made of silk (about 200dh a pair). Mohammed speaks English, and you can accept his offer of tea without feeling cornered into buying.

Artisanat Berbère

33 Souk El Attarin (024 44 38 78). **Open** 9am-8pm daily. **Map** p56 B4 **11**

A charmingly dusty old place, filled with heaps of largely useless items fashioned from brass, copper, pewter and other pliable metals. There are lots of trays, pots and lamps on offer, plus ancient flat irons and giant sculpted animals. And you've got to love a place that promises 'small margin profit' on its business card.

Atelier Moro

NEW *114 place de Mouassine, Mouassine (024 39 16 78/ 060 54 35 20/ateliermoro@menara.ma).* **Open** 9am-1pm, 3-7pm Mon, Wed-Sun. **Map** p55 F4, p56 A4 **12**

This L-shaped first-floor space by the Mouassine fountain contains a cool, eclectic selection of homeware, clothes, accessories and carpets chosen by Viviana Gonzalez of Riad El Fenn (p153). Some of the clothes are designed by Viviana herself and a few other items are from her native Colombia, but most of the stock is Moroccan, often the work of nameless artisans that would otherwise be lost in the souks. There's everything from inexpensive handmade scissors and Tuareg cutlery to pricey rugs, lamps made from ostrich eggs and suede or Egyptian cotton tops. The door is to the west of the fountain, just right of the arch that leads into the Souk des Teinturiers. Ring for entry.

Bazaar Ikhouan

15 marché Sidi Ishak, off rue Sidi Ishak (024 44 36 16). **Open** 10am-7pm daily. **Map** p56 B4 **13**

Just how antique most of these pieces are is open to debate – antiquity is in the eye of the beholder. Anyway, curious excavators can sift through piles of tarnished jewellery, dull-bladed daggers, trays and teapots, greening brass lanterns, fancy-headed walking sticks, silver Koranic carry-cases, gunpowder flasks and ivory-handled muskets. Owner Khalid is a real charmer and speaks fluent English.

Bazaar les Palmiers

145 Souk Dakkakine (024 44 46 29). **Open** 9am-7pm Mon-Thur, Sat, Sun. **Map** p56 B4 ⑭

Hamid is a fourth-generation carpet dealer. His passion is carpets from the High Atlas, characterised by their beautiful colouring. Pieces here take in the old and not-so-old, with prices starting at an affordable 100dh (although all that is likely to get you is a cushion). He speaks English, and is happy to expound on his favourite subject over a glass of mint tea.

Bazaar du Sud

117 Souk des Tapis (024 44 30 04). **Open** 9am-7pm daily. **Map** p56 B4 ⑮

This place has possibly the largest selection of carpets in the souk, covering all regions and styles, new and old. The owners say they have 17 buyers out at any one time scouring the country for the finest examples. Although considerable effort goes into supplying collectors and dealers worldwide, sales staff are just as happy to entertain the novice. Prices range from 2,000dh to 350,000dh. Ask for Ismail, who speaks perfect English.

Beldi

9-11 Soukiat Laksour, Bab Fteuh (024 44 10 76). **Open** 9.30am-1pm, 3.30-8pm daily. **Map** p55 F5 ⑯

Toufik studied fashion in Germany and now, back in Marrakech, he and his brother Abdelhafid have transformed the family tailoring business into what is probably the most talked-about boutique in town. They offer both men's and women's ranges in the most beautiful colours and fabrics, fashioned with flair and an eye to Western tastes. Beautiful velvet coats lined with silk start at around 1,600dh; men's shirts in fine linen cost from 400dh. Collections change seasonally.

Bellawi

Kessariat Lossta No.56, off Souk El Attarin (024 44 01 07). **Open** 9am-7pm Mon-Thur, Sat, Sun. **Map** p56 B4 ⑰

At this closet-like jewellery store there's just about room for Abdelatif, his workbench and one customer. The walls are hung with beads clustered like bunches of berry fruits, along with a fine selection of traditional Moroccan-style silver bangles, necklaces and rings set with semiprecious stones. There's no sign in English, but just ask for Abdelatif. Everyone knows him – he's been here for over 40 years.

Caverne d'Ali Baba

17A Fhal Chidmi, Mouassine (024 44 21 48). **Open** 9am-8pm daily. **Map** p55 F4, p56 A4 ⑱

This huge shop is stocked with an incredible array of goods in all imaginable colours, from egg cups to lamp bases. In fact, just about any pottery trend that has hit the Medina will very quickly be copied and put on sale here. Especially attractive are the *tadelakt*-finish items, which have an almost soft, leather-like appearance.

Cherkaoui

120-122 rue Mouassine (024 42 68 17). **Open** 8.30am-7.30pm daily. **Map** p55 F3, p56 A3 ⑲

Opposite the Mouassine fountain is this glittering Aladdin's cave, full of everything imaginable in the way of home decoration Moroccan-style (with the exception of carpets). The proprietors, one local (Jaoud) and one German (Matthias), use their own local artisans, working in various media including wood, leather, metal and clay, to supply the store. Customers include the famed restaurant Dar Yacout and the Hotel les Jardins de la Koutoubia. Any piece can be made up in eight weeks, and shipping can be arranged.

Chez Aloui

52 rue des Ksour, Mouassine (062 08 48 71). **Open** 9am-8pm daily. No credit cards. **Map** p55 F4, p56 A4 ⑳

Caverne d'Ali Baba

The smell of leather

There are two reasons why the tanneries are located so far from the centre of the Medina that they fall off the edge of our map. First, they were built where there was access to water (a small stream, dry in summer, runs outside the nearby ramparts). Second, they stink.

The easiest way to get there is a taxi to Bab Debbagh (Tanner's Gate) on the Medina's north-eastern side. The tannery quarter is behind it. Some loitering youth will offer to be your guide and this is one place where it makes sense to accept – the individual tanneries can be tricky to find.

There are several, some supposedly Berber, others allegedly Arab. Each comprises a large yard filled with open vats of various liquids, all aligned in rows. Of different colours, they can look pretty from a distance, like a giant paint set. Close up, they are scummy and noxious. The tanning process involves lime, pigeon shit, and assorted natural and, latterly, chemical dyes. The unfortunate tanners have to work knee-deep in this stuff, soaking and scouring the hides of sheep, goats and, occasionally, camels. The work makes them prone to arthritis and most must retire around 40, at which point they induct their sons into the family trade.

If you're lucky, your guide will be able to explain some of what is going on. Even luckier, and he'll proffer a sprig of mint to help block out the stench. The smell is worse when it's hot, but even in winter it's inescapable. In compensation you will witness a pre-industrial process, carried on in much the same way it has been for centuries.

You won't want to linger too long. The finished leather can be seen shaped into bags, belts and sandals at the many nearby leather shops. Your guide will steer you to the one where he gets a kickback. Tip him 20dh-30dh if you don't buy anything. If you want to walk back, rue de Bab Debbagh runs west from the gate towards the Medersa Ben Youssef and Musée de Marrakech.

A great place to look for ceramics in a variety of styles including Berber (which looks African, with bold, clean shapes) and both old and new pieces from Safi, one of Morocco's main pottery-producing centres. Our favourites are the traditional green ceramics from Tamegroute near Zagora. The green glaze never comes out quite the same, so each piece is unique. Some of the plates and bowls are marked with a spiral motif, the Berber circle of life.

Chez Brahim

101 Rahba Lakdima (024 44 01 10). **Open** 9.30am-6.30pm daily. **Map** p56 B4 ㉑

Brahim offers an almost overwhelming selection of fabulous Moroccan textiles, with a collection that covers all regions and styles. Many of his textiles are antique, and hard to find elsewhere. Visiting Chez Brahim is rather like going to a museum where everything is for sale; prices are steep, but these are collectors' pieces.

Chez Climou et Ahmed

2 Souk Lebbadine (070 94 94 00). **Open** 9am-8pm daily. No credit cards. **Map** p56 A3 ㉒

Using a small, rudimentary lathe that he spins with his bare feet, Ahmed carves chess pieces from cedar, olive and lemon wood. His designs are pleasingly solid and simple, the black pieces created using burnt olive oil as a stain. He also sells boards and other woodcraft items, but only makes the pieces himself – a process well worth watching.

Chez Moulay Youssef

Souk El Kchachbia, off rue El Hadadine (024 44 34 01). **Open** 10am-8pm daily. No credit cards. **Map** p56 A3 ㉓

One of our favourite shops in the souk, Moulay Youssef does beautiful, richly coloured and stripy bedspreads in sabra, cotton or raffia. There are also homeware items such as jewellery boxes, napkin rings and pillow cases, plus fashion accessories like belts and hand-embroidered bags. It isn't the easiest place to find, but if you can locate the general neighbourhood, just ask – everybody round here knows Moulay Youssef.

Chez Said

155 Souk Chkairia (024 39 09 31). **Open** 9.30am-7.30pm daily. **Map** p56 B3 ㉔

Chez Moulay Youssef

MARRAKECH BY AREA

Said specialises in fashionable leather bags, decorated with coins or beads, or just a simple metal disc on the front. Designs come in both modern and vintage styles. The leather is either natural or dyed; when the latter, colouring is properly fixed and doesn't come off on your clothes. Said speaks English, and also sells his bags in bulk to certain well-known stores in the UK.

Costumes 1001 Nuits
97 Souk Semarine (061 87 26 87). **Open** 8am-8pm daily. **Map** p56 A4 ㉕
In a prime position on a busy street corner, Abdelaziz Elouissi's shop specialises in beautiful vintage kaftans and *djellebahs*, all from Marrakech and some of them over a century old. In addition to the stock displayed in his small shop, he has still more stashed nearby, and will hurry off to find other examples of whatever you seem to want. Prices start at around 500dh, but can climb very high for more elaborate pieces.

Création Chez Abdel
17 Souk des Teinturiers (024 42 75 17). **Open** 9am-9pm daily. No credit cards. **Map** p56 A3 ㉖

Another good outlet for *tadelakt* pottery, this small shop is packed from floor to ceiling with ceramics in simple shapes in rich, luminous colours. There are great bowls and lamps, but also lighter and more portable items such as candlesticks and ashtrays. Quality is excellent and prices are reasonable. There's no name on the shop so it can be difficult to spot – walk east past the Mouassine fountain and there's a sharp right, then a left; Abdel's is behind the pine-framed door on the right.

El Yed Gallery
66 Fhal Chidmi, rue Mouassine (024 44 29 95). **Open** 9.30am-12.30pm, 1.30-6.30pm Mon-Sat. **Map** p55 F4 ㉗
Opposite the side of the Mouassine Mosque, El Yed is a real collectors' haunt, specialising in beautiful antique Moroccan jewellery and pottery. Much of it comes from the deep south, and it's not for the delicate of frame – bracelets look like great silver sprockets and the favoured stone is amber by the hunk. The owner speaks English and is highly knowledgeable about his stock. He's happy to discuss details

Dar Cherifa p74

and provenance, but probably less willing to talk prices, which are fixed and pretty expensive.

Eva/Adam

144 Souk El Hanna (024 44 39 69).
Open 10am-12.30pm, 3.30-6.30pm Mon-Thur, Sat, Sun. **Map** p56 B4 ㉘
No high fashion or class cuts, just practical and genuinely comfortable warm-weather clothes in neutral colours. Made from cotton and lightweight wool, the styles are loose-fitting yet elegant. It's the kind of stuff you might actually wear on a day-to-day basis, and prices are reasonable enough. To find it, walk north up Souk El Attarin just past the entrance to the mosque on the left. Look to the right for the word 'Lacoste' painted on a whitewashed arch: Eva/Adam is first on the right, with barely more than a door by way of shop frontage.

Au Fil d'Or

10 Souk Semmarine (024 44 59 19).
Open 9am-1pm, 2.30-7.30pm Mon-Thur, Sat, Sun; 9am-1pm Fri.
Map p55 F5, p56 A5 ㉙
Au Fil d'Or is worth homing in on for the finest quality *babouches* and wool *djellabas*, plus fantastic own-label hand-stitched shirts (400dh) in gorgeous deep hues, and finely braided silk-lined jackets (2,200dh) – just the thing should one be invited to the palace. Note that the bulk of the stock is kept in the cellar-like space downstairs, accessed via a trapdoor behind the counter. Watch your head (and your spending).

Founoun Marrakech

28 Souk des Teinturiers (024 42 62 03). **Open** 10am-7pm daily.
Map p55 F3, p56 A3 ㉚
This is the place to come if you want a lantern (*founoun*) of quality. At first glance it's tiny, but walk through to the back room to find an impressive choice of truly beautiful things. Ask owner Rachid El-Himel to take you through to the workshop; here, a team of men and young boys hammer and cut at sheets of copper, fashioning the goods to fill the shop. To find it, walk

east past the Mouassine fountain then through the arch, and it's the first lantern shop on the left.

Haj Ahmed Oueld Lafram

51 Souk Smafa (024 44 51 27).
Open 10am-6.30pm Mon-Thur, Sat, Sun. No credit cards. **Map** p56 B3 ㉛
Most of the souk's slipper shops are much of a muchness – look into one and you've pretty much seen them all; the same styles pop up again and again. But Haj Ahmed Oueld Lafram offers a selection of *babouches* in a variety of styles from all over Morocco – embroidered leather ones from Tafraoute, for example – and in a variety of materials that include the likes of dyed goat fur, Italian horse leather and python skin. They're not the cheapest, but the quality is excellent.

La Maison du Kaftan Marocain

65 rue Sidi El Yamami (024 44 10 51). **Open** 9am-7.30pm daily.
Map p55 E4 ㉜
La Maison may have the unloved, run-down look of a charity shop, but it also has the widest selection of Moroccan clothing for men, women and children in the souk, housed in a vast mausoleum of a place. Stock ranges from *pantalon turque* (traditional men's trousers) to beautiful velvet jackets and vintage kaftans that go for 20,000dh. Scouts for international fashion houses often drop by to place orders and look for inspiration.

Maktabet El Chab

Rue Mouassine (024 44 34 17). **Open** 8.30am-8.30pm daily. No credit cards.
Map p55 F4, p56 A4 ㉝
Aka the 'FNAC Berbère' bookshop, this corner kiosk claims to be '*La première librairie à Marrakech*', founded in 1941. Stock is pitifully limited, but full marks for perseverance.

Michi

[NEW] *19-21 Souk Lakchachbia (061 86 44 07/aitelaloud2001@yahoo.fr).*
Open 9am-7pm daily. No credit cards.
Map p56 A3 ㉞

MARRAKECH BY AREA

Owned by a Japanese-Moroccan couple, this small shop near the slipper souk has a small but appealing selection of well-made Moroccan items, chosen with a Japanese aesthetic. The collection includes simple slippers and jewellery, as well as delicate wooden spoons and spatulas, and raffia shoes from Essaouira.

Miloud Art Gallery

NEW *48 Souk Charatine (024 42 67 16/070 41 76 61).* **Open** 9am-8pm daily. **Map** p56 B4 **35**

This new venture, opened by Miloud El Jouli in early 2007, is a one-stop shop for competitively priced versions of modern Moroccan design. A generous space is packed with large furniture pieces and smaller, more transportable items to take back home. Armchairs and coffee tables, ceramics and textiles, pouffes and picture frames are all specially made and are very good quality. There's also a selection of kaftans and handbags. With no shop front, this place can be a litle hard to find; call to arrange a visit.

Miloud El Jouli

6-8 Souk Smat El Marga, off Souk El Kebir (024 42 67 16). **Open** 9am-7.30pm daily. **Map** p56 B3 **36**

Join buyers from boutiques in Chelsea and New York's Upper East Side to rifle through an impressive selection of patterned *babouches*, vibrantly coloured shirts and blouses in Indian silks, dyed-leather and silk sequinned handbags, beaded belts with heavy silver buckles and *djellabas*. Some of the wares are Miloud's own designs, some cleverly crafted local copies of high-fashion pieces, as in the Hermès sandals that fill one shelf. Prices are less than you'd pay back home – but not that much less. Miloud has now applied this same approach to homeware and furnishings at Miloud Art Gallery (p73). Souk Smat El Marga is in the Kissaria, the third narrow alley from the northernmost end of Souk El Kebir.

Ministerio del Gusto

22 Derb Azouz El Mouassine, off rue Sidi El Yamami (024 42 64 55). **Open** 9.30am-noon, 4-7pm Mon-Sat. **Map** p55 E4 **37**

The Ministero is HQ to ex-*Vogue Italia* fashion editor Alessandra Lippini and her business partner Fabrizio Bizzarri. It's a surreal space – sort of Gaudi goes Mali with a side trip to Mexico. As well as filling the role of informal social centre for friends and assorted fashionistas and creatives blowing through town, the two floors act as an occasional gallery and a showcase for funky 'found' objects (sourced from house clearances) such as African-inspired furniture, Eames chairs and Bernini glassware.

MOHA

5 Laksour Sabet Graoua, Mouassine, (068 94 90 97). **Open** 9am-8pm daily. No credit cards. **Map** p55 F4 **38**

One of several objets d'art shops around Mouassine, this place offers a good selection of choice, if not always particularly old, doors, large vases, armoires and chests. Moha himself speaks English and will happily hold court in his modest showroom and serve mint tea while discussing purchases. He also has a second shop nearby.

Mohammed Ouledhachmi

34 Souk El Hararin Kedima (066 64 41 05). **Open** 9am-6pm Mon-Thur, Sat, Sun. No credit cards. **Map** p56 B3 **39**

Mohammed does copper – copper trays, copper pots, copper kettles, copper you-name-it. Some of the pieces are new, but the bulk of the stock is older and sometimes includes pieces by well-known metalsmiths whose work is prized by collectors. To find the shop, head north up Souk El Attarin and take the second right after passing the entrance to the mosque on your left.

Mustapha Latrach

7 Souk Labbadine (061 74 34 58). **Open** 9am-7pm daily. **Map** p56 A3 **40**

The amiable Mustapha Latrach runs this small shop, located near the slipper souk. It's filled with authentic antique teapots, including quite a few with old English hallmarks – highly collectible and becoming ever-harder to find. Prices start at around the 1,000dh mark.

Rahal Herbes

43-47 Rahba Kedima (024 39 14 16). **Open** 9am-8pm daily. No credit cards. **Map** p56 B4 ④

The west side of Rahba Kedima is lined with herbalists and 'black magic' stores; we recommend Rahal for owner Abdeljabbar's fluency in English and wickedly dry sense of humour.

Tapis Akhnif

6 rue Mouassine (024 42 60 96). **Open** 9am-8pm daily. **Map** p55 F4, p56 A4 ④

A small family business, run by a father and his two sons, Akhnif offers a wide array of carpets, raffia and wool rugs, pillow cases and pouffes, without any sales hassle. Prices are fair, and there's good *café au lait* on request.

Arts & leisure

Dar Cherifa

8 Derb Charfa Lakbir (024 42 64 63/ www.marrakech-riads.net). **Open** 9am-7pm daily. No credit cards. **Map** p55 E4 ④

This gorgeous townhouse is the Medina's premier exhibition space. Parts of the building date back to the 16th century and it has been lovingly restored by owner Abdelatif Ben Abdellah, who's taken great pains to expose the carved beams and stucco work while leaving walls and floors bare and free of distraction. Regular exhibitions lean towards resident foreign artists, but there have also been shows by Moroccan artists Hassan Hajjaj and Milaudi Nouiga. The space also includes a small library; tea and coffee are served, and there's a light lunch menu too.

Ministerio del Gusto

22 Derb Azouz El-Mouassine, off rue Sidi El-Yamami (024 42 64 55). **Open** 9am-noon, 4-7pm Mon-Sat. **Map** p55 E4 ④

This is the showroom for the design talents and eclectic tastes of owners Alessandra Lippini and Fabrizio Bizzarri. The eccentric space also hosts art exhibitions; when these are over Alessandra and Fabrizio source and sell work by the artists they like. These include Essaouira-based English artist Micol, the American photographer Martin H M Schreiber, Italian Maurizio Vetrugno, who creates multimedia installations, Indonesian painter Ribka and Marrakchi Pop artist Hassan Hajjaj.

Elsewhere

Sights & museums

Bab Doukkala Mosque

Map p54 C2 ④

The Bab Doukkala Mosque was built in 1558 by the mother of the Saadian sultans Abdel-Malek and Ahmed El-Mansour. The mosque is fronted by the Sidi El-Hassan fountain, which is now dry, fenced around and used as an occasional exhibition space. Across from the fountain, a small white-washed building houses a 400-year-old hammam (men only) with a fantastic cedarwood ceiling in the reception area. Behind the fountain a faint hand-painted 'WC' signposts the city's oldest toilets, built at the same time as the Bad Doukkala Mosque opposite. They're still in use.

Dar El-Bacha

Map p55 D/E2 ④

West of the Mouassine quarter is the high-walled former residence of the most unsaintly Thami El-Glaoui, self-styled 'Lord of the Atlas' and ruler of Marrakech and southern Morocco throughout much of the first half of the 20th century. Known locally as Dar El-Bacha ('House of the Lord'), and also as Dar El-Glaoui, the residence is where the Glaoui entertained luminaries such as Churchill and Roosevelt, as well as the women his agents collected for him, scouring the streets for suitable prizes. The

The personal touch

Laetitia Trouillet

A native of Bordeaux who divides her time between Morocco and London, Laetitia Trouillet first arrived to produce the bags and accessories she still designs for her own Lalla label. Along the way, though, she also got to know the city's designers and artisans, souks and boutiques.

A request to help some people from Victoria's Secret on an 'inspiration' trip led to other work pointing professional shoppers – wholesalers, designers – in directions they might find interesting. Soon there were also calls from ordinary visitors, seeking a shortcut to the bargains, pursuing a particular interest, or simply up for a bit of good old-fashioned 'girlie shopping'. Almost by accident, Laetitia had morphed into modern Marrakech's answer to the traditional guide: a personal shopper.

Here's the difference. When it comes to shopping, an old-school guide will steer you to any old place where they happen to get a kick-back – often to disappear while you fend off the hard sell. It's more about what they've got than what you want. A personal shopper looks at things the other way around, bringing a European sensibility to the search for stuff you might find interesting, haggling on your behalf, and not accepting kickbacks.

Laetitia is good at her work, both expert and excellent company. She charges €200 a day, doesn't take groups, and might lead you far beyond the souks to distant corners of the Medina, obscure markets, specialised Guéliz showrooms, or out to the industrial quarter of Sidi Ghamen. Her bags are pretty good too.

complex dates from the early 20th century and is disappointingly dull to visit, given its lurid past. Visitors pass through several mundane administrative chambers (the complex now belongs to the Ministry of Culture) into a large courtyard, overwrought with carved plaster and woodwork, and excessive tiling. A passage snakes through to a second courtyard, which once served as the Glaoui's harem. The decor is similarly ornate, with particularly ornate details around the column capitals. At the time of writing Dar El-Bacha was closed to visitors; past dates for its reopening have been repeatedly postponed.

Facing the side wall of the Dar El-Bacha is another property with pedigree – owned previously by the chamberlain of the Glaoui, later by French couturier Pierre Balmain ('dressmaking is the architecture of movement') and now the premises of Dar Moha, one of the finest restaurants in Marrakech.

Eating & drinking

Dar Moha

81 rue Dar El-Bacha (024 38 64 00/ www.dar moha.ma). **Open** noon-3pm, 7.30pm-late Tue-Sun. Alcohol served. **$$$**. **Fusion**. Map pp55 D2 🄸
Owner Moha Fedal is the closest thing Marrakech has to a home-grown celebrity chef. He learned his trade over 14 years in Switzerland and the result is a kind of Moroccan fusion cuisine – traditional dishes with a twist. We recommend sampling a standard tagine or couscous elsewhere first, then coming here to delight in the difference. Both lunch and dinner are set-course affairs but there is some choice of dishes. Service is good; gregarious Moha is often found flitting from table to table, and the gnawa musicians who play nightly are among the best we've encountered in Marrakech restaurants. Book well in advance, and try to get a table outside by the pool – the interior is dull by comparison.

Dar Yacout

79 rue Ahmed Soussi, Arset Ihiri (024 38 29 29). **Open** 7pm-1am Tue-Sun. Alcohol served. **$$$$**. **Moroccan**. Map p55 D1 🄸
Dar Yacout's fame rests more on its style of decor and performance than it does on the food. The building is all show, a madcap mansion designed by Bill Willis, complete with flowering columns, candy striping and fireplaces in the bathrooms, topped off by a yellow crenellated rooftop terrace. Guests are led up to the latter on arrival or invited to take a drink (included in the price, so feel free) in the first-floor lounge, before being taken down, past the swimming pool and across the courtyard, to be seated for dinner at great round tables, which are inset with mother-of-pearl. On comes the food, delivered with maximum pomp by teams of costumed waiters, course after course, quickly passing the point where you'd wish it would stop. It's perfectly adequate stuff, but then you wouldn't come to Dar Yacout for the cooking alone. Reservations are essential.

Ksar Es Saoussan

3 Derb El-Messaoudyenne, off rue des Ksour (024 44 06 32). **Open** 8pm-1am Mon-Sat. Alcohol served. **$$$**. **Moroccan**. Map p55 E4 🄸
Yet another historic house/fixed menu combination, but one possessed of a peculiar old-world charm. The tone's set by the elderly French gentleman who greets guests with an invitation to ascend to the roof for the fine view of the Koutoubia Mosque. Then it's back downstairs to be seated in silk-cushioned corners with gentle piano concertos filling the space where other diners' conversation would be (the number of covers barely reaches double figures). Tall Africans take the orders from a choice of three set dinners; all but the most ravenous should be satisfied by the three-course '*petit*' option (350dh), which comes with an aperitif, a half-bottle of wine and bottled water.

Station to station

Since the French first built the railway line in the 1930s, trains have arrived in a small, colonial-era station that has few facilities but oodles of charm. There's a basic kiosk, an aged café, faded photos of vintage locomotives and Moroccan monarchs, past and present. It was here that Graham Nash arrived in 1966 and, apparently so stoned that he imagined 'ducks and pigs and chickens' running around, was inspired to write the song 'Marrakesh Express'.

But by early 2008, all that will have changed. As part of the huge expansion of tourist infrastructure – and an upgrading of train stations throughout Morocco – a new terminus is being built just 200 metres south of the old one. It fronts rather grandly on to avenue Mohammed VI, diagonally opposite the Théâtre Royal, rather than depositing passengers on a dusty stretch of avenue Hassan II.

From 2.5 million travellers in 2006, traffic is slated to rise to around 4.5 million by 2010. They will arrive in a 1,250-square-metre hall, equipped with shopping galleries, escalators, banking facilities and electronic arrival boards. There will even be video surveillance. It's as big an indication of how Marrakech is changing as any of the city's other new structures. And no matter how stoned the passengers, few will be likely to imagine pigs running around.

Maison Arabe

1 Derb Assehbe, Bab Doukkala (024 38 70 10). **Open** 7-11pm daily. Alcohol served. **$$$**. **Moroccan**. **Map** p54 C3 **50**

Other than the address, the house restaurant of the hotel of the same name (p155) has no connection to the original and legendary Maison Arabe. But the food is commendable and, as with the hotel, the surroundings are beautiful. The setting comprises a grand dining room under a brilliant blue-hued Persian-style ceiling. The heavily draped tables are generously spaced and discreetly attended by liveried staff. In fact, the place feels more like an exclusive private club than a restaurant – if you want to glam it up, this is a good place to do so. The restaurant offers a prix fixe menu but there are choices between some wonderful tagines (including the excellent lamb and pear) and several different kinds of couscous. Lighter European dishes are served at the bar. Afterwards, take tea or coffee in the charming courtyard which features lovely a trompe l'oeil façade. Reservations are recommended.

Palais Soleiman

NEW *Route de Fès, Kaa Machraa (024 37 89 62/www.palais-solei man.com).* **Open** 7.30pm-1.30am Mon-Sat. Alcohol served. **$$$**. **Moroccan**. **Map** p54 B1

This serious 19th-century palace, owned by the Segueni family from Casablanca, opened as a restaurant in June 2006 after years as a private event location. Those who make the schlep (or short taxi ride) from the souks are rewarded with a truly spectacular setting, with tables scattered around an immense and beautifully lit courtyard. Decorative highlights include huge pillars and fine tiling and woodwork, topped off by antique chandeliers. The whole place is covered by a clear electric retractable roof. The experience is a bit like eating on the set of a Bond film; you half expect a missile to rise from the central fountain and soar off into the night. The traditional Moroccan food is fine, if a little pricey (and wine comes extra), but you get whatever you're given and the setting remains the main reason to visit. Entertainment is provided in the form of alternating *gnawa* and Arabo-Andalucian musicians. There are also occasional piano recitals.

Pavillion

Derb Zaouia, Bab Doukkala (024 38 70 40). **Open** 7.30pm-midnight Mon, Wed-Sun. Alcohol served. **$$$**. **French**. Map p54 C2 ⑤②

The setting is superlative: the courtyard of a splendid old house where tables are squeezed under the spreading boughs of a massive tree. Several small salons provide for a more intimate dining experience. The day's menu is scrawled out on a white board presented by the waiter. Offerings change regularly but expect the likes of *agneau*, *canard* and *lapin*, all exquisitely presented with seasonal vegetables and rich wine sauces. The staff can be supercilious, but otherwise this is a truly classy affair. The restaurant is a little difficult to find, but if you can locate the alley leading to the Maison Arabe, which is well signposted, then Pavillion is approximately 100 metres north, tucked down the next alley but one. Reservations are recommended.

Shopping

Ensemble Artisanal

Avenue Mohammed V (024 38 67 58). **Open** 8.30am-7.30pm daily. Map p54 C4 ⑤③

The second major tourist stop after photo ops at the Koutoubia, the EA is a state-sponsored crafts mini-mall, popular because of its central location. All the artisans selling within are purportedly here by royal appointment, selected as the best in their field (a licence therefore to charge higher prices, and these are completely non-negotiable). Expect to find everything from fine embroidered table linen (first floor at the back) to jewellery, clothing, lamps and maybe even the odd 'brand-name' handbag.

Kifkif

8 rue des Ksour, Bab Laksour (061 08 20 41). **Open** 9.30am-7.30pm daily. No credit cards. Map p55 D5 ⑤④

Ksar Es Saoussan p77

This is a quality knick-knack shop with an eclectic array of goods, including unique bangles, belts, earrings and other accessories, little towelling dressing gowns for kids, embroidered napkin sets and own-designed glasses, electric lights, vases and table decorations. Stephanie is the owner, and almost everything she stocks is made in Morocco. Unfortunately some things are simply too expensive, like the set of Momo's Arabesque CDs at 350dh (buy the bootleg in Jemaa El Fna), but others, like the charming white cotton baby romper suits at 100dh a throw, or the attractive beaded cigarette lighter covers for tabletops, are good value.

Kulchi

1 rue des Ksour, Bab Laksour (no phone). **Open** 9.30am-1pm, 3.30-7pm Mon-Sat. No credit cards. **Map** p55 D5 ⑤

Florence Taranne's small boutique stocks a quirky hand-picked collection of boho Moro chic, including leather shopping bags with the *khamsa* (hand of Fatima) motif, lovely ruffly silk dresses as well as chiffon blouses in flowery prints by Spanish designer Lola, T-shirts by Hassan Hajjaj, Zinalabel plastic shopping bags with brightly coloured flowery designs and delicate jewellery, including rose petals laminated as earrings. It's pricey, at around 1,200dh-1,600dh for a silk and chiffon blouse, although you can find the odd bargain kaftan for 65dh or less. Our biggest beef is that a lot of the clothes are too small around the bust and would suit only the likes of Kate Moss or Sienna Miller – both of whom have been seen here. The store was closed for a while, but has recently reopened.

Librairie Dar El Bacha

2 rue Dar El Bacha (024 39 19 73). **Open** 9am-1pm, 3-7pm daily. No credit cards. **Map** p55 E2 ⑤

This small shop's main stock consists of coffee table books about Morocco and Marrakech, but there's also a decent selection of guide books and reproductions of old tourist posters.

Mustapha Blaoui

142-144 rue Bab Doukkala (024 38 52 40). **Open** 9am-8pm daily. **Map** p55 D2 ⑤⑦

This is the classiest, most beloved 'best of Morocco' depot in town. It's a warehouse of a place that's crammed, racked and piled with floor-to-ceiling irresistibles – lanterns, dishes, pots, bowls, vases, candlesticks, chandeliers, chests, tables and chairs… If Mustapha doesn't have it, then you don't need it. He supplies a lot of the furnishings for local riads; even people who don't own a hotel will find it almost impossible to visit here and not fill a container lorry. Added to which, Mustapha is an absolute sweetheart, his staff are ultra-helpful and shipping from here is a cinch.

Arts & entertainment

Hammam El Bacha

20 rue Fatima Zohra (no phone). **Open** *Men* 7am-1pm daily. *Women* 1-9pm daily. **Rates** 7dh men; 7.50dh women; massage 50dh. No credit cards. **Map** p55 D4 ⑤⑧

Hammam El Bacha is probably the best-known hammam in Marrakech, thanks largely to its historic role as local soak for the servants and staff of the Dar El Bacha opposite. It boasts impressive dimensions, including a 6m (20ft) high cupola, but unfortunately it's very badly maintained – best not to count on coming out much cleaner than you went in.

Maison Arabe

1 Derb Assehbe, Bab Doukkala (024 38 70 10/www.lamaison arabe.com). **Open** by appointment only. **Map** p54 C3 ⑤⑨

The ultimate in self-indulgence – a hammam with rubdown (*gommage*) administered by a vicious pro, followed by an all-over body treatment. Another package includes the most-thorough of massages.

Badii Palace p87

South Medina

Almost since the founding of Marrakech, the **South Medina** has been the domain of sultans and their retinues. Today it houses the museum-palaces of the city plus the **Kasbah** and the **Mellah**, historically Marrakech's Jewish quarter. The present **Royal Palace** is built on the site of the earliest Almohad palaces and covers a vast area. Morocco's new king, Mohammed VI, a little more modest in his requirements, has had a much smaller residence built nearby. Neither of these two modern-day royal precincts is open to the public, but visitors are allowed to explore two 19th-century viziers' palaces, the **Bahia Palace** and the **Dar Si Said Museum**, as well as the impressive ruins of the **Badii Palace** and the ornate **Saadian Tombs** to the west.

Kasbah

The traditional entrance to the Kasbah is via the gorgeous **Bab Agnaou** (Gate of the Gnawa), named after the black slaves brought from sub-Saharan Africa. The gate was built on the orders of the Almohad sultan Yacoub El-Mansour in 1185. It's one of the very few stone structures in this otherwise mud-brick city, and has weathered in such a way that the aged limestone now resembles heavily grained wood.

Across the street from Bab Agnaou is the original southern gate to the Medina, the **Bab Er Rob**, now filled by a pottery shop and bypassed by traffic, which exits through a modern breach in the walls.

A

B

C

1

Jemaa
El Fna

Mosque

See
p56

DERB DEBBACHI

Mosque

RUE DES BANQUES

25

42

DOUAR
GRAOUA

36

RUE BAB AGNAOU

2

29

40

23

27

RIAD ZITOUN
EL KEDIM

38

39

Dar Si Said
Museum

13

3

15

35

14 Maison
Tiskiwin

AVENUE
HOUMANN

EL
FETOUAKI

RUE RIAD ZITOUN EL KEDIM

34

32

RIAD ZITOUN
EL JEDID

Bahia
Palace

10

4

Marché
Couvert

Bab Es Salam
Market

MELLAH

5

PLACE DES
FERBLANTIERS

12

4 11

Bab
Berrima

See
p84

PLACE
SOUWEKA

D RUE SIDI BOULABADA **E** See p57 **F**

ARSET MOULAY BOUAZZA

1

2

RUE BA HMAD

Moulay Idriss Palace

JNANE BEN CHEGRA

	Sights & museums
	Eating & drinking
	Shopping
	Nightlife
	Arts & leisure
	Hotels

3

RUE IMAM EL RHEZALI

4

Cemetery

| 0 | 200 m |
| 0 | 200 yds |

© Copyright Time Out Group 2008

Jewish Cemetery

See p85

5

South Medina (north)

ARSET EL MAACH

A

See p82

B

AVENUE HOUMANN EL FETOUAKI

RUE RIAD ZITOUN EL KEDIM

C

RUE OQBA BEN NAFIA

RUE IBN RACLID

1

Marché Couvert

PLACE DES FERBLANTIERS

12

4 11

BAB AGNAOU

Bab Berrima

37

Kasbah Mosque

2

Badii Palace

Bab Agnaou

7

3 Saadian Tombs

2

9

Market

RUE DE LA KASBAH

6

Centre Artisanal

3

30

Royal Palace

KASBAH

31

26

4

RUE DU MECHOUAR

DERB CHTOUKA

5

28

8

5

Grand Méchouar

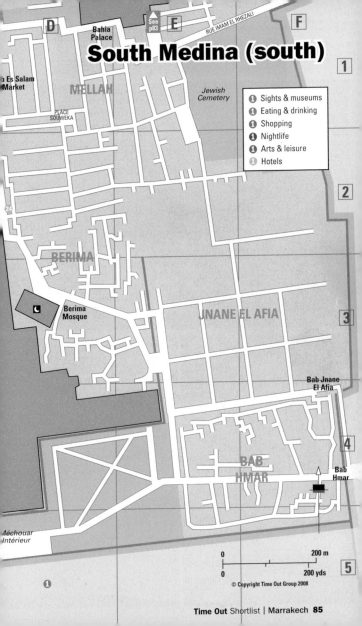

South Medina (south)

D   Bahia Palace   See p83   E   RUE IMAM EL RHEZALI   F

1

Es Salam Market

MELLAH

Jewish Cemetery

PLACE SOUWEKA

1	Sights & museums
1	Eating & drinking
1	Shopping
1	Nightlife
1	Arts & leisure
i	Hotels

2

24

BERIMA

Berima Mosque

JNANE EL AFIA

3

Bab Jnane El Afia

4

BAB HMAR

Bab Hmar

Méchouar Intérieur

| 0 | | 200 m |
| 0 | | 200 yds |

© Copyright Time Out Group 2008

5

1

A short distance inside the Agnaou gate is the **Kasbah Mosque**, constructed in 1190, again during the reign of Sultan Yacoub El-Mansour (hence its alternative name of El-Mansour Mosque). It has been renovated on numerous occasions since (most recently during the reign of Hassan II, father of the current king), but the cut-brick-and-green-tile decoration on the minaret is original. The plaza in front is usually busy with guide-led tourist groups. They're not here for the mosque, which, of course, they're forbidden to enter, but for what lies hidden in the lee of its southern wall: the **Saadian Tombs**.

Sights & museums

Agdal Gardens

Path off south-western corner of Méchouar Intérieur. **Open** usually on Fri & Sun; closed if the king is in residence at the Royal Palace. **Admission** free. **Map** p85 D5 ❶

Stretching for a few kilometres south of the Medina, essentially the huge back garden of the enormous Royal Palace, the Agdal Gardens cover a vast 16 hectares (40 acres). Laid out in 1156-57 by the Almohads, they are several hundred years older than those most celebrated of Islamic gardens at the Alhambra. They cover a vast 16 hectares (40 acres), stretching south for a couple of kilometres from the palace.

At the centre of the Agdal is a massive pool, the Sahraj El-Hana. In 1873 Sultan Mohammed IV drowned in it while boating with his son; the servant who managed to swim to safety was executed on the spot for failing to save his lord. The rest of the area is divided into different kinds of orchards and gardens, including an orange grove, vineyards, areas of pomegranates and figs, masses of walnut trees and palm groves. There are several ornamental pavilions, and it's possible to climb on to the roof of one of them, the Dar

El-Hana, beside the pool, for an impressive view of the gardens and the High Atlas beyond.

Badii Palace

Place des Ferblantiers (no phone). **Open** 8.30-11.45am, 2.30-5.45pm daily. **Admission** 10dh; 20dh minbar pavilion. **Map** p84 B/C2 ❷

Constructed by Sultan Ahmed El-Mansour (1578-1607) and funded by wealth accrued through victories over the Portuguese, the Badii Palace stands as one of the two principal monuments of the Saadian era (the other is the Saadian Tombs). Today it survives only as a denuded ruin, but once it was a model of triumphal ostentation. Walls and ceilings were encrusted with gold from Timbuktu (another of the sultan's conquests), while the inner court had a massive central pool with an island, flanked by four sunken gardens filled with scented flowers and trees. At the centre of each of the four massive walls were four pavilions, also flanked by arrangements of pools and fountains. It took some 25 years to complete the palace and barely were the inaugural celebrations over before the ageing ruler passed away. His palace remained intact for less than a century before the Merenid sultan, Moulay Ismail, had it stripped bare and the riches carted north for his new capital at Meknès.

The palace is entered at the south end of place des Ferblantiers via a canyon-like space constricted between two precipitous walls; the outer one was intended to keep the Medina at a respectful distance from the royal domains. The former main gate is collapsed and gone, and entrance is through a gaping hole in the fortifications directly into the great court. It's a vast empty space the size of a couple of football pitches, ringed around by pockmarked mud-brick walls that act as apartment blocks for pigeons and have stork nests along the battlements. The sunken areas that were once gardens still exist, as does the great dry basin that was the ornate central pool. On the west side are the ruins of the

Pavilion of Fifty Columns; a small area of mosaic is on the floor, colours badly dulled by exposure to the elements.

In the south-east corner, a gate leads through to a newly reconstructed pavilion housing the Koutoubia Mosque minbar (20dh admission). This was the original minbar (stepped pulpit) in the city's great mosque. It was fashioned in the early 12th century by Cordoban craftsmen, and the 1,000 decorative panels that adorn the sides supposedly took eight years to complete – the word 'ornate' falls somewhere short. It was removed from the mosque in the early 1960s for restoration and after a spell at the Dar Si Said Museum has ended up here. Next to the minbar pavilion are the excavated remains of troglodytic chambers and passages: a small underground labyrinth opened up for visitor exploration.

One of the palace bastions remains intact at the north-eastern corner of the great central court. Steps lead up to a rooftop terrace with fine views of the site and the surrounding quarter. You can also get up close and personal with the many nesting storks.

The palace comes back to life once a year when a giant screen is set up on the central island for the International Film Festival (p25).

Saadian Tombs

Rue de Kasbah, Bab Agnaou (no phone). **Open** 8.30-11.45am, 2.30-5.45pm daily. **Admission** 10dh. **Map** p84 A2 ❸
In the early 1920s the French authorities noticed two green-tiled roofs rising above the shanty quarters. Inquiries made of the locals were met with evasive answers. The persistence of one curious official was rewarded when he discovered a narrow, dark lane that ended in a tiny arched door. He pushed through to enter a courtyard garden and saw what apparently no infidel had ever seen before – the holy tombs of the Saadian sultans. According to the account in a 1928 travelogue, *The Magic of Morocco*, the Frenchman was then accosted by a wizened guardian

who said, 'You have discovered our secret, but beware what you do with the knowledge. You cannot make it a mere show for your people to come and gaze at.' Well, that's exactly what has happened: the tombs are possibly the most visited site in Marrakech.

Flanking the south side of the Kasbah Mosque, the tombs are easier to find today. The site is basically an ancient walled garden, the use of which far predates the Saadian era. Dotted around the shrubbery are a great many early mosaic graves; the identity of those interred is long lost. Attention instead focuses on the three pavilions built during the reign of Saadian sultan Ahmed El-Mansour. Despite drawing so many visitors, it's not spectacular – the modest setting reminds one of an English parish churchyard.

First on the left is the Prayer Hall, which was not intended as a mausoleum but nevertheless holds numerous graves, mainly of Alaouite princes from the 18th century. Their resting places are marked by what look like marble offcuts from a mason's yard. Next to it is the Hall of Twelve Columns, a far more ornate affair with three central tombs surrounded by a dozen marble pillars. The tomb in the middle is that of Ahmed El-Mansour, flanked by those of his son and grandson. A third, stand-alone pavilion has ornate Andalucian-style entrance portals.

Eating & drinking

Kosybar

NEW *47 place des Ferblantiers (024 38 03 24).* **Open** meals noon-2.30pm, 7.30pm-11pm; drinks only 2.30pm-7.30pm Tue-Sun. Alcohol served. **$$**. **Moroccan/Sushi. Map** p84 C1 ❹
The decor is funky Moroccan, and there are tables on the ground and first floors as well as the roof. The place belongs to the son of the owner of some of Morocco's best wine estates, so it won't come as a surprise to learn that the list here includes a number of rarities and the cellar has quite a few others that are not listed. The menu features

Staff of life

Wandering around the Medina, you may catch a whiff of woodsmoke and baking bread. Locate the source – kids with trays of dough or fresh loaves on their heads offer another clue – and you'll encounter one of the institutions found in every traditional quarter: a communal bread oven.

Bread is eaten with every Moroccan meal. How else do you mop up a chicken tagine without those chewy, soft-crusted wedges, both accompaniment and utensil? Its price is controlled by the state, and has been a source of strife in the past, responsible for riots in the 1980s and bakers' strikes in the '90s. The standard, small, round loaves are called khubz, cost 1dh each to buy ready-made and are on sale everywhere.

But lots of people still make their own bread, and most poor families don't have their own ovens. They make the dough at home – white flour, sometimes mixed with barley or semolina – and take it to the neighbourhood oven, where it joins dozens of similar loaves to be

baked for a pittance. Families mark their dough with a special stamp, so there's no confusion about whose loaves are whose, and might also bring along a tagine or bastilla to cook too.

Morocco's collision with French culture means bread doesn't stop with the traditional khubz. You can also find croissants and pain au chocolat, crusty baguettes and pain de campagne – especially in Guéliz, where there are also some excellent French-style pâtisseries. Places like Table du Marché (p123) or Adamo (p100) offer fine cakes and delicate quiches – just one of which, at 15dh-30dh, would wipe out a family's bread-baking budget for a month.

But there are also Moroccan pâtisseries, where a cornucopia of small, spiced biscuits and sweetmeats, mostly based on almonds, are piled high and sold by the kilo. A box of these, excellent with mint tea, is a fitting gift if someone invites you to their home. The best place to buy them is Pâtisserie Al Jawda (p114).

MARRAKECH BY AREA

a number of appealing fish and meat dishes, and there is also a skilled sushi chef, who produced an fine selection of very fresh sushi and sashimi on a recent visit. At weekends a piano player accompanied by a drummer create a great atmosphere. The other entertainment is watching the storks nesting in the ruins of the Badi Palace opposite.

Tatchibana

NEW *38 Derb Bab Ksiba (024 38 71 71/www.tatchibana.com).* **Open** 7.30-10.30pm Tue; noon-2.30pm, 7.30-10.30pm Wed-Sun. Alcohol served. **$$**. No credit cards. **Japanese**. **Map** p84 A5 ❺

The German owner has worked hard to make this old Kasbah house look Japanese – to the point where it can be disorientating to walk into its comfortable, clean-lined interior, all latticed screens and simple wood surfaces. Its Moroccan aspects reveal themselves on closer inspection – lampshades that would be paper in Tokyo are here made of camel-skin. The food is similar: Japanese ideas with local ingredients. It's all tasty and well prepared, even if it bears only a vague resemblance to the Japanese food you'll have eaten elsewhere. The tempura served with lemon, salt and green tea powder is particularly good, and the kiwi

sorbet memorable. There are three menus, one vegetarian. Take a taxi to Bab Ksiba, walk through the gate, and Tatchibana is on the right.

Shopping

Centre Artisanal

7 Derb Baissi Kasbah, off rue de Kasbah (024 38 18 53). **Open** 8.30am-8pm daily. **Map** p84 A3 ❻

Don't let the humble entrance fool you – this is the closest thing to a department store in Marrakech, albeit one selling nothing but handicrafts. It's the ultimate souvenir store, with everything from trad clothing (*babouches*, *djellabas*, kaftans) to jewellery, and home furnishings to carpets. Prices are fixed at slightly above what you would pay in the souk, but this at least does away with tiresome haggling. The stalker-like behaviour and rudeness of the sales assistants can irritate.

Arts & leisure

Bains de Marrakech

Riad Mehdi, 2 Derb Sedra, Bab Agnaou (024 38 14 28/www.lesbains demarrakech.com). **Open** 9am-1pm, 3-8pm daily. **Rates** treatments from 200dh-400dh; day packages up to 1600dh. **Map** p84 A2 ❼

Jewish cemetery p93

Sultana

Attached to the Riad Mehdi, just inside the Bab Agnaou, is this extensive spa complex occupying several rooms and a courtyard of an old Medina house. An array of treatments include all manner of baths and body wraps – with essential oils, algae, refreshing mint and orange blossom milk – as well as various massages. It's one of the only places in town that does a shiatsu massage.

Light Gallery

NEW 2 Derb Chtouka, Kasbah (072 61 42 10/light.marrakech@gmail.com). **Open** 11am-7pm Tue-Sun. No credit cards. **Map** p84 B5 ❽

The newest arrival on the Marrakech scene is an internationally oriented contemporary art gallery in the Kasbah, just down the derb from Les Jardins de la Medina. Founded by Marcelle Danan, Julie Caignault and Nicolas Carré, it kicked off in early 2007 with photographs by Gilles Coulon, then moved on to drawings by Swiss painter Mathias Schauwecker. It's a big, bright, modern space. A few clothes are also sold, along with a few small photos from

the likes of Robert Mapplethorpe, Helmut Newton and Martin Parr.

Sultana

Rue de la Kasbah, Kasbah (024 38 80 08/www.lasultana marrakech.com). **Open** 10am-8pm daily. **Rates** treatments from 275dh; day packages from 1,100dh. **Map** p84 A2 ❾

The five-star Sultana hotel has a lovely little spa complex with an intimate, grotto-like feel. We particularly like the free Jacuzzi that comes with all treatments. Hammam treatments come with a special aromatic body massage; body wraps with argan oil also feature.

The Mellah

Hugging the eastern walls of the Badii Palace are the narrow gridded alleys of the Mellah, the old Jewish quarter. The name translates roughly as 'Place of Salt', a reference either to the Jews' historic monopoly on the trade in mineral salts from the Atlas Mountains, or to their landing the job of salting the heads of decapitees before they were hoisted on spikes. Although the number of Jews in Marrakech is now negligible (around 120 still live in the Mellah), evidence of Jewish heritage is abundant to anyone who knows where to look. Several houses in the neighbourhood have external balconies, which was peculiar to Morocco's Jewish population. Some have Hebrew letters on the metal grills above the doors and there's even an occasional Star of David.

Across the road from the Rose Garden, a green-painted arch leads through into the **Bab Es Salam Market**, also known to locals as the Jewish market. Following this south and east, past stalls of gaudy beaded necklaces (made in Hong Kong), bright pyramids of spices (the tallest of them are actually clever cardboard fakes), and windows of the lurid sweets known as Pâte Levy, leads deep into the Mellah. The streets here are some of the narrowest in the Medina and in places crude scaffolding keeps the houses from collapsing.

At the heart of the quarter is a small square, **place Souweka**, now disfigured by a badly sited concrete building. At No.36 along the street that runs north just beyond the square is one of the Medina's three last working synagogues (once there were 29). It occupies a large hall off the open courtyard of a well-maintained community centre. Knock, and someone from the Muslim family that looks after the place will let you in to have a look around. The ageing congregation gathers for prayer every morning.

On the very eastern edge of the Mellah is the extensive Miâara **Jewish cemetery**; the sheer number of modestly marked graves

(tens of thousands – no one knows exactly how many are buried here) is probably the best remaining testament to the one-time importance of Jewish life in Marrakech. Scattered among them are a few larger mausoleums erected for revered rabbis.

Sights & museums

Bahia Palace

Riad Zitoun El-Jedid (024 38 92 21). **Open** 8.45-11.45am, 2.45-5.45pm Mon-Thur, Sat, Sun; 8.45-11.30am, 3-5.45pm Fri. **Admission** 10dh; 5dh children. **Map** p82 C4 ⑩

On the northern edge of the Mellah is the Bahia Palace. If you've read Gavin Maxwell's *Lords of the Atlas* this place will mean much more to you but even if you haven't, its shady courtyards and blue mosaic walls make a pleasant break from the hot bustling streets outside. The palace was built principally by Bou Ahmed, a powerful vizier to the royal court in the 1890s and a man of 'no particular intelligence, but of indomitable will, and cruel' (*Morocco That Was*, Walter Harris; 1921). Entered via a long garden corridor, it's a delightful collection of paved courtyards, arcades, pavilions and reception halls with vaulted ceilings. The walls are decorated in traditional Moroccan *zelije* tiling, with sculpted stucco and carved cedarwood doors. The fireplace on your left as you enter is quite impressive too. The palace includes extensive quarters that housed Bou Ahmed's four wives and twenty-four concubines. On Bou Ahmed's death – he was probably poisoned by the sultan's mother, along with his two brothers – the palace was completely looted by Sultan Abdel-Aziz. Caravans of donkeys bearing furniture, carpets and crates made their way from the Bahia to the Royal Palace. Between then and now it served as the living quarters of the French *résident généraux* (Edith Wharton stayed here at this time, described in her *In Morocco*; 1927) and it's still used by the current royal family occasionally.

Eating & drinking

Le Tanjia

NEW *14 Derb J'did (024 38 38 36/ www.letanija. com).* **Open** 10am-1am daily. Alcohol served. **$$$.**
Moroccan. Map p82 B5 ⑪

This new Moroccan à la carte venture by the owners of the successful Marrakchi occupies a house on the edge of the Mellah, with a comfortable bar on the ground floor lit by candles and chandeliers, and a variety of dining spaces on the balconies and terraces above. It's named after a local speciality (a *tanjia*, like a tagine, is a kind of cooking pot) and there are both chicken and beef *tanjias* on the menu, but the real gastronomic selling-point is the *mechoui* (360dh for two), a lamb barbecue dish that in most places has to be ordered a day in advance, but here can be had on the spot. There's a light international menu at lunch, tea and shisha on the terrace in the afternoon, and belly dancers and musicians every night.

Shopping

Dinanderie

6-46 Fundouk My Mamoun (024 38 49 09). **Open** 8am-8pm Mon-Sat.
Map p82 B5/p84 C1 ⑫

Moulay Youssef is one of the country's handful of elite artisans. If you need something extravagant wrought from metal – and you have the money – then Moulay is your man. The bulk of his work is made to order, but next to his workspace is a crowded gallery of smaller pieces. A little difficult to find, the Dinanderie atelier fills an alley immediately west of the small rose garden across from the place des Ferblantiers.

Elsewhere

Sights & museums

Dar Si Said Museum

Riad Zitoun El-Jedid (024 38 95 64). **Open** 9am-12.15pm, 3-6.15pm Mon, Wed-Sun. **Admission** 20dh.
Map p82 C3 ⑬

The Dar Si Said Museum is the former home of the brother of Bou Ahmed, builder of the Bahia Palace. Now open to the public, it is home to a large collection of crafts and woodwork. Among the kitchen implements, musical instruments and weapons are numerous beautiful examples of carved cedar, rescued from the city's lost dwellings – among them, polychromic painted doors, window shutters and fragments of ceilings. There's also one room devoted to 'rural' woodwork that includes some primitively worked and painted Berber doors. Such items are very much in vogue with collectors these days and change hands for vast amounts of cash. The exhibits here are captioned in French only.

Maison Tiskiwin

8 Derb El-Bahia, off Riad Zitoun El-Jedid (024 38 91 92). **Open** 9.30am-12.30pm, 3.30-5.30pm daily. **Admission** 15dh; 10dh reductions.
Map p82 C4 ⑭

This private house owned by veteran Dutch anthropologist Bert Flint contains his fascinating collection of crafts and decorative arts from southern Morocco and the Sahara. The exhibition is designed to highlight Morocco's cultural connection to sub-Saharan Africa and is organised geographically, taking you on a journey across the Sahara, as if you were following an old desert trade route from Marrakech to Timbuktu. Exhibits include masks from as far afield as Mali, and an entire Berber tent made of camel hair.

Shopping

Cordonnerie Errafia

Rue Riad Zitoun El Jedid (mobile 062 77 83 47). **Open** 9am-1pm, 3-9pm daily. No credit cards.
Map p82 B3 ⑮

In a little workshop opposite the Préfecture de la Medina, artisan Ahmed cobbles together classic loafers made out of raffia for gents, with more extravagantly coloured and cut stylings for women. Given three or four days, he can also make to order.

Guide to the guides

Marrakech can be a bewildering place when you first arrive. The crowded alleys of the Medina defy one's sense of direction, little is signposted, maps are incomplete, sights are buried in obscure corners, and everyday things just don't always work the same way they do in Europe or the US.

Looking to get their bearings, make the most of a short visit, explore a specialised interest, or simply have some company on a first walk around town, many will consider hiring a guide. For any of those reasons, it can be a good idea.

You don't really need a guide, though. Sure, you'll get lost – but that's half the fun, and most Marrakchis will happily set you back on track. Beware the 'faux guides', however – locals who pester to show you around. Most will just hang around uselessly, or steer you straight to a shop owned by a relative.

Official guides have a licence from the Ministry of Tourism, and wear a laminate with picture ID when on duty. They have to be born and bred in Marrakech, and pass tests in languages and local knowledge. This doesn't mean that everything they tell you is true. And many aren't much different from their unlicensed counterparts when it comes to guiding you to businesses where they'll get a kickback. (If shopping is your main objective, you're better off with a personal shopper; see box p75). But some are very good, they all know their way around, and you know you won't get hassled on the way.

An official guide costs 200dh for a half day. There's no centralised number, but any hotel can arrange one, or you can call one of the numbers on page 11. Sit down first and discuss what you want to do. The more specific you can be, the less likely they are to slip into the kind of lazy routine that is their trade's most common failing. So ask questions, and when it comes to carpet shops, just say no.

Galerie Rê p117

Guéliz

North-west of the old city walls is the nouvelle ville or 'new city', a French colonial creation of the 1930s, which goes by the name of **Guéliz** (pronounced 'gileez'). Old city and new are connected by the broad, tree-lined avenue Mohammed V (pronounced 'M'hammed Sanc'). Named for the king who presided over Morocco's independence, it's the main street of Guéliz. Few visitors bother with this part of town but middle-class Marrakchis and expats favour it for its car-friendly streets, modern apartment blocks and decent restaurants and shops, plus most of what passes for nightlife.

Home to some interesting modernist buildings and known for its 1930s elegance, Guéliz has more recently been marred by new concrete blocks, tourist coaches and a McDonald's. Still, ladies who lunch promenade their poodles on quiet streets lined with orange trees, (fairly) respectable gents grab a beer at the famous Café Atlas, and local youths rev up their Vespas on the street corners. Guéliz is where you find restaurants with airs and graces, pizza and pasta joints, and seedy bars with girls who try to catch visitors' eyes.

The rise of the riad hotel in the 1990s made the Medina the place to stay, and with an increasing number of decent restaurants there too, Guéliz has been pushed off the tourist map. But while the area is devoid of big sights, it does have a pleasant, unhurried atmosphere. This is the part of town where you can go to an art gallery, shop at fixed prices, or find a liquor store. It's a good break when everything has been getting just a little bit too Moroccan.

Things weren't always this way. Back in the 1970s it was the Medina that was run down and few visitors ventured into the alleys away from the Jemaa El Fna. Foreigners would hang out in Guéliz, with its broad avenues, European-style buildings, old-fashioned hotels and continental bistros. The big hangout was the rooftop bar of the Café Renaissance (now closed). The jetset dropped in on the Villa Taylor, while William Burroughs and Brion Gysin invoked demons in the Hotel Toulousain (still standing, just behind the site of the former Marché Central).

Central Guéliz

The focal point of Guéliz used to be the Marché Central on avenue Mohammed V, and it was here that the expats and middle-class Marrakchis gathered for groceries, booze, flowers and gossip. However in a mystifying piece of town planning, it was demolished in 2005. It has been replaced by a much more sterile affair just behind the new buildings on nearby place du 16 Novembre.

At the junction of avenue Mohammed V and rue de la Liberté is an elaborate colonial building with pavement arcades, art deco lines and Moorish flourishes. It dates to 1918 and is just about the oldest surviving building in Guéliz. This was the address (30 rue de la Liberté) of the city's first tourist office. A fading gallery of ancient hand-painted scenes of Morocco decorates the hallway.

The eastern stretch of rue de la Liberté is the local maid market, busy with poorly dressed women hanging around on the chance of some cleaning work. At the western end of the street, beyond the **Kechmara** bar and where it meets rue de Yougoslavie, is a forgotten bit of Marrakech history: a narrow alley planted with mulberry trees and crammed with single-storey dwellings daubed in many colours (it may be the only non-pink street in Marrakech). This is the old Spanish quarter, a reminder of the city's once significant Hispanic population.

Bright lights, little city

Towards the northern end of Mohammed V is place Abdel Moumen, which is about as close as this town gets to Piccadilly Circus. It's the hub of an area of cafés, bars, restaurants and nightclubs; it's even got neon. At **Café les Négociants** grouchy uniformed waiters generate an air of efficiency while being brusquely indifferent to the customers. It's pleasing to find that almost 100 years on, the ground rules laid by the French are still so lovingly adhered to. Across the intersection, the **Café Atlas** is the place for beer with added entertainments. North of the Atlas is the boarded-up building that was formerly the infamous Café Renaissance. From place Abdel-Moumen, it's a 20-minute walk to the delightful **Majorelle Gardens**.

In the beginning...

The 'new city' came into being shortly after December 1913 – the arrival date of Henri Prost, the young city planner imported to assist in the schemes of French résident général Marshal Lyautey. One of Prost's early sketches shows how he took the minaret of the Koutoubia as his focal point and from it extended two lines: one north-west to the Guéliz hills; the other south-west to the pavilion of the Menara Gardens. In the pie slice between these lines (which have since become **avenue Mohammed V** and **avenue de la Menara**) is the original nucleus of the new European city.

Guéliz

- ❶ Sights & museums
- ❶ Eating & drinking
- ❶ Shopping
- ❶ Nightlife
- ❶ Arts & leisure
- ❶ Hotels

To Semlalia &
Route de Casablanca

A B C

1

2 Cemetery

RUE ABDELOUAHAB DERRAQ

3 Polyclinique
du Sud

RUE IBN AICHA

BOULEVARD

Cinema
Colisée CTM
Office PLACE
ABDEL
MOUMEN

AVENUE MOHAMMED

BD MOHAMMED ZERKTOUNI

AVENUE

MOHAMMED V

RUE DE LA LIBERTE

RUE TAREK IBN ZIAD

ABDELKARIM

EL KHATTABI

BOULEVARD EL

AVENUE MOHAMMED EL BKAL

MANSOUR EDDAHBI

BOULEVARD MOULAY RACHID

RUE DE MAURITANIE

RUE CADI AYAD

AVENUE HASSAN II

Théâtre Royal &
Opera House

Train Station

Sadly, instead of developing as the grand *rondpoint* of Prost's vision, **place du 16 Novembre**, the hole in the middle of Guéliz's spider-web street pattern, has been disfigured by some plug-ugly structures, including a totalitarian central post office and two mammoth apartment blocks. Until the 1970s there were two lines of parking down the centre of the avenue, but the increase in traffic has done away with them. Shame, because standing in the middle of Mohammed V presents one of the city's best views: in one direction the Koutoubia minaret, sometimes with snowy Atlas mountains in the background; in the other a high rocky outcrop topped by the pink wall of a former French Foreign Legion fortress.

Sights & museums

Majorelle Gardens
Avenue Yacoub El-Mansour (no phone). **Open** 8am-5.30pm daily. **Admission** 30dh. *Museum of Islamic Art* 15dh. **Map** p99 E2 ❶
Now privately owned by Yves Saint Laurent – but open to the public – the gardens were created in the 1930s by two generations of French artists, Jacques and Louis Majorelle. Although small in scale and out on the edge of the New City, the glamour of the YSL connection ensures that the gardens are usually packed well beyond comfort by coachloads of visitors. The juxtaposition of colours is striking; plants sing against a backdrop of the famous Majorelle blue, offset with soft yellows and terracottas. Bamboo groves rustle in the soft breeze and great palms tower over all, sheltering huge ancient cacti. Rills lead into pools floating with water lilies and flashing with golden carp, terrapins paddle languidly and frogs croak. Great pots overflow with succulents and birds sing. For the botanically curious, everything is clearly labelled.

Jacques Majorelle's former studio has been turned into a fine little Museum of Islamic Art, recently renovated and reorganised to display a collection of traditional jewellery, fine embroidery, illuminated manuscripts, carved wooden doors and Majorelle lithographs of the High Atlas. Air-conditioned and dimly lit, the museum is a welcome refuge from the intensity of light and colour outside; exhibits have English labelling. Beside the museum is a small boutique selling books, T-shirts, leather goods, *babouches*, pottery, cushions…

To get to the garden walk from central Guéliz (it's about two kilometres, or just over a mile, east along boulevard Mohammed Zerktouni) or take a *petit taxi*. Note that picnics, children and dogs are not allowed; it's a shame that the prohibitions don't extend to coach parties.

Eating & drinking

Adamo
44 rue Tarik Idn Ziad (024 43 9419/ www.traiteur-adamo.com). **Open** 7.30am-1pm, 4-9pm Mon-Sat. **$$$**. **Café**. **Map** p98 C4 ❷
This quiet, air-conditioned *salon de thé* serves wonderful French patisserie items to consume on the premises with coffee or tea, and there are good baguettes to take away. Their small quiches are particularly mouth-watering and the ice-cream is excellent.

Al Fassia
Résidence Tayeb, 55 boulevard Zerktouni (024 43 40 60/alfassia@ menara.ma). **Open** noon-2.30pm, 7.30-11pm daily. Alcohol served. **$$$**. **Moroccan**. **Map** p98 C4 ❸
One of the few posh Moroccan restaurants in town that allows diners to order à la carte, Al Fassia is also unique in being run by a women's co-operative – the chefs, waiting staff and management are all female. It recently moved from avenue Mohammed V into this quieter location, where excellent versions of Moroccan standards are

Amandine p102

Grand Café de la Poste p105

served. It's a classy place. We'd come here for the Moroccan salad alone, but there are also ten tagines, five couscous dishes and a couple of pastillas, all in very un-ladylike portions. Reservations are recommended.

Amandine

177 rue Mohammed El-Bekal (024 44 96 12). **Open** 6am-11pm daily. **$$.** No credit cards. **Pâtisserie/ Café.** Map p98 B4 ④

Amandine comes in two parts: there's the smart pâtisserie with a long glass display cabinet layered with delicious continental-style cakes and pastries and a few chairs and tables in front; or next door there's the proper café space with a high bar counter, fewer cakes and far more atmosphere. Both spaces are air-conditioned but we prefer the café, where efficient and friendly table service provides the usual coffees and (mint) teas, plus a mix of tasty hot savouries and goodies such as buttery croissants and French toast.

Bar L'Escale

Rue de Mauritanie (024 43 34 47). **Open** 11am-10.30pm daily. **$$.** No credit cards. **Bar.** Map p98 C4 ⑥

The menu claims that L'Escale opened in 1927; the window says it was '47. Either way, most of the customers look as if they've been settled in place since opening night, nursing bottles of Flag Spéciale, half an eye on the big, boxy wall-mounted TV, while engaging in sporadic chat with the red-jacketed, grey-haired old gent who patrols the big, bare paddock behind the high bar counter. Though all male – or perhaps because it is all male – Bar L'Escale is a totally non-threatening environment (although hygiene freaks might have a tough time of it). Beers can be taken out to the pavement tables and there's food in the form of grilled meats.

Boule de Neige

Corner of rue de Yougoslavie, off place Abdel-Moumen (024 44 60 44). **Open** 5am-11pm daily. **$$.** No credit cards. **Café.** Map p98 B3 ⑦

Don't come particularly for the coffee or food, but do come for a look. The large room is a fetching mint green and pink, with tables laid out canteen style. There's a food counter at one end with things shiny, gelatinous and best left well alone. There's also a breakfast menu but it baffles the staff if you order from it. Instead, nip next door to the Pâtisserie Hilton and bring something back – this is permitted, even encouraged. Then settle in and watch the sitcom-like spectacle of staff chasing cats chasing other cats dodging men eyeing single girls… Huge fun.

Café Atlas

Place Abdel-Moumen, avenue Mohammed V (024 44 88 88). **Open** 8am-10pm daily. **$$**. **Café**. Map p98 B4 ⑧

You used to be able to take your beer at one of the outside tables but this is no longer the case. Its role as a rendezvous for foreign gents and local gigolos does Café Atlas few favours, but obviously uninterested parties are left alone. A beer costs 13dh-20dh depending on the mood of the waiter, and patrons are also offered the chance to purchase anything from peanuts to lotto cards to carpets by itinerant salesmen. Leaving your cigs in view on the table invites a steady stream of supplicants, including those boys in their snug white trousers.

Café du Livre

44 rue Tarek Ibn Ziad (024 43 21 49). **Open** 9.30am-9pm Mon-Sat. Alcohol served. **$$$**. **Café**. Map p98 C4 ⑨

So quickly did Sandra Zwollo's bookshop café become a favourite hangout for anglophone expats, it's hard to believe that nothing like it existed before. It's a comfortable first-floor space (accessed from the courtyard of the Hotel Toulousain) with a (mostly second-hand) bookshop (p111) at one end and café tables at the other. Breakfast is served until 11.30am, high tea from 4pm to 6pm, and an all-day

African chic

Have a snack at Le Guepard, inspect the new lounge in Grand Café de la Poste (p105), drink a beer in Afric'n Chic (p200). A fad is sweeping the town, a rage for 'Africa' reflected in zebra-skin upholstery, ebony masks, 'colonial' chairs, engravings of gorillas and leopards. Furniture from Laurence Corsin's African Lodge (p111) can be found in riads all over the Medina, and at Essaouira's L'Heure Bleue (p169) you can stay in a colonially themed suite and sip a pink gin in a 'clubroom' decked with mounted animal heads.

The *gnawa* have long represented the black African aesthetic in Moroccan culture, and perhaps the increasing popularity of their music is part of the phenomenon. But mostly the fad is to do with decor. The imagery chiefly derives from big-game hunting. This isn't alien to Morocco, but there isn't much game left. Hunters shot the last Atlas bear in the 1870s, the last Barbary lion in 1922, and are now busy polishing off the few remaining gazelles.

And that doesn't explain the zebra skin, nor the ebony masks. In part, what's being evoked is colonialism, a fantasy of when white men were waited on hand and foot. A reflection of the new tourist economy perhaps?

But, looked at in reverse, it's perhaps also a way of asserting a non-European identity that avoids the over-used clichés of Moroccan traditionalism and ducks the question of Islam while still remaining nicely exotic. This is Africa. Get used to it.

Kechmara

menu includes a handful of dishes devised by celebrity chef and erstwhile Marrakech resident, Richard Neat. Popular attractions include the excellent traditional hamburgers and the lemoniest lemon tart this side of the Mediterranean.

Café les Négociants

Place Abdel-Moumen, avenue Mohammed V (024 43 57 82). **Open** 6am-11pm daily. **$$**. No credit cards. **Café**. Map p98 B4 ⑩

Far classier than the endearingly sleazy Café Atlas, which it faces across the road, Les Négociants is a Parisian boulevard-style café with acres of rattan seating and round glass-topped tables crowded under a green-and-white striped pavement awning. We like it for breakfast: café au lait, orange juice and croissants, plus the papers from the international newsagent across the road.

Casanova

NEW *221 avenue Yacoub El-Mansour (024 42 37 35/ristorantecasanova @menara.ma).* **Open** noon-3pm, 8-11pm daily. Alcohol served. **$$$**. **Italian**. Map p99 D3 ⑪

Housed in one of the splendid modernist villas that are scattered around Guéliz, this Venetian-run restaurant (though, surprisingly, with a Moroccan chef) serves up Italian food to international standards. The surroundings are unpretentious and comfortable, though cultural overload is sometimes reached with both televisions showing Serie A football and a pianist knocking out (by Marrakech standards) relatively uncheesy interpretations of 'Feelings' and 'Windmills of Your Mind'. The menu includes home-made pasta and familiar grill standards as well as specials such as pappardelle with wild boar and some salads. There's also a good wine list and a nice choice of digestifs.

Catanzaro

42 rue Tarek Ibn Ziad (024 43 37 31). **Open** noon-2.30pm, 7.30-11pm Mon-Sat. Alcohol served. **$$**. **Italian**. Map p98 C4 ⑫

It's a simple rustic-style neighbourhood French-run Italian (red-checked tablecloths, faux-woodbeam ceiling) with a homely air and reliable cooking, but Catanzaro is one of the most popular eateries in town. White-hatted chefs work an open kitchen with a big wood-fired oven turning out excellent pizzas. Alternatives include various grills and steaks, with a selection of salads and a good choice of wine by the bottle or half-bottle. The dessert list includes a tip-top crème brûlée. Customers all seem to be regulars – most are greeted by name as they arrive – and, although the place seats 60 or more, reservations are recommended in the evenings. It's easy to find: one street back from avenue Mohammed V, behind the site of the old Marché Central.

Chesterfield Pub

Hotel Nassim, 1st floor, 115 avenue Mohammed V (024 44 64 01).
Open 9am-1am daily. **$$$. Bar.**
Map p98 C4 🚇

Also known as the 'Bar Anglais', though there's nothing particularly English about this little first-floor hotel bar. A tiny lounge is cast in an eerie glow by a luminously underlit pool on the other side of a glass wall, while a larger back bar is an equally twilit gents' hangout. In between is a polished mahogany counter area dispensing bottled and draught beers, spirits and cocktails at reasonable cost. Best of all is the open-air, pool-side patio – a popular Friday night venue for expats on the razz.

Grand Café de la Poste

🆕 *Corner boulevard Mansour Eddahbi and avenue Imam Malik (024 43 3038/www.grandcafedela poste.com).* **Open** 8am-1am daily.
$$$. European. Map p98 C5 🚇

Just behind the main post office on Place Novembre 16, one of the oldest buildings in Guéliz (a hotel when it opened surrounded by trees) is now a sophisticated brasserie serving breakfast, lunch and dinner. The charm of the terrace, cooled by misters in summer, isn't wrecked by traffic noise, and there's a generous interior with a mezzanine 'colonial' lounge. The steaks are enormous, the calamari and artichoke starter is worthy of attention, and the oysters are fantastic when they have them. Great service too.

Jacaranda

32 boulevard Mohammed Zerktouni (024 44 72 15/www.lejacaranda.ma).
Open noon-3pm, 6.30-11pm daily.
Alcohol served. **$$$. French.**
Map p98 B4 🚇

With large picture windows looking on to the traffic tango of place Abdel-Moumen, Jacaranda is the place for an urban dining experience. Inside it's hardly less busy: a crush of furniture, chintzy table settings and assorted paintings spill down from the mezzanine gallery cluttering all available wall space. Despite the frenzy, it has a friendly and comfortable atmosphere. The kitchen specialises in *cuisine française* with plenty of *viande* and *poisson*, but it's hardly haute cuisine and as such is a bit overpriced. However, decent value is offered by a lunchtime two-course *menu rapide* at 85dh or the *menu tourisme*, three courses for 105dh. In the evenings there's a *menu du marché* for 180dh. In addition to beer and wine, the tiny bar counter also stretches to aperitifs and a small selection of cocktails.

Kechmara

3 rue de la Liberté (024 42 25 32).
Open 7am-midnight Mon-Sat.
Alcohol served. **$$. European.**
Map p98 C4 🚇

Its name a reversal of 'Mara-kech', this is a hip young café-bar-restaurant. The stylish decor is all white and clean-lined with chrome fittings and white moulded plastic chairs. Lunch and dinner are a *prix fixe* continental menu; choice is a little limited (soup, salads, meat in sauces, grills and desserts) but the food is generally of a high standard and well presented. Unfortunately there is absolutely nothing here for vegetarians, however. The drinks menu includes *bière pression* at a reasonable 25dh and a good line-up of cocktails to be drunk at the bar counter or, better still, up on the fine first-floor terrace – which makes Kechmara one of the few places in Marrakech where you can legitimately booze al fresco.

GRAND CAFÉ RESTAURANT DE LA POSTE
Angle boulevard El Mansour Eddahbi et avenue Iman Malik
Guéliz - Marrakech
Tél. : 00 212 (0) 24 43 30 38
Resa@grandcafedelaposte.com
www.grandcafedelaposte.com

Lolo Quoi

Lolo Quoi

NEW 82 avenue Hassan II (072 56
98 64). **Open** 7.30pm-midnight daily.
$$$. **Italian**. Map p98 C5 ⑰
Reopened in the same old location after
an unexplained two-year absence, this
is a relaxed and funky Italian-interna-
tional restaurant twinned with the own-
ers' other establishment in Lyon. The
vibe is fashionably dark and un-
parochial, with a spectacular manager-
ess, sociable bar and passable pasta.
Try the artichoke carpaccio.

Le Lounge

24 rue Yougoslavie (024 43 37 03).
Open 9pm-1am Mon-Sat; 6pm-1am
Sun. $$. **Bar**. Map p98 B3 ⑱
Just north of place Abdel-Moumen on a
short stretch of pedestrianised street, Le
Lounge is a small bar-restaurant. While
a simple Moroccan and international
menu (main courses 70dh-130dh) is
served downstairs, beers and cocktails
are imbibed on the big sofas and throne-
like armchairs of an orange-accented
mezzanine. Naturally, the music is
lounge-like – a selection of ironically
tasteful cover versions on our last visit.
The outdoor terrace where you were
once allowed to drink seems to have
been banished, but may yet reappear.

Montecristo

20 rue Ibn Aicha (024 43 90 31).
Open 8pm-2am daily. $$$$. **Bar**.
Map p98 B3 ⑲
On the ground floor is the Bar African,
a world music venue, where French
musicians indulge in interminable
twiddly solos. Upstairs is where a
smart set of foxy chiquitas and macho
hombres slink and strut to samba and
salsa. Off to the side of the dancefloor
is a small area of non-ergonomic seating, made all the more uncomfortable
by the inevitable crush of bodies. For
elbow room and aural respite head up
to the cushion-strewn rooftop terrace,
which is peaceful and pleasant until
the drinks menu arrives and you note
that a small bottled beer goes for a
staggering 70dh (almost five of your
English pounds).

El-Moualamid Bar

Hotel El-Moualamid, 6th floor,
avenue Mohammed V (024 44 88 55).
Open 5pm-2am daily. $. No credit
cards. **Bar**. Map p98 B3 ⑳
It has all the charm of a Mongolian bus
station waiting room – with added
drunkenness – but the beer is cheap
and there are great views from the
outdoor terrace (six floors up) south

down Mohammed V to the Koutoubia minaret. A resident band with a frightening way with a synth brings the elderly boozy males to their unsteady feet, while the hard-faced local 'ladies' patiently bide their time. On the right night it could pass for fun. To ascend to these tawdry heights, enter the uninviting corner bar just north of place Abdel-Moumen and take the lift.

Musica Bar

Boulevard Mohammed Zerktouni (no phone). **Open** 7pm-midnight daily. **$.** No credit cards. **Bar**. Map p98 C3 ㉑

Its gaping black hole of an entrance, signed with a desultory scrawl of neon, looks as if it belongs on the Reeperbahn. But the Musica Bar isn't as classy as that. Enter – if you dare – into a huge tiled hall of swimming pool acoustics that nightly reverberates to the mad cacophony of a five- or six-piece mini Arab orchestra. Fuelled by cheap bottled beer, punters are too far gone to dance but they bang their hands on the tabletops and wail along with the chorus. Downstairs is a nightclub of sorts that kicks off as the bar closes, but we're not that brave.

Rôtisserie de la Paix

68 rue de Yougoslavie (024 43 31 18). **Open** noon-3pm, 6.30-11pm daily. Alcohol served. **$$$.** **European**. Map 98 C5 ㉒

Flaming for decades, the 'peaceful rôtisserie' is a large garden restaurant with seating among palms and bushy vegetation. Simple and unpretentious, it's utterly lovely whether lunching under blue skies (shaded by red umbrellas) or dining after sundown when the trees twinkle with fairy lights. (In winter, dining is inside by a crackling log fire.) Most of the menu comes from the charcoal grill (kebabs, lamb chops, chicken and merguez sausage) but there are also delicacies such as quail, and a selection of seafood. We recommend the warm chicken liver salad, listed as a starter but easily a meal in itself.

Salam Bombay

1 avenue Mohammed VI (024 43 70 83). **Open** noon-2.30pm, 7pm-12.30am daily. **Main courses** 80dh-180dh. Alcohol served. **$$$.** **Indian**. Map p98 A3 ㉓

Not only was this Marrakech's first Indian restaurant, it was also the first in Morocco, set up by four guys from Madras who already had a successful Indian restaurant in Toulouse. They've adapted to local sensibilities by going over the top with the design – it's all very big, ornate and pink, and there's a row of painted elephant heads studding the road-side wall. The serving girls wear shimmery *kurtas* and *bindis* dot their foreheads but they're all Moroccan and the biriyani is served in a *tanjia* clay pot. The Rajasthani chefs have been careful to tone down the spicing to the extent that anyone familiar with Indian food as eaten in India (or even the UK) is liable to find their curries a little bland. The wide-ranging menu is heaven for vegetarians, though.

Samovar

133 rue Mohammed El Bekal (no phone). **Open** 7pm-2am daily. **$.** No credit cards. **Bar**. Map p98 B5 ㉔

Possibly the most raucous saloon in town. Two rooms heave with a crush of slurry young men in cheap leather jackets, rambling old soaks and ageing prostitutes. Every table teeters beneath the weight of squadrons of Stork empties. Body contact is frequent, unavoidable and occasionally opportunistic. It's a place where 'too much to drink' is the natural state of being and the underlying threat of violence is periodically realised before being quickly smothered by laconic bar staff. You don't want to go to the toilets. Visit, if you will, and take a walk on the Marrakech wild side, but don't come crying to us afterwards.

La Strada

90 rue Mohammed El Bekal (061 24 20 94). **Open** 7pm-2am daily. **$$.** No credit cards. **Bar**. Map p98 B5 ㉕

The Palmeraie

Nikki Beach Hotel

North-east of the Medina is the **Palmeraie** district, an area defined by a vast oasis of palm trees. While not particularly attractive, its distance from the hoi polloi, low population density, lack of pollution, and lavish new houses have made it a favourite home of the rich – both Moroccans and foreigners.

Legend has it that the Palmeraie was born of the seeds cast away by date-chomping Arab warriors centuries ago. A nice story but it fails to accord due credit to the clever minds that designed an underground irrigation system to carry melted snow all the way from the High Atlas to water the palm oasis of several hundred thousand trees. The ancient *khettra* system now has only historical curiosity value because the water supply is guaranteed by several reservoirs and a network of artesian wells.

It's not what you'd call a pretty oasis: many of the palms are worse for wear and the ground is dry, dusty and lunar-like. Even so, this is probably the most prime real estate in all North Africa. Ever since the 1960s, when King Hassan II first granted permission for it to be sold, Palmeraie land has been the plot of choice for the rich. This is the Beverly Hills of Morocco. Land is available only in parcels of more than one hectare and buildings must not interfere with the palms. Narrow lanes slalom between copses, occasionally squeezing by high walls surrounding the massive grounds of discreet residences.

Other than expensive accommodation, (see box p161) there isn't much to see in the Palmeraie (think ramshackle villages, grazing camels, building sites). You might venture out here for a combination lunch and swim at **Nikki Beach** (a pool/bar in the grounds of the Royal Golf Palace; 024 36 87 27, www.nikkibeach. com). It's also a good area for cycling. The ideal half-day ride is to head east out of town along the main route de Fes and take a left on to the route de Palmeraie (look for signs for the Tikida Gardens hotel), which winds through the oasis to exit north of the city on the Casablanca road. For details of where to hire bikes, see p174.

By day this is a local take on a pizza restaurant, but by night the oven goes cold, the heavy drapes are drawn across the windows and place settings are pushed aside to accommodate steadily growing collections of empty bottles. Upstairs is a small air-conditioned lounge with cushioned seating, which is where the 'ladies' hang out. We feel safer staying down on the ground floor, watched over by a grimacing, bare-chested Anthony Quinn in a large, framed film poster of Fellini's *La Strada*.

Trattoria de Giancarlo

179 rue Mohammed El-Bekal (024 43 26 41/www.latrattoriamarrakech.com). **Open** 7.30-11.30pm daily. Alcohol served. **$$$**. **Italian**. **Map** p98 B5 ●

Just about clinging on to its reputation as Marrakech's finest Italian restaurant, Trattoria de Giancarlo serves good food in enchanting surroundings. The Felliniesque interiors (lush, occasionally lurid and more than a little louche) are designed by local legend Bill Willis and are a delight – in fact, they are alone worth a visit. The best tables are those overhung by oversized greenery out on the tiled garden terrace. The latter is situated beside a large luminous pool. In the evening the place is lit by lanterns and candles to ridiculously romantic effect. While the menu is hardly extensive, it holds plenty of broad appeal (a variety of salads, several vegetarian pastas, and an array of meat and seafood dishes). Service is excellent, verging on obsequious: 'Would sir like his beer with a head or without?' Reservations are recommended.

Shopping

ACR Libraire d'Art

Résidence Tayeb, 55 boulevard Mohammed Zerktouni (024 44 67 92). **Open** 9am-12.30pm, 3-7pm Mon-Sat. **Map** p98 C4 ●

ACR is a French publishing house, notable for its lavish art books. The company is seemingly dedicated to photographing every last mud brick and orange blossom in Marrakech and publishing the results in a series of coffee-table volumes. Get them all here, along with other (non-ACR) titles on the art and architecture of Morocco and the Islamic world, guides, cookery books and art cards. What little English-language stock the shop used to have seems to have disappeared. You'll find some Acr books for sale at the Musée de Marrakech bookshop.

Café du Livre

African Lodge

NEW *1 rue Loubnane (024 43 95 84/laurencecorsin@yahoo.fr).* **Open** 10am-1pm, 3-7.30pm Mon-Sat. **Map** p98 C4 ㉘

'African', as opposed to North African, style is currently the fashionable thing in Marrakech, and unique furniture pieces by designer Laurence Corsin, whose shop this is, have started to appear in many a restaurant and riad. There's a selection of his work downstairs, along with sub-Saharan ornaments and figurines. Much of Corsin's work is in metal; we liked the shelves and tables fashioned out of old bedsprings, like a high-style version of those toys made from old olive oil or sardine cans. A small mezzanine hosts a colourful cornucopia of knick-knacks from around the world, including lacquer-bound Japanese photo albums, Chinese thermos flasks, Lebanese jewellery and an assortment of crockery.

Amazonite

94 boulevard El Mansour Eddahbi (024 44 99 26). **Open** 9.30am-1pm, 3.30-7.30pm Mon-Sat. **Map** p98 C4 ㉙

This is a cramped, three-storey repository of all manner of objets d'art, top quality Berber jewellery, early 20th-century oil paintings (displayed in the basement), a stunning collection of ancient silk carpets, plus miscellaneous ethnic trappings, including old marriage belts. A place for serious buyers in search of rare finds. Ring the doorbell for entry.

Atika

35 rue de la Liberté (024 43 64 09). **Open** 8.30am-12.30pm, 3-7.30pm Mon-Sat. **Map** p98 C4 ㉚

This is where well-heeled residents and enlightened tourists flock for stylish and affordable men's and women's ranges – everything from classic loafers to natural leather sandals and stylish beige canvas mules. Prices start at 300dh and rarely go beyond 750dh. It also carries children's shoes and a small selection of handbags.

There's also a second branch a few hundred metres south at 212 avenue Mohammed V.

Bazaar Atlas

129 boulevard Mohammed V (024 43 27 16). **Open** 9.30am-1pm, 3.30-7.30pm Mon-Sat; 9.30am-1pm Sun. **Map** p98 B4 ㉛

This small but eye-catching boutique in central Guéliz comprises one room lined from floor to ceiling with cabinets full of jewellery: antique, antique-styled, ethnic (Berber and Touareg) and modern. In among it all is a smattering of odd gift items, including ceramics, tiny silver pill boxes and sculpted gazelle-horn and camel-bone ink wells and letter openers. The owner speaks fluent English.

El Badii

54 boulevard Moulay Rachid (024 43 16 93). **Open** 9am-7pm daily. **Map** p98 C5 ㉝

Two floors packed with museum-quality antiques, hand-picked by owners Najat Aboufikr and his wife, featuring a dazzling array of gold and silver jewellery, unusual lamps, carved Berber doors, ornate mirrors and a huge choice of carpets. In pride of place are ancient ceramics from Fes, in traditional yellow and cobalt blue. They display photos of Brad Pitt, Tom Cruise and Hillary Clinton browsing here, but happily the fixed prices and warm welcome are for everyone.

Café du Livre

NEW *44 rue Tarik Ben Ziad (024 43 21 49).* **Open** 9.30am-9pm Mon-Sat. **Map** p98 C4 ㉜

The only English-language bookshop in town has a reasonably good stock of second-hand books and a small selection of new books about Morocco. It also occasionally hosts readings and signings – John Hopkins, a Tangier resident through the 1960s and 1970s, was a recent guest, signing copies of his novel, *All I Wanted was Company*. Bibliophiles should be thankful for the café component of the operation (p103), not only because of the excellent light meal it serves up, but because without it the book business wouldn't survive. A few laptop-toting Moroccan students make the most of the free Wi-Fi internet. The shop's entrance is in the courtyard of the Hotel Toulousain.

Entrepôt Alimentaire

117 avenue Mohammed V (024 43 00 67). **Open** 8am-noon, 3-10pm Mon-Sat; 8am-noon Sun. No credit cards. **Map** p98 C4 ③④

This dusty little place may appear disorganised, but it does have one of the best selections of wine (Moroccan and French) in town. If you can't see what you're looking for, ask.

Galerie Birkemeyer

169 rue Mohammed El Bekal (024 44 69 63). **Open** 8.30am-12.30pm, 3-7.30pm Mon-Sat; 9am-12.30pm Sun. **Map** p98 B4 ③⑤

A long-established haunt for leather goods, from handbags and luggage to shoes, jackets, coats and skirts, with a sportswear section of international designer labels. The sales assistants aren't usually particularly helpful, and founder Ms Birkemeyer no longer has anything to do with the place (she now owns Intensité Nomade), but you still might stumble across a good bargain, such as a beautifully crafted purse for 600dh.

Jeff de Bruges

17 rue de la Liberté (024 43 02 49). **Open** 9am-1pm, 3.30-8pm Mon-Sat. **Map** p98 C4 ③⑦

Not real Belgian chocolates, but still the best chocolates in Marrakech. They make a great gift if you're invited to dinner at a local home (Moroccans are notoriously sweet-toothed), but don't expect to get a share because they'll be hoarded away for later.

Librairie Chatr

23 avenue Mohammed V (024 44 79 97). **Open** 8am-1pm, 3-8pm Mon-Sat. **Map** p98 B3 ③⑧

These days Librairie Chatr is mainly a stationers, the long bar counter perpetually swamped by short-trousered

fiends in search of marker pens and notebooks. However, there is a large back room where a heavy patina of dust fogs the titles of what's mainly Arabic and French stock. A single shelf represents the English-language world, and much of what it contains is heavier on pictures than words.

Marrakech Maille Sarl

69 boulevard El Mansour Eddahbi (024 43 95 85). **Open** 8am-1pm, 3-7pm Mon-Sat. No credit cards. **Map** p98 C4 ③⑨

A well-kept secret among Moroccan royalty and the chic wives of diplomats, this small and unprepossessing boutique contains some very wearable clothes which will also make that all-important transition home to a colder climate. In winter, the owner and designer Khadija Daaraoui stocks lovely woollen shawls and scarves, quality wool and mohair suits and *djellabas* in natural fibres. In summer, expect lightweight cotton T-shirts in all colours (think John Smedley) and cotton and linen skirts, trouser suits and kaftans. Classic.

Mysha & Nito

NEW *Rue Sourya, corner rue Tarik Ibn Ziad (024 42 16 38/www.mysha-nito.com).* **Open** 9am-1pm 3.30-8pm, Mon-Sat. **Map** p98 C4 ④⓪

On the ground floor you'll find womenswear by 12 local designers (11 Moroccan, one Belgian). The focus is kaftans and *djellebas*, reinvented as eveningwear in a variety of fabrics – including chiffon, gingham, simulated leather and imitation snakeskin – and priced anywhere between 1,000dh and 25,000dh. There are also T-shirts, bags, slippers and belts for those on a smaller budget. Downstairs is an assortment of antiques and sculpture.

L'Orientaliste

11 & 15 rue de la Liberté (024 43 40 74). **Open** 9am-12.30pm, 3-7.30pm Mon-Sat; 10am-12.30pm Sun. **Map** p98 C4 ④①

A small street-front boutique and a huge basement space hidden round

Charles Boccara

He's usually described as 'Tunisian-born', some people say he's from Uzbekistan, and when we visit Charles Boccara in his Guéliz office, he tells us, 'I am French, by the way.' Whatever the mystery of his origins, Morocco's most famous architect completed his studies at the École des Beaux Arts in Paris in 1968, and moved to Marrakech shortly afterwards. He has since designed dozens of houses and hotels, such as the Tichka Salam and the Dar Les Cigognes (p142), as well as the still unfinished Théâtre Royal on avenue Mohammed VI (p122).

The man who, along with American interior designer Bill Willis, kicked off the whole modern-ideas-with-Moroccan-materials philosophy that still underpins Marrakech style, first arrived 'to make modern architecture. I try different windows, like this, and like this.' He draws polygons on a sheet of paper. 'Invention is necessary, but I do it without *plaisir*.' After five years of that, he became more interested 'in the plan of the tradition' and the typical contrast between interior and exterior. 'Outside it smells bad, busy, crowded, but inside it is not only a home, but a paradise. This is Marrakech. We are lucky it's not like Malaysia or Abu Dhabi.'

An amiable man, he speaks English with a heavy French accent. While known for launching – with his design of Les Beaux Tours in the Palmeraie – the now-widespread use of *tadelakt* (a kind of polished plaster traditionally used in hammams) as a cheap and versatile material for creating whimsical forms, Boccara is keen to point out how his work is based on classical architecture. He speaks of 'mosaics of patios', compares Moroccan groundplans to those of French palaces, points to a common vocabulary of arcades, domes and arches.

Some of Boccara's ideas, especially the use of *tadelakt* in interiors, have now become so common they are almost cliché. We wonder whether he ever wishes he could put the genie back in the bottle. He's having none of it. 'We are lucky,' he repeats. 'The Medina is lovely again.'

the corner make up L'Orientaliste. The former is stuffed with stacks of inexpensive items – Fès ceramics, filigree metal containers, painted glasses, scented candles and perfume bottles, some filled with essences. The latter is crammed with pricey antique furniture, early 20th-century Moroccan paintings and engravings, and leatherbound notebooks with original watercolours.

Pâtisserie Al Jawda

11 rue de la Liberté (024 43 38 97/ www.al-jawda.com). **Open** 8am-8pm daily. **Map** p98 C4 ㊷

The best Moroccan pâtisserie in town has glass display cases full of plates piled high with small biscuits, bite-sized pastries, tiny macaroons, miniature scones, candied orange slices, chocolates and lots of things made from almonds. It's all priced by the kilo (160dh for pastries, 180dh for chocolates) and they'll box your selection after weighing it. If you want to sit down and sample rather than take away, try their new *salon de thé* around the corner: Al Jawda Plus (84 boulevard Mohammed V, 024 43 46 62).

Pharmacie Centrale

166 avenue Mohammed V, corner of rue de la Liberté (024 43 01 58). **Open** 8.30am-12.30pm, 3.30-7.30pm Mon-Thur; 8.30am-noon, 3.30-7.30pm Fri; 8.30am-1pm, 3.30-7.30pm Sat. **Map** p98 C4 ㊸

The most conveniently central pharmacy in the New City. On the door is a list of the city pharmacies that are on 24-hour duty that particular week.

Place Vendome

141 avenue Mohammed V (024 43 52 63). **Open** 9am-12.30pm, 3.30-7.30pm Mon-Sat. **Map** p98 C4 ㊹

Owner Claude Amzallag is known for his custom-designed buttery leather and suede jackets, and sleek line of handbags and wallets, which come in every colour from forest green to hot pink. The suede shirts for men and stylish luggage are also big hits with the fortysomething crowd.

La Porte d'Orient

6 boulevard El Mansour Eddahbi (024 43 89 67). **Open** 9am-7.30pm Mon-Sat. **Map** p98 B4 ㊺

The most mind-blowing of shopping experiences occurs when a door at the rear of this modest shop is opened to a back room, revealing a space of warehouse-like proportions. The enormous room houses an impressive panoply of Berber jewellery, ancient carved doors of fantastic size and patterning from Fès and Meknès, irridescent lanterns, beautiful glass cases of illuminated manuscripts and gilded lion thrones. The only thing you won't find is too many bargains. English is spoken.

La Savonnerie

NEW *Marché Central, rue Ibn Toummert (068 51 74 79/ram bad5@yahoo.com).* **Open** 9.30am-7pm Mon-Thur, Sat; 9.30am-2pm Fri, Sun. No credit cards. **Map** p99 D5 ㊻

Among the horse butchers and grocers of the new Marché Central, this soap-maker's stall is a fragrant highlight. As well as colourful bars and lozenges of soap, with a variety of scents such as almond, rosemary, orange, musk or green tea, the owner also sells lovely terracotta soap dishes to put them in.

Scènes de Lin

70 rue de la Liberté (024 43 61 08). **Open** 9.30am-12.30pm, 3.30-7.30pm Mon-Sat. **Map** p98 C4 ㊼

Scènes de Lin is a chic fabric store that specialises in linens, and also offers a huge range of brilliant hues in striped woven cloth or delicate pastel organdie. Any combination can be ordered for custom-made curtains, tablecloths or place settings. There's plenty of other top-quality stuff besides, including luxurious fringed hammam towels, cushions with Fès embroidery, natural essential oils (including argan oil) and unusual contemporary lamps. Downstairs you'll find a small selection of interesting Moroccan couture.

Tinmel

38 rue Ibn Aicha (024 43 22 71).
Open 9am-7.30pm Mon-Sat.
Map p98 C3 ⑱
A highly browseable mini-museum of Islamic art with a staggering variety of antiques: aged silver swords, Tuareg earrings and pendants, 18-carat-gold jewellery from the early 20th century, colossal bronze lanterns that once adorned palaces, decorative oil jars, mirrors with cedar and camel-bone frames, silk-embroidered camel-skin bags and a variety of marble fountains. Don't miss the exquisitely crafted backgammon tables displayed in the upstairs room.

De Velasco

4 rue le Verdoyant, avenue Hassan II (024 43 03 27). **Open** 9am-1pm, 3-8pm daily. **Map** p98 C5 ⑲
Adolfo de Velasco was a kaftan designer and colourful raconteur who, until a few years ago, held court in a Mamounia boutique, fitting splendid one-off kaftans to royals and flogging a few *objets* on the side. Now Adolfo has gone to the great salon in the sky, the shop still bearing his name has moved to Guéliz. There's still a rack of

kaftans in the back, but mostly it's an ornate orientalist clutter of outsize vases, lacquer cabinets, silver rhinos, chaises longues, paintings of souks, ceramic leopards and the occasional mounted pair of tusks – everything you might need to furnish a camp fantasia of the colonial era. It's pricey stuff and not much fun to browse; charmless staff pursue in packs.

Vita

58 boulevard El Mansour Eddahbi (024 43 04 90). **Open** 8.30am-12.30pm, 3-7.30pm Mon-Sat; 9am-1pm Sun. No credit cards. **Map** p98 C4 ⑳
A Western-style florist and garden centre with a decent stock of cut flowers and ready-made bouquets. It also does delivery (local and Interflora), and sells potted plants, seeds and compost.

Wrédé

142 avenue Mohammed V (024 43 57 39). **Open** 8.30am-12.30pm, 2.45-7.30pm Mon-Sat. **Map** p98 C4 ㉑
Staff are friendly in this photography shop and lab; the quality of processing is fine. Slide film is sent to Casablanca and returns in three days. Staff speak some English.

Cinéma le Colisée p116

Galerie 127

Yahya Creation

49 passage Ghandouri, off
rue de Yougoslavie (024 42
2776/www.yahyacreation.com).
Open 10am-12.30pm, 2.30-7pm
Mon-Sat. **Map** p98 B4 🏷️

Yahya Rouach's mother is English
and Christian, his father is a Jew from
Meknès, and he's a Muslim convert
brought up in the UK and now resident in Marrakech. He designs extraordinary items, such as lanterns,
torches and screens, all made from
finely crafted metals. His pieces are
unique, often stunning one-offs. Most
of them are big too: conversation
pieces for a chic sheikh's Dubai pent-
house, perhaps. This arcade outlet is
a showroom rather than a shop, where
customers drop in to place commis-
sions, joining a client list that includes
Harrods and Neiman Marcus.

Yves Rocher

157 avenue Mohammed V (024 44
82 62). **Open** 9am-1pm, 3-7pm Mon-
Sat. No credit cards. **Map** p98 C4 🏷️

This French beauty chain has several
sites, but this branch is the easiest to
find. All offer moderately priced beauty
products, plus manicures, pedicures,
facials and epilation.

Arts & leisure

Cinéma le Colisée

Boulevard Mohammed Zerktouni
(024 44 88 93). No credit cards.
Map p98 B4 🏷️

This place trumpets itself as 'the best
cinema in Morocco' and it's certainly
the best in downtown Marrakech – a
comfortable, modern venue with
excellent sightlines. Movies are usually dubbed into French and shown
with Arabic subtitles.

Galerie 127

🆕 *127 avenue Mohammed V*
(024 43 26 67/galerie127moha
mmedV@hotmail.fr). **Open** 11am-
7pm Tue-Sat. No credit cards.
Map p98 C4 🏷️

When Natalie Locatelli opened Galerie
127 in 2006 it became the very first
photo gallery in the Maghreb and only
the third in all Africa (the other two
are in Dakar and Bamako). It's an
appealingly simple space – a converted apartment with tall windows and
walls left unsurfaced – and it got off
to a very good start with an opening
show by Tony Catany. The king
bought 30 of the photographs.
Locatelli has continued with work by
other big names in contemporary

photography, mostly French or France-based, such as portraits by Carole Bellaiche and Gérard Rondeau, Alejandra Figueroa's images of ancient statues, and Bernard Faucon's 'staged photography'.

Galerie d'Art Lawrence-Arnott

NEW *Immeuble El-Khalil, avenue Hassan II (024 43 04 99/gallery@ arnott-lawrence.com).* **Open** 9.30am-12.30pm, 3.30-6.30pm Mon, or by appointment. **Map** p99 E4 ❺❼

Just as art follows money, so do estate agents. Both arrived together in June 2005 when Philip Arnott and John Lawrence set up their second gallery in Morocco – along with an adjacent branch of Moroccan Properties, their real estate company. It's hard to escape the feeling that the artists they exhibit, mostly native or expatriate painters of 'Moroccan' subjects – neo-Orientalist noble savages, villages set in hazy landscapes, scurrying figures in *djellabas* – are simply chosen to adorn the walls of the half-million-euro second homes they're also trying to flog next door. The Moroccan Properties website even suggests as much. In Tangier, where there's been a Lawrence-Arnott gallery since 1991, there is some connection with the local art scene. In Marrakech, they're outsiders. And it shows.

Galerie Rê

NEW *Résidence Al-Andalus III, angle rue de la Mosquée and Ibn Touert No.3 (024 43 22 58).* **Open** 9.30am-1pm, 3-8pm Tue-Sat; 3-8pm Sun. **Map** p99 D4 ❺❽

With a background of collecting Berber textiles and running a New York gallery specialising in Egyptian art, Lucien Viola opened this serious and lavishly designed contemporary gallery in late 2006. His intention was to pick up where the now closed Les Atlassides left off – with the involvement of that gallery's Christine and Alain Gorius. A splendid staircase rises through the centre of the space

to a small mezzanine. Downstairs is for changing exhibitions by mostly 'Moroccan and Mediterranean' artists. An opening show by French painter Sébastien Pignon was followed by recent work from M'Barek Bouchichi, who lives near Zagora, and sculptures by the Marrakech-based American, Lori Park. Upstairs is work from established Moroccan artists such as Abdelkarim Ouazzani, Tibari Kantour and Mohammed Lagzouli. Lucien Viola's next project is to open a museum of ancient textiles and Moroccan art in the souks (see p62).

Matisse Art Gallery

61 rue Yougoslavie, No.43 passage Ghandouri (024 44 83 26/www.matisse-art-gallery.com). **Open** 9am-1pm, 3.30-8pm Mon-Sat. **Map** p98 B4 ❺❾

A decent space devoted to solo shows by young Moroccan artists such as calligraphy painters Nouredine Chater and Nouredine Daifellah, and figurative painter Driss Jebrane. More established names are also exhibited, such as Farid Belkahia and Hassan El-Glaoui (the late son of the former 'Lord of the Atlas' was devoted to painting horses). Upstairs are some vintage Orientalist canvases.

Nakhil Gym

75 rue Ibn Aicha (024 43 92 90). **Open** 8am-10pm daily. No credit cards. **Map** p98 C3 ❻⓪

This place also offers aerobics classes for women three days a week.

Secrets de Marrakech

62 rue de la Liberte (024 43 48 48). **Open** 10am-8.30pm Mon-Sat. **Rates** treatments from 400dh; day packages from 650dh. No credit cards. **Map** p98 C4 ❻❶

A small establishment and more personal than other spas in Marrakech, it's something of a rarity in that it is not attached to a hotel; it offers correspondingly fewer treatments. A menu of light snacks and fruit salads is served on the terrace.

Menara Gardens

Hivernage

South of Guéliz and immediately
west of the city walls is
Hivernage, a small, low-density
neighbourhood of villas and
international five-star hotels.
Out this way lie the city's civic
trappings such as the sports
stadium, opera house, the
enormous convention centre and
beyond them all, the airport.

Avenue Mohammed VI (formerly
known, and still often referred to,
as the avenue de France) is the
central artery of Hivernage (see
box p122). The area it bisects is a
veritable showcase of colonial
planning. On curving suburban
streets, hidden in greenery, hotels
sit next to modernist villas. In the
shade of a well-groomed hedge,
machine-gun toting soldiers
indicate a royal in residence.

There's an attractive little
colonial-era **railway station**. A
new but less charming station is
under construction. The junction
with avenue Hassan II is lorded
over by the monumental **Théâtre
Royal & Opera House**, designed
by local star architect Charles
Boccara (see box p113). More than
14 years after it was begun the
interiors have yet to be completed
due to the spiralling costs.

Here also sits the squat red
mass of the **Palais des Congrès**.
Constructed in 1989, it's a mammoth
five-storey edifice used for the
signing of GATT agreements in
1994. It has been mainly empty
ever since, although it is used for
the Marrakech Film Festival.

Sights & museums

Church of St Anne
Rue El-Imam Ali (024 43 05 85).
Map p121 D2 ❶
This Catholic church is barely a commu-
nion queue from the Medina's northern
walls. It is a modest affair with a bell
tower very deliberately overshadowed

MARRAKECH BY AREA

by the taller minaret of a mosque built next door after independence. One of the first buildings in the area, the French word for church, *église,* was corrupted into the name of the district, Guéliz. It wasn't the first church in Marrakech; in 1908 a French priest consecrated a house in the Medina near what is now the Dar Si Said Museum. A cross fashioned into the wrought-iron grill over one of the windows survives as evidence. Mass is in French, but there is an interdenominational service in English at 10.30am on Sundays (9.30am during July).

Jnane El Harti Park

Map p120 C2 **2**

The Jnane El Harti park was originally laid out as a French formal garden and a zoo. In a 1939 essay titled 'Marrakech', George Orwell writes of feeding gazelles here and of not being able to look at the animals' hindquarters without thinking of mint sauce. The park was relandscaped recently and now boasts fountains, ponds and a children's play area; a big blue dinosaur is the only reminder of the former menagerie.

Menara Gardens

Avenue de la Menara (024 43 95 80). **Open** 5am-6.30pm daily. *Marvels & Reflections* box office 9am-8pm daily; show Mar-Dec 9.45pm Wed-Sat. **Admission** free; picnic pavilion 15dh. Marvels and Reflections 250dh. Map p120 A5 **3**

Coming in to land at Marrakech Menara Airport, alert passengers may notice a large rectangular body of water to the east. This is the basin of the gardens from which the airport takes its name. The Menara Gardens were laid out by the Almohads in the 12th century. Later they fell into neglect and their present form is a result of 19th-century restoration by the Alouites. The green-tile-roofed picnic pavilion that overlooks the basin was added in 1869. Climb to the upper floor for a view over the water, or stroll around to the opposite side for a view of the pavilion against a backdrop of the Atlas. The bleachers that disfigure the view are there to accommodate the audiences for the 'Marvels and Reflections' show, which four nights a week presents the history of Morocco through contemporary dance and fireworks. To get to the Menara Gardens take a *petit taxi,* which should cost about 30dh from the Medina. They'll try to charge you more coming back.

Eating & drinking

Afric'n Chic

NEW *6 rue Oum Errabia (061 43 04 45/www.africnchic.com).* **Open** 6pm-1am daily. **$$. Bar. Map** p121 E1 **4**

Taking the fashion for all things 'African' to a raucous extreme, this is a big space with a party atmosphere. There's a small stage for occasional live music, lots of sub-Saharan figurines and a crowd of nattily dressed young men, along with middle-aged beer drinkers and good-time girls clustering around tables and massing at the long, busy bar. Flag beer, unusually, on tap.

Alizia

Corner of rue Ahmed Chouhada Chawki (024 43 83 60). **Open** noon-2.30pm, 7-11pm daily. Alcohol served. **$$$. Italian. Map** p121 E3 **5**

An intimate and well-established Italian-flavoured venture popular with the old-school expat crowd. As well as pizzas, pastas, fillets and steaks, it serves wonderful fish dishes, such as a starter salad of red mullet fillets flamed in balsamic vinegar, followed by fillet of John Dory served in a prawn bisque sauce. Ask about the special of the day – a roll of plaice stuffed with salmon and spinach on a recent visit. Save room for the dessert selection, one of the best in town. There's a decent wine list too. Prices are reasonable and the atmosphere relaxed, especially in the bougainvillea-draped garden.

La Casa

Hotel El Andalous, avenue Président Kennedy (024 44 82 26/www.eland alous-marrakech.com). **Open** 8pm-2am daily. **$$$. Bar. Map** p121 D4 **6**

A bar that thinks it's a club, La Casa mixes food, music and dance to great

Hivernage

PLACE EL
MOURABITENE

Bab
Doukkala

D   E   F

1

GUELIZ

Main
st Office

AVENUE DES NATIONS UNIES

PLACE DU
16 NOVEMBRE

AVENUE MOHAMMED V

8

RUE OUED EL MAKHAZINE

RUE OUM ERRABIA

AVENUE JACOUB EL MARINI

4

16

RUE MOHAMMED

EL MELLAKH

Bab
Larissa

oyal
is Club

25

Hôtel de
Police

1

Church of
St Anne

20

PLACE DE
LA LIBERTÉ

Bab
Nkob

2

14

Kawkab
Centre

9
13

AVENUE MOULAY HASSAN

AVENUE MOHAMMED V

3

AVENUE ECHOUADA

RUE ABOU EL ABBES SEBTI

AVENUE DE PARIS

5

AVENUE DU PRESIDENT KENNEDY

7

AVENUE EL QADISSIA

10 22

4

6

Sofitel
Marrakech

19 23 46

Hotel
Es Saadi

12 24 50

17

To Jemaa El Fna

AVENUE DE LA MENARA

Le Meridien
N'Fis

47

0   300 m

0   300 yds

© Copyright Time Out Group 2008

5

To Pasha & Rô Zin

Time Out Shortlist | Marrakech **121**

King's road

Avenue Mohammed VI

The longest avenue in Africa? It's a strange claim to fame, but that's how they're billing the Avenue Mohammed VI these days. While Avenue Mohammed V is the new city's commercial spine, Avenue Mohammed VI – running parallel, more or less, to the west – is its processional drag. Strewn with civic and municipal structures, prestige offices and big hotels, its old name was Avenue de France. But as his father and grandfather already have their own avenues, why not the current king too? It's certainly the thoroughfare that most clearly reflects the way his policies are reshaping the city.

And yes, it's long – eight kilometres (five miles) from its northern intersection with the Route de Targa to its southern extremity in the middle of what is currently still nowhere: the designated *zone touristique.*

Motoring north to south, the first kilometre is unremarkable. But at the junction with Avenue Hassan II, the new railway station is taking shape. Over the road, the white elephant that is Charles Boccara's still unfinished Théâtre Royal overstates the city's cultural aspirations – just as the Palais de Congrès to the south is about five sizes too large for the workaday conference trade. On the same stretch there are local government offices, banks, chain hotels, and some vast new premises for Royal Air Maroc.

But it's the southern extension that really points at the shape of things to come: a whole new 'touristic city' is in accelerated development. Barren lots are fenced off and ramshackle hamlets brushed aside for dozens of resort hotels and luxury apartment complexes. The Pasha franchise, the city's first multiplex, and a few hotels are all that's standing now, but in a few years there'll be beds and amusements for tens of thousands.

The result will perhaps be somewhat soulless, but hey, there's a nice view of the Atlas. And if anything in Marrakech will stand as a monument to the current king's ambition, this vast new quarter is likely to be it.

effect. It is primarily a bar, dominated by a huge central serving area, surrounded on all sides by tables. Above the counter hangs a giant rig of multi-coloured lights fit for a Pink Floyd gig. Much flashing and strobing occurs in accompaniment to a heavy Arab/Latin beats soundtrack. There's no dancefloor, but then none is needed, as everyone just lets go where they are. Around the stroke of midnight expect a dance performance from the chefs in the corner kitchen area. Berber columns cloaked in purple drapes and characters from the ancient Tifinagh alphabet highlit in ultraviolet add the thinnest veneer of Moroccan theming.

Comptoir

Avenue Echouada (024 43 77 02).
Open 4pm-1am Mon-Thur, Sun; 4pm-2am Fri, Sat. Alcohol served.
$$$. Moroccan/French/Bar.
Map p121 E4 **7**

Inevitably, Comptoir's exotic-East-meets-moneyed-West style has become diluted by overexposure. What began as a hangout for hipsters, fashionistas and models now seems to cater largely for coach parties from Club Med. The menu is divided between *saveurs d'ici* (Moroccan) and *saveurs d'ailleurs* (French). Quality varies wildly, but what's constant is a party atmosphere, aided by a four-piece of elderly fez-wearing musicians and brought to a raucous climax each weekend evening with the arrival of belly dancers. The bar upstairs is a sizeable lounge, packed every weekend. The crowd is a mix of good-looking locals, sharper expats and wide-eyed tourists delighted to have stumbled on the Marrakech they'd always heard about – but with pricier drinks.

Le Guépard

NEW *Residence Al Mourad, avenue Mohammed V (024 43 91 48).*
Open 11am-5pm, 6pm-1am Tue-Sun. Alcohol served. **$$. French/Bar.**
Map p121 D1 **8**

Opened in June 2006, this restaurant and bar decorated in faux African colonial style (leopardskin upholstery, pictures

of gorillas) has quickly become one of the most fashionable spots in the district. Many will find it of more use for a drink than a meal – chef Laurent Agredano's menu is full of over-rich dishes leaning heavily on foie gras and caviar – but the light lunch menu (50dh-80dh) is useful, and the croque monsieur (60dh) is probably the best in town.

Kawkab Jeu

1 rue Imam Chafii, Kawkab Centre (024 43 89 29). **Open** 8.30am-10pm daily. **$$$.** No credit cards. **Café.**
Map p121 D2 **9**

Next door to the Royal Tennis Club, Kawkab Jeu is a coffee shop (big on crêpes and fancy ice-creams) that's particularly good for families, with both an indoor play area for the really little 'uns, plus an outdoor playground with swings, slides, climbing frames and so on. For big kids there's table football, table tennis and video games.

Table du Marché

Corner of avenue Echouda & rue du Temple (024 42 12 12).
Open 7am-11pm daily. **$$.**
Café. Map p121 E4 **10**

Attached to the Hivernage Hotel & Spa, the Table du Marché is a dependable French-style pâtisserie and café with outdoor patio seating. The view isn't up to much but the wickerwork furniture is attractive and the maroon canopies offer welcome shade (there are a handful of seats in the air-conditioned interior). The tarts, croissants and breads are excellent, and there are sandwiches and panini. While it's off-route for most visitors, the local middle classes have taken to the place, driving over to exit with a baguette tucked under one arm.

La Villa

NEW *Avenue Kennedy (024 42 19 69).* **Open** 8-11pm Mon; noon-2.30pm, 8-11pm Tue-Sat. Alcohol served. **$$.**
French. Map p121 D3 **11**

Chef Didier Beckaert came to Marrakech from Lille, bringing with him a good reputation and the intention of presenting 'affordable gastronomy'. This he has been doing since December

2006, in a comfortable tented dining area on the edge of the Hivernage, decorated with warm accents by Léon L'Africain, and with a roof that opens to the sky in summer. There's a lot of choice in the three-course French menu (five starters, five mains, six desserts) and it's solid, sensible stuff: well presented with an eye for detail and all very decent for the price.

Shopping

Salon Jacques Dessange

Sofitel Marrakech, rue Harroun Errachid (024 43 34 95). **Open** 10am-8pm daily. **Map** p121 E4 ⑫
A French hairdresser, formerly at the Meridien, whose salon has a growing reputation among the moneyed set.

Ikram Photo Lab

Centre Kawkab, 3 rue Imam Chafii (024 44 74 94). **Open** 9am-noon, 3-9pm Mon-Sat. **Map** p121 D2 ⑬
A smart Fuji lab near the Jnane El Harti, offering 24-hour print processing, plus slide and video services.

Yacout Services

2 rue Yakoub El Marini (024 43 19 41). **Open** 8am-9pm daily. No credit cards. **Map** p121 E2 ⑭
Just south of place du 16 Novembre in Guéliz and not far from the church, Yacout is a fantastically well-stocked mini-market that incorporates a basement store devoted to booze – local and imported wines, beer and spirits. Next door is a shop selling own-made pasta.

Nightlife

Actor'S

NEW *Hotel Medina Spa, avenue Mohammed VI (reservation 067 52 63 92/061 06 41 16).* **Open** 11pm-4am daily. No credit cards. **Map** p120 C3 ⑮
Opened in December 2006, this place was still struggling to find its feet in mid 2007. Music is a mix of '80s hits, rock, Spanish stuff and the odd trance or techno number, which suits a club that isn't yet sure who its audience

ought to be. The circular bars are a nice touch; you can look across and meet the glance of whoever's waiting to be served on the other side, making it a good place to meet people. But only time will tell what kind of people those are likely to be.

Diamant Noir

Hotel Marrakech, place de la Liberté, avenue Mohammed V (024 43 43 51). **Open** 10pm-4am daily. No credit cards. **Map** p121 E2 ⑯
Spurned by the smart set, Diamant Noir nevertheless remains popular with party boys and girls and a smattering of expats, including the Euro queens. It's a non-judgemental crowd, making it something of a refuge for Moroccan gays. Scout out the talent going in from the vantage of the neighbouring house pizzeria before descending to the sub-basement dancefloor (passing a couple of bar levels and pool area en route). Music is a better-than-average mix of Arabesque and electrobeats, spun by competent DJs.

Palais Jad Mahal

10 rue Haroun Errachid (024 43 69 84). **Open** *Bar* 7am-3pm. *Club* midnight-4am daily. **Map** p121 F4 ⑰
Almost too big for its own good, this complex just outside Bab Jedid has a nice restaurant and bar with (usually) a boring live band band playing rock covers on the ground floor, and a club down below (separate entrance along the street, admission 100dh) that today houses a nightly 'oriental cabaret' frequented mostly by Moroccans.

Paradise Club

Kempinski Mansour Eddahbi, avenue de France (024 33 91 00). **Open** 10.30pm-4am daily. **Map** p120 B3 ⑱
Before the Pacha franchise opened to the south of the town in the new *zone touristique*, Paradise was the largest club in Marrakech. It always attracted an unexciting, moneyed crowd, which was predominantly Moroccan. These days it's even less happening than ever. A grand flight of steps leads down to the main arena, where spacious enclaves of

seating encircle a small dancefloor. A vast upper level offers pool and table football, as well as prime viewing of the occasionally impressive light show.

Théâtro

Hotel Es Saadi, avenue El-Qadissia (024 44 88 11/www.essaadi.com). **Open** 11.30pm-5am daily. **Map** p121 E4 ⑲

Théâtro opened in 2004 and quickly established itself as the club least dependent on out-of-towners. This is where you'll find the hippest, best-informed locals. The venue was once a theatre; now, the stalls are filled with sofas, while the balcony is tiered with throw cushions. A series of semi-private, gauze-veiled crash crèches fill the stage, while the former orchestra pit houses a long curved bar. The sound system is thunderous, and psychedelic cinema projections entertain the eye.

VIP Room

Place de la Liberté, avenue Mohammed V (024 43 45 69). **Open** 9pm-4am daily. **Map** p121 E2 ⑳

Hailed as the Studio 54 of Marrakech when it opened several years ago, VIP Room falls an abyss short of those ambitions – but it's still worth a visit. Flounce down the neon-striped tunnel to the upper-basement level, where a jobbing Arabic orchestra saws away at Middle Eastern classics while couples canoodle in the semi-gloom. Down in the nightclub proper is a circular dancefloor, overhung by a sci-fi spider-like light rig. Equally alarming are the leather-clad local ladies who, between sultry demands of random men to 'light their cigarettes', shoot a mean game of pool.

Arts & leisure

El-Harti Stadium

Jnane El-Harti (024 42 06 66). **Map** p120 C2 ㉑

Home to the Kawkab and Najm football teams. It seats just 15,000 and facilities are sparse. Tickets are usually purchased on the day, but sometimes in advance for big games.

Hotel Hivernage & Spa

Angle avenue Echouhada & rue des Temples (024 42 41 00/www. hivernage-hotel.com). **Open** 9am-10pm daily. **Rates** treatments from 150dh-750dh; day packages 1,500dh. **Map** p121 E4 ㉒

The Hotel Hivernage is a smart, mid-range new build just a few minutes walk from the Bab Jedid and Mamounia. It has a dedicated spa with a separate section for men and women, both kitted out with state-of-the-art equipment. Staff are notably smiley and welcoming and most of them speak English. It's a great place to come to as a couple.

L'Oriental Spa

Hotel Es Saadi, avenue El-Qadissia (024 44 88 11/www.essaadi.com). **Open** 9.30am-12.30pm, 2.30-7.30pm daily. **Rates** treatments from 250dh; day packages from 1,300dh. **Map** p121 E4 ㉓

The Hotel Es Saadi (p165) is a long-standing Marrakech fixture, now with a stunning-looking spa. Day packages are available.

Sofitel Marrakech

Rue Harroun Errachid (024 42 56 00, www.sofitel.com). **Open** 9am-9.30pm daily. **Rates** treatments 500dh-1,000dh; day packages from 2,000dh. **Map** p121 E4 ㉔

This is the number one spa in Marrakech. Staff are well trained (diploma-holders, the lot) and thoroughly professional, and the world-class facilities are cleverly grouped into a series of appealing packages. It's essential to book well in advance; weekends are reserved exclusively for hotel guests.

Royal Tennis Club de Marrakech

Rue Oued El-Makhazine, Jnane El Harti (024 43 19 02). **Open** 7am-8pm daily. No credit cards. **Map** p121 D2 ㉕

As much a social club as a sports centre, this is where Marrakech's well-heeled families come to play. There are only six courts and the place is very popular, so reservations are essential.

Port p128

Essaouira

Southern Morocco's most interesting coastal town – and the one most easily reached from Marrakech – offers both a contrast and an escape. There's a point on the road, about two-thirds of the way there, where the villages stop being pink and green and start being blue and white – the colours of earth and vegetation replaced by the colours of sea and sky. This elemental reorientation is matched by a change in climate. Where Marrakech is hot and arid, Essaouira is subject to winds that keep at bay the searing temperatures of the interior.

It's around three hours from Marrakech by bus, quicker by car or taxi, and, while just about doable as a day trip, travellers tend to linger here. Out on a limb from the rail network and until recently with no airport (it now has a small one with flights to Paris and Casablanca), Essaouira long managed to retain a laid-back timelessness all of its own. That's now changing, a victim of the town's accelerating popularity amid the same mix of foreign investment and state-encouraged development of tourist infrastructure that is pumping up Marrakech.

That said, it's still a relatively relaxing place, and a charming one too. Sandy-coloured ramparts shelter a clean and bright Medina built around French piazzas, carved archways and whitewashed lanes and alleys. The fishing port provides a constant fresh catch for local restaurants, while the wide, sandy beaches to the south, combined with high winds of up to 40 knots, have put Essaouira on the international windsurfing map.

It's also probably the best place to be in Morocco during Ramadan.

Many cafés and restaurants remain open through the day, unlike in most Moroccan towns, and the atmosphere in the evening is crowded but fairly calm when locals come out to socialise in the streets and cafés. Essaouira can also claim to be one of the cleanest and freshest Moroccan towns, with no vehicles in the Medina, regular street sweeping, and the Alizés winds keeping the temperature to an equable average of 22°C (72°F).

Despite the town's increasing popularity, all the renovations going on, and its designation as a UNESCO World Heritage Site, there is high unemployment and considerable poverty. Factories lie empty in the industrial quarter north of the Medina and the port no longer provides a living. Meanwhile, over ten per cent of the Medina's 16,000 houses – some 1,700 properties – are now owned by Europeans. The accompanying upswing in property prices is pushing the poorest Souiris out to the city limits. But locals know that the town is now largely dependent on tourism and this reinforces their instinctive tolerance – only occasionally tested by behaviour considered inappropriate in a Muslim country.

As in Marrakech, Essaouira has next to nothing in the way of formal sights such as monuments and museums. The Medina itself is one big sight, with highlights including the ramparts, the **souks** and the **Mellah**. You can march from one end to the other in ten minutes; a more leisurely exploration, however, can take days. The **port** is a separate entity, worthy of at least a stroll. Connecting the two is the **place Moulay Hassan**, the town's social nexus, which you'll pass through at least a dozen times a day as you explore the town.

Orientation

Arriving by car from Marrakech, you'll most likely enter the Medina through the arch of **Bab Sbaâ**, one of five gates. (By bus, you'll enter thriough **Bab Marrakech**.) Beyond Bab Sbaâ, avenue du Caire has the town's useless **tourist information office** on the left, and the **police station** further down on the opposite side. The few cross streets around here also contain several hotels, galleries and restaurants and a rowdy Moroccan bar, but it's a strangely detached corner of town, separate from both the Kasbah area and the rest of the Medina.

The narrow, shady avenue du Caire intersects the broad, open avenue Oqba Ibn Nafia, spine of the Medina. Left, this leads out to the port. Right, it dips under an arch, changes its name to **avenue de l'Istiqlal**, and becomes Essaouira's main commercial thoroughfare. Opposite avenue du Caire, the arch in the wall leads into the Kasbah district and, bearing left, to the place Moulay Hassan.

Sights & museums

Beach

Essaouira's beach is wonderful, but the north-westerly winds, known as the Alizés, make it cold and choppy for bathing. It's ideal for windsurfing, though, and the beach stretches for miles to the south, backed by dunes once the town peters out. Closer to the Medina it serves as a venue for local youths to play football. There's always a game going on and at weekends there are several played simultaneously, their kick-offs timed by the tides. You'll also find guys with camels, or they will find you, insistently offering rides. It can be fun to trek around the bay to the ruined old fort of Borj El Berod, but wait until you find a camel guy you feel comfortable with, and agree a firm price before setting off.

Mellah

Essaouira's old Jewish quarter, the Mellah, can be found just inside the ramparts beyond the Skala de la Ville – or by walking along avenue Sidi Mohammed Ben Abdellah. When the shops and businesses start to peter out, the Mellah begins.

During the 19th century, British merchants outnumbered other nationalities to the extent that 80 per cent of the town's trade was with Britain and sterling was the favoured currency. Muslims were not permitted to conduct financial transactions, so the sultan brought in Jews from all over the kingdom; by 1900 they outnumbered the locals. All but the wealthiest lived in the Mellah district between the North Bastion and Bab Doukkala. The area has been so neglected since mass emigration to Israel in the 1950s and 1960s that many buildings have fallen down or been demolished due to disrepair.

At one time Essaouira was known as the Sanhedrin (Jewish cultural centre) of North Africa. As recently as the 1950s the city still claimed 32 official synagogues. One of those that still functions remains at 2 Derb Ziry Ben Atiyah, which is the last lane on the west off rue Derb Laâlouj before it intersects with avenue Sidi Mohammed Ben Abdellah. The synagogue was founded by British merchants from Manchester; at the height of Essaouira's importance this section of the Kasbah was the location of various consulates and administrative buildings.

These days there are perhaps two dozen Jews left in Essaouira, some still distilling fiery *eau de vie de figues*, but they don't necessarily live here. The Mellah's alleys have become grubby and dilapidated, with big gaps where buildings have gone. It was always a gloomy quarter; until the end of the 19th century it was even locked up at night.

Musée Sidi Mohammed Ben Abdellah

7 Derb Laâlouj (024 47 23 00).
Open 8.30am-6pm Mon, Wed-Sun.
Admission 10dh.

This renovated 19th-century mansion was used as the town hall during the Protectorate and hosts a fairly boring collection of weapons, woodwork and carpetry. There are also gnawa costumes and musical instruments and a few pictures of old Essaouira.

Place Moulay Hassan

Connecting the Medina to the port, place Moulay Hassan is Essaouira's social centre. Early in the morning, fishermen pass by on their way to work, and the first wave of itinerant musicians and shoe-shine boys appears. By mid morning the café tables have begun their secondary function – as al fresco offices from which most Souiris conduct business at some time or another. Purveyors of sunglasses, watches and carpets sweep from table to table, only occasionally selling something. It's a popular spot for tourists, who can be found sitting at any of the cafés watching the theatre of the town unfold or buying the previous day's international newspapers from Jack's Kiosk.

Port

Essaouira's port, although pleasant at any time of day, is most interesting in the late afternoon when the fishing fleet rolls back into the harbour. Essaouira is Morocco's third-largest fishing port after Agadir and Safi. The catch is auctioned between 3pm and 5pm at the market hall just outside the port gates, and fresh fish are grilled and served up at stalls on the port side of place Moulay Hassan (see box p129).

If you want to go fishing yourself, you can hire a boat from the kiosk of the Societé Navette des Iles (064 32 64 93/www.mogador-iles.com) on the quayside near Chez Sam (p131) for 200dh per person for three hours. The Societé also offers a 'promenade en mer' – an hour-long drift around the bay on a 70-seater tourist boat – for 80dh a head; fizzy drinks and junk food extra.

Skala de la Ville

The Skala de la Ville is the only place where you can walk on top of the

Something fishy

Essaouira is no gourmet paradise, but in one department it bows to no man: fresh fish. At the fish market on the harbour side of place Moulay Hassan, there's a fresh catch on offer twice a day. The first lot arrives around 10am, just in time to be bought and prepared for lunch. The second catch appears around 4pm, ready for the evening meal.

There are various specialist fish and seafood restaurants, such as Chez Sam (p131) and Le Patio (p132), and most other places will have fish on the menu. But nowhere is the produce fresher or cheaper than at the fish stalls, clustered in an L-shape on the Medina side of the fish market.

OK, there are few trimmings. But with open-air tables overlooking the square, and prices ranging from 10dh for a plate of sardines to 400dh for a kilo of 'spiny lobster', there's also not much to bemoan. It's the best budget lunch option in town.

The catch varies by season. January to March is the time for sea urchins and shrimp. The sardines are at their best in July and August. Shark, sole and turbot are good all year round, and there's also a lot of red snapper. You can sample a selection for 60dh.

Choose what you want from the produce on display, and it will be sprinkled with salt, grilled over charcoal, and served on a plastic plate with a slice of lemon, salad, soft drink and a chunk of baguette. These are included in the fixed prices, displayed on a notice board as you approach the stalls. Chips are extra, and you'll have to wait while they run off to get them from one of the cafés on the square.

Stall-owners can get a little hassly when trying to usher you into their joint, but this shouldn't deter you from comparing what's on offer before choosing where to sit. We favour Ali's stall at No.33, Les Bretons du Sud (067 19 42 34), but they're all pretty much the same, and open from around 11am to 4pm daily.

Elizir p132

ramparts. There is one ramp up to the top near the junction with rue Ibn Rochd at the southern end, and another can be found near the junction with rue Derb Laâlouj at the northern end. Locals gather here to watch the sunset and lovers cuddle in the crenellations, where ancient cannons offer places to perch. At the far end is the tower of the North Bastion, the top of which offers good views across the Mellah and Kasbah.

Painters lay out their work for sale on and around the ramparts. Artisans sculpting *thuja* – a local coniferous hardwood with a smell like peppery cedar – have their workshops in the arches below and here you can find all manner of carvings and marquetry.

Souks

The souks can be found at the centre of the Medina, in cloistered arcades around the intersection of avenue Mohammed Zerktouni and avenue Mohammed El-Qouri. On the eastern side, just south of the arch from avenue Zerktouni is the grain market. Slaves were auctioned here until the early 20th century. The neighbouring cloistered square, the Joutiya, comes to life between 4pm and 5pm for a daily auction. The auctioneers walk in a circle holding up old alarm clocks, fishing reels, slippers, transistor radios – like a demented Moroccan version of *The Generation Game*.

On the west side of the avenue, the fish and spice souk is lively and interesting, but beware of unscrupulous stallholders, expert at the hard sell. It is here that Souiri women come to buy chameleons, hedgehogs and various weird and wonderful plants for use in sorcery and magic.

The jewellery souk curls around the outside of the mosque to the south-east of the junction. It's a surprisingly quiet corner where it's possible to browse in peace and pick up pieces of traditional silver jewellery.

Eating & drinking

Les Alizés Mogador

26 rue Skala (024 47 68 19). **Open** *lunch* noon-3pm, *dinner* 1st service 7pm, 2nd service 9pm, daily. **$**. No credit cards. **Moroccan**.
Opposite the wood workshops under the ramparts, and thus sheltered from the winds that lend the restaurant its name, this is one popular restaurant. It is known for its stone-arched interior, friendly, candlelit atmosphere, and above all for hearty portions of good and reasonably priced Moroccan home-cooking from a set menu. You can't

make reservations, so expect to wait for a table sometimes $ – especially when it's feeding time for backpackers from the Hotel Smara upstairs.

Bar

Boulevard Mohammed V (no phone). **Open** 9am-8pm daily. $$. No credit cards. **Bar**.

Attached to the beachfront restaurant Chalet de la Plage (below) on the side furthest from the port, and accessed by a discreet entrance signed only with the single word 'Bar', this is a simple drinking den where Moroccans gather over cold bottles of Flag Spéciale either on a small terrace overlooking the sands or indoors in the cosy saloon. It's a friendly place, but it's their place.

La Cantina

NEW *66 rue Boutouil (024 47 45 15).* **Open** 11am-8pm daily. No credit cards. $. **Mexican/British**.

Whatever possessed the congenial Steve Murphy and Sharon Hallom from South Yorkshire to open a 'vaguely Mexican' café on this square near the Mellah, the result is good news for those bored with couscous and tagines – especially vegetarians, who are catered for with understanding and flexibility. Jacket potatoes, burgers, chilli, stews, stir-fries and wonderful home-made cakes and desserts form the spine of a menu that is constrained by the availability of local ingredients. Guacamole is served only in late autumn when avocados are in season.

Chalet de la Plage

1 boulevard Mohammed V (024 47 59 72/www. lechaletdelaplage). **Open** 6.30-10pm Mon; noon-2.30pm, 6.30-10pm Tue-Sat; noon-2.30pm Sun. $$. **Moroccan**.

Built in 1893 entirely out of wood, this Essaouira beachside institution – just outside the Medina, opposite place Orson Welles – has been a restaurant forever. Good fish dishes are the highlight of a solid, unfussy menu, there's beer and a small wine list, and the overall vibe is friendly and efficient. It's at its best for lunch, when the terrace

affords a tremendous panorama of the bay, from the guys touting camel rides and the kids playing football in the foreground to the ruins of the Borj El-Berod on the headland. The owners have also opened a terrace café on the harbour side of the building, where coffee, tea and soft drinks can be enjoyed with an ocean view.

Chez Driss

10 rue El-Hajali (024 47 57 93). **Open** 7am-10pm daily. $$. No credit cards. **Pâtisserie**.

The pâtisserie at the end of place Moulay Hassan, founded in 1925, serves mouth-watering selection of croissants, tarts and cakes at prices everyone can afford. You can eat them with coffee here in the small, sheltered courtyard, or take them to one of the cafés with tables on the square (waiters are quite happy for you to consume food from off the premises).

Chez Sam

Port de Pêche (024 47 62 38). **Open** 12.30-3pm, 7.30-10pm daily. $$$. **Seafood**.

Right by the harbour, the building is a waterside wooden shack, designed like a ship, cramped and full of clutter. Continuing in the nautical vein, you can even peer out of the portholes to see fishing boats bringing in the catch. It's a no-nonsense kind of restaurant where you'll always find some local seafood, even if you rarely get anything exceptional, but the staff seem to know what they're doing. The new balcony out the back, overlooking the entrance to the harbour, is a nice spot for lunch.

Côté Plage

Boulevard Mohammed V (024 47 90 00). **Open** noon-3pm, 7-10.30pm daily. $$$. **French**.

On the promenade opposite the Sofitel, by which it is owned and operated, this is a good spot for mildly upmarket beachside lunches and interminable menu descriptions, both epitomised by the likes of *duo de melon du pays au jambon cru de parme et pain tomate* or *escabèche d'ombrine et saumon frais aux epices de la médina et herbes fraîches de l'Atlas, toast chaud*. It's about a ten-minute stroll from the Medina. Barbecue on Sundays.

Elizir

NEW *1 rue de Agadir (024 47 21 03). Main courses 90dh-120dh.* **Open** noon-3pm, 7.30pm-1am daily. **$$$**. No credit cards. **Moroccan/Fusion**.

Elizir opened back in June 2006 with a Moroccan-Mediterranean menu and an atmosphere of idiosyncratic cool; it has already become one of the best restaurants in town. Young owner Rharbaoui Abdellatif, who lived in Italy for a few years, still tinkers keenly with the stylish interior, where a few traditional elements set off an impressive retro-futurist collection of 1960s plastic furniture and fittings in orange and white – all of them sourced in Moroccan flea markets. Meanwhile, he's serving a menu that veers from a camel tagine via home-made pasta to organic chicken and the catch of the day. In winter, ask for a table in the room with the open fire; in warmer months, go for the sheltered roof terrace. The louche, jazzy playlist sounds good wherever you're sitting.

Fanatic

NEW *Boulevard Mohammed V (024 47 50 08).* **Open** 8am-11pm daily. Alcohol served. **$$$**. No credit cards. **French**.

This seafront seafood restaurant opened by what was otherwise a surfer operation is a surprisingly formal place offering a cheaper beachside lunch than the nearby Côte Plage. The kitchen is competent if unimaginative, but you can enjoy a drink with your *loup de mer* on the terrace and there are plenty of inside tables if it's too windy for al fresco dining.

Ferdaouss

27 rue Abdessalam Lebadi (024 47 36 55). **Open** 12.30-2.30pm, 6.30-10.30pm Tue-Sun. **$$**. No credit cards. **Moroccan**.

Ferdaouss is a cute and cosy place where traditional Moroccan food is served with an imaginative twist at prices so reasonable that you usually need to book a couple of days in advance. It's quite a way down an alley off rue Sidi Mohammed Ben Abdellah in the central Medina, from which it is signposted. At the time of writing it was undergoing renovations.

Gelateria Dolce Freddo

25 place Moulay Hassan (063 57 19 28). **Open** 7.30am-10pm daily. **$$**. No credit cards. **Café**.

A prime location around the corner and facing across the open part of the town's main square is one reason why this is the most fashionable of the central cafés; good Italian coffee is another. A selection of garish ice-cream adds colour to the proceedings and helps keep outdoor tables full.

Le Patio

W *28 rue Moulay Rachid (024 47 41 66).* Open tapas 5.30-11pm, dinner 6.30-11pm Tue-Sun. **$$$**. **French/Moroccan**.

Fish dishes are the highlight of a French-Moroccan menu, presented on a blackboard that can be hard to read in the dingy, candlelit interior. The venue is an old house with a roofed-over courtyard, dark red palette, and fabrics hanging to create a tented effect. Tables are cramped, though the room is spacious; music so insipid you almost don't notice it adds little to a rather bland atmosphere. That said, it's a good place to sample a selection from the day's catch, and there's a beautiful bar where you can order from a small but respectable tapas selection (around 35dh per item).

Silvestro

70 rue Derb Laâlouj (024 47 35 35). **Open** 11am-3pm, 7.30-11pm daily. **Main courses** 60dh-150dh. **$$$**. No credit cards. **Italian**.

Silvestro is a cool and unpretentious first-floor Italian restaurant. Run by Italians, it feels authentic, with an open kitchen, an espresso machine and a basic but sensible menu of antipasta, pasta and pizza. The food's all very well prepared and served with a smile.

Accompany it with something from the short but reassuring list of Italian wines.

Taros

Place Moulay Hassan (024 47 64 07/ www.taroscafe. com). **Open** 11am-4pm, 6pm-midnight Mon-Sat. **$$$**.

Bar/European.

Perched above the town's main square on a corner overlooking the sea, Taros is a multi-purpose venue with a prime location. It has a first-floor salon and library, where you can drink tea and read quietly during the afternoons or have a beer and listen to live music in the evenings (from Thursday to Saturday nights). Then there's a cocktail bar on the fine roof terrace (serving Mojitos, Margaritas, Caipirinhas and the like) with tables and bar stools. Food is served in either area, and the menu includes a modest vegetarian selection, complemented by the best steaks in town. An art gallery and small shop round off this much-loved institution.

Le Trou

Rue Mohammed El Ayachi (no phone). **Open** 11am-11.30pm daily. **$**. No credit cards. **Bar**.

At the cul-de-sac opposite and beyond the restaurant El-Yacoute, the entrance to 'the hole' is obvious at night, with a small barrow selling cigarettes and snacks outside, and a beery glow emanating from within. It's a disreputable sort of place, full of fishermen in djellabas drinking bottles of Stork beer, with a drunken hubbub and the occasional row. Tourists are tolerated rather than welcomed.

Shopping

Afalkay Art

9 place Moulay Hassan (024 47 60 89). **Open** 9am-8pm daily.

The one-stop shop for all your Essaouiran woodcraft needs. Searching the wood workshops under the ramparts might turn up the odd different item, but pretty much anything they can make out of fragrant *thuja* wood – from tiny inlaid boxes to great big

Orson's nose

At the centre of a small square on the south-west corner of Essaouira's Medina stands a stone bas-relief of a burly, bearded figure. Someone has knocked the nose off. Even if they hadn't, it's still hard to recognise as Orson Welles.

The legendary actor and director arrived in June 1949 to shoot a substantial portion of his *Othello*. Despite financial problems with the film, Welles would remember working in Essaouira as 'one of the happiest times I've ever known'.

Locals pitched in as extras as Welles strode the ramparts, caped and in blackface as the jealous Moor. To get over a lack of costumes, he staged the murder of Roderigo in a steamy hammam, to brilliant effect. He lost his false nose, and so shot remaining scenes without it.

Despite dodgy dubbing, a terrible soundtrack, the variable nose and at least four different Desdemonas, the result bagged a Palme d'Or at Cannes in 1952. Only limited distribution ensued, however, and the original negative was lost for decades. It turned up in 1990 and was brilliantly restored – along with the film's reputation.

In 1992, in a ceremony following a special screening, King Mohammed V (then Crown Prince) renamed the square place Orson Welles, and unveiled local craftsman Samir Mustapha's curiously un-lifelike memorial. But hey, at least the lost nose is appropriate.

treasure chests, toy camels to bathroom cabinets – can be found somewhere in this big barn of a place opposite the cafés of place Moulay Hassan. Staff speak English and are used to shipping larger items.

Azurrette

12 rue Malek Ben Morhal (024 47 41 53). **Open** 9.30am-8pm daily.
No credit cards.
At some remove from the hassle and hustle of the spice souk, this traditional Moroccan pharmacy has the largest herb and spice selection in the Medina and also offers perfumes, pigments, remedies, incense and essential oils. The big, cool space is lined with shelves of common condiments, exotic ingredients, mysterious herbs and colourful powders, all in glass jars or baskets. English is spoken by amiable young owner Ahmed, who's happy to explain what's what.

Bazaar Mehdi

5 rue de la Skala (024 47 59 81). **Open** 9am-8pm daily.
As good a place as any to buy a Moroccan carpet. It's no match for the big dealers of Marrakech, but there are literally heaps of rugs, with floorspace to lay them out and nimble helpers to unfurl them. The owner, Mustapha, is a good sort, speaks excellent English, and will provide detailed biographies of each carpet. Don't expect any bargains, though. If nothing here takes your fancy, there are other carpet shops further up rue de la Skala.

Chez Aicha

116 place aux Grains (024 47 43 35). **Open** 9am-8pm daily.
Moroccan ceramics can be a pretty standard affair – and much Essaouiran pottery is poorly glazed and chips easily. Aicha Hemmou's stock is a cut above. It's mostly Berber pottery, made near Marrakech. Some of the designs are a bit fussy, but others are cleanlined in warm, solid colours. There's also a bit of glassware and argan oil in gift bottles.

Chez Boujmaa

1 avenue Allal Ben Abdellah (024 47 56 58). **Open** 8am-midnight daily.
No credit cards.
Expats call this small, central grocery 'Fortnum & Mason's'. That's a bit of a stretch, but Chez Boujmaa is the place to find English teas and biscuits, plus a range of Italian pasta and parma ham, French cheeses and tinned haricots. At the basic deli counter they'll make up a sandwich to your specifications.

Galerie Aida

2 rue de la Skala (024 47 62 90).
Open 10am-1pm, 3-8pm daily.
A big place filled to bursting with an intriguing selection of old jewellery, paintings, glassware, crockery and other Moroccan antiques, plus a small but good (and pricey) selection of secondhand books.

Galerie Jama

22 rue Ibn Rochd (024 78 58 97).
Open 9am-noon, 1-9pm daily.
The brother of Mustapha from Bazaar Mehdi offers an interesting and nicely displayed selection of antiques and old pieces – silver jewellery, select ceramics, ancient wooden doors, vintage kaftans, treasure chests and old portraits of King Mohammed V.

The Gallery

NEW *19 rue Moulay Ismael (067 96 53 86).* **Open** by appointment only.
No credit cards.
In a small apartment space (with lots of stairs) Emma Wilson of Dar Beida (p168) offers an intriguing selection of clothes, accessories and artworks from a variety of sources. There are bags by Lalla from London and clothes in reworked vintage fabrics by Lola from Morocco, also some furniture, 'wonky donkeys' made of wood, and boxframed 'assemblages' by French artist Anne Marie Duprés.

Hassan Fakir

181 Souk Laghzel (070 23 00 17).
Open 9am-8pm daily. No credit cards.
Second on the right among the row of babouche stalls as you turn into the

Souks p130

fish and spice souk from rue El-Fachtaly, Hassan sells the usual Moroccan slippers and sandals and speaks decent English.

Jack's Kiosk
1 place Moulay Hassan (024 47 55 38). **Open** 9.30am-10.30pm daily. No credit cards.

In a key location on the square, Jack's is the place to find the previous day's international newspapers and other foreign periodicals, complemented by a small selection of new and second-hand English, French, German and Spanish books – mostly guides and bestsellers. Jack also rents sea-view apartments by the ramparts.

Kifkif
NEW *204 place du Marché aux Grains (061 08 20 41/www.kifkifbystef.com).* **Open** 10am-noon, 4-8pm Mon-Sat. No credit cards.

This smaller sister shop to the Kifkif in Marrakech (p78) sells the same eclectic assortment of colourful bags and purses, along with nice notebooks, electric lamps, jewellery and lots of things for children.

Mogador Music
52 avenue de l'Istiqlal (070 72 57 79). **Open** 10am-noon, 4-8pm Mon-Sat. No credit cards.

Gnawa, arabo-andalucian, grika, belly-dance, rai, desert bles – Mogador Music is well stocked with all varieties of North African and West Saharan music on CD and cassette. If you can't find it here you probably won't find it anywhere: owners Youssef and Azza know their stuff and distribute to all the other music shops. They have another store at 1 place Chefchaouen (061 72 83 62).

Ouchen Mohamed
4 rue El Attarine (024 47 68 61). **Open** 9am-9pm daily. No credit cards.

On a corner by the Riad Al Madina, Ouchen Mohamed is our favourite of the various leatherwork shops. It's good for pouffes, bags and belts, but there's also a big slipper selection and a few non-leather items, such as boxes, mirrors and old musical instruments.

Trésor
57 avenue de l'Istiqlal (064 84 17 73). **Open** 9am-8.30pm daily.

On the Medina's main avenue, jeweller Khalid Hasnaoui speaks good English and offers a more discerning selection than that found in the nearby jewellers' souk. His stock is a mixture of Berber, Arab, Tuareg and other pieces – some of it old, some new, and some new but using old designs. Look out for work in the local filigree style, made by Essaouiran Jews.

Arts & leisure

Espace Othello
9 rue Mohammed Layachi (024 47 50 95). **Open** 9am-8pm daily.

The extremely mixed bag of work by artists from Essaouira and beyond includes some small pieces as well as large paintings and sculptures. There's some interesting stuff, but you have to poke around a bit to find it. The gallery's architecture is a worth a look in its own right. It's behind the Hotel Sahara.

Galerie Damgaard
Avenue Oqba Ibn Nafiaa (024 78 44 46). **Open** 9am-1pm, 3-7pm daily.

Danish expat Frédéric Damgaard opened Essaouira's only serious commercial gallery in 1988 and helped to develop the work of around 20 local artists – known as the 'Essaouira school'. It's bright and colourful, almost hallucinogenic work, heavy with folk symbolism and pointillist techniques. Gnawa artist Mohammed Tabal is the star: his 'paintings of ideas' are inspired by the gnawa trance universe of colour-coded spirits. We also like the paint-splattered wooden furniture sculptures of Saïd Ouarzaz and the dreamlike canvases of Abdelkader Bentajar. We're worried, following Damgaard's recent retirement, that things might stagnate under new ownership.

Essentials

Riad Samarkand p149

Hotels

The piecemeal conversion of the Medina into a vast complex of boutique hotels continues apace. Marrakech probably boasts more of these per square mile than any other city in the world. At press time there were 370 establishments registered with the local authorities as *maisons d'hôtes*, with another 150 places awaiting classification. In some districts, such as the R'mila area in the north-western Medina – more developed than most because of good vehicle access – there already seem to be more guesthouses than houses. And though rocketing property prices mean there are few real bargains left on the market, all the signs are that this trend will continue, if a little more slowly than in the last few booming years. And it all makes a certain sense. If your city is low on conventional sights, then it makes sense to make the accommodation the destination. It's just that Marrakech has taken this further than most places.

'Riad' means garden house, though for 'garden' you can usually read 'courtyard'. The city's riad guesthouses are organised around one or more of these courtyards, reflecting the traditions of Moroccan domestic architecture, which are inward-looking with thick blank walls to protect the inhabitants from heat, cold and the attentions of the outside world. Grander riads involve two or more houses knocked together, but many consist of just half a dozen or so rooms around a single courtyard. Most are privately operated affairs, which generally means excellent personal service and a high degree of individuality.

In all but the cheapest riads, rooms have en-suite bathrooms, but air-conditioning, TVs, telephones, hairdryers and other mod cons are often dispensed with in the name of authenticity and getting away from it all. Marrakech can be decidedly chilly during the winter; anyone who is travelling then and feels the cold should check the heating situation before booking. Breakfast is commonly taken on a roof terrace shielded from the sun under tent-like awnings, while lunch and dinner are often provided on request. Many riads have excellent cooks, producing food as good as, if not superior to, anything dished up in the city's restaurants.

In deference to local aesthetics, most riads forgo any kind of tell-tale frontage, signboard or even nameplate. Given that they often lie deep within the obscure twists of narrow alleys, this makes them a swine to locate. Guests are generally met at the airport (for which there may or may not be

ESSENTIALS

Jnane Tamsna
Country Guesthouse
24 bedrooms spread over 5 villas
on 9 acres in the Palmgrove
Tel: 212 24 329423   Fax: 212 24 329884
Email: meryanne@jnanetamsna.com
www.jnanetamsna.com

an additional charge in the region of 80dh-150dh), but after that it's just you and your sense of direction. With that in mind, it's always wise to carry your riad's business card to show locals in case you get lost.

Get a room

When it comes to making a reservation, even though most hotels boast websites, bear in mind that Moroccan servers are prone to meltdown. Book through the website by all means, but it's wise to follow up with a phone call.

A new internet booking service, www.so-maroc.com, is a particularly useful resource to check on last-minute room availability, and to make online bookings.

Whichever way you choose to go, we highly recommend pushing the budget. Marrakech is not a place to scrimp on the accommodation – not when your hotel could turn out to be the highlight of the trip.

Money matters

There are significant seasonal variations in room rates, with prices at some hotels rising by up to 25 per cent at peak periods. What constitutes peak period varies by establishment, but generally speaking you'll pay considerably more for a room any time over Christmas/New Year and Easter, plus from late September through to October, when the fierceness of the summer heat has abated and temperatures are near perfect. Rooms are scarce at peak times and booking well in advance is a must.

Breakfast is usually included in the price of a room. Payment is typically cash only, and made in local currency. Even places that purport to take credit cards usually prefer cash – you might too, given that a five per cent surcharge may be added on top to cover the transaction costs.

Jemaa El Fna

Grand Tazi

Corner of avenue El-Mouahidine & rue Bab Agnaou (024 44 27 87/fax 024 44 21 52). **$**. **Map** p45 C5 **1**

A well-known two-storey, two-star establishment that retains its popularity because of its plum location just a minute's walk from Jemaa El Fna, combined with cheap room rates and the added benefits of a swimming pool and bar. The rooms vary wildly in quality: it's best to ask to view a few before settling. Up on the first floor, what must be the longest corridor in Marrakech leads to the good-sized outdoor swimming pool, bordered by sun loungers. In the evening the area beside reception takes on a life of its own as a lounge bar (p48), the only place in the central Medina for a cheap beer. We have heard less-than-favourable reports about the food in the in-house restaurant.

Jardins de la Koutoubia

16 rue de la Koutoubia (024 38 88 00/fax 024 44 22 22/hoteljardin koutoubia@menara.ma). **$$$**. **Map** p45 C2 **2**

If you want to be in the Medina but prefer the relative impersonality of a hotel over the intimacy of a *maison d'hôte*, then this comfortable, well-run establishment is the place. It's brilliantly located, two minutes from the Jemaa El Fna in one direction, two minutes from the Koutoubia mosque and a steady stream of taxis in the other. The courtyard pool is heated, they can shake a proper cocktail in the Piano Bar (p49), the patio restaurant is a fine spot for lunch, and everything is nicely spacious. The faux traditional design may be nothing for the style supplements, but it isn't too shabby and both beds and bathrooms are big and welcoming. A huge new extension has brought the total number of rooms up to around 100 and added another garden, a couple more swimming pools and a subterranean fitness centre.

Riad Lotus Ambre

22 Fhal Zefriti, Bab Laksour (024 44 14 05/fax 024 44 14 07/www.riads lotus.com). $$$. **Map** p45 B2 ❸

In contrast to most riads, where the gone-native aesthetic means you're lucky to get a table lamp in your bedroom, let alone a TV, the Lotus lays on the extras big time. The four doubles and one suite all come with logo'd bed linen, towels and toiletries, high-speed internet access and a Bang & Olufsen plasma screen, sound system and DVD player. Not to mention the huge Warhol-copy Pop Art pieces (Jackie O, Marilyn, Goëthe and Mao) that dominate each room. All the lighting is touch-sensitive B&O, the crystalware comes from Italy and there's a jacuzzi on the roof. If bling's your thing, then here's your Marrakech home from home. Rooms, however, vary greatly in size (Marilyn, in particular, is a bit mean). Owner Reda Ben Jelloun, Marrakech-born but previously a travel agent working in Florence, says his aim is to offer five-star service in intimate, stylish surroundings. In 2005 he opened the Lotus Perle, on similar lines (neo-classical columns, black and white marble floors, gadgetry and a retro American theme reflected in room names like Kennedy, Gatsby and Coco Chanel). He's now also opened the even more upmarket Lotus Privilege near the Dar El Bacha, with a similar array of gadgets, five suites around an enormous courtyard where mirrored obelisks flank a huge plunge pool, and rather too much black marble throughout. See the website for details of the Perle and Privilege.

Riad de l'Orientale

8 Derb Ahmar, Laksour (024 42 66 42/www.riadorientale.com). $. **Map** p45 C2 ❹

In the quarter behind Bab Fteuh, just a few minutes' walk from the Jemaa El Fna, this 250-year-old house has been a seven-room guesthouse since 2000. The owners are English but the style is traditional Moroccan – no radical design concepts here, just small but comfortable rooms ranged around the

usual courtyard with fountain. The best deal, though, is the rooftop suite, which has two rooms, a bathroom, an open fire and a private terrace with its own fountain. It sleeps up to four.

North Medina

Dar Atta

28 rue Jebel Lakhdar, Bab Laksour (024 38 62 32/ fax 024 38 62 41/ www.daratta.com). No credit cards. $. **Map** p54 C3 ❺

At first sight it seems an unpromising location – a not very picturesque part of the Medina, opposite the gaudy Alanbar. But you can get a taxi to the door, or walk to the Jemaa El Fna or Koutoubia in ten minutes, and once you're inside, this Italian-owned *maison d'hôte* reveals itself to be a very pleasant place indeed. Seven stylish double rooms and three spacious suites are ranged around a sunken patio and two terraces. We liked the big and faintly ramshackle-looking wooden partitions that separate the comfortable double beds from the wardrobe areas, and the generally unobtrusive design – it's cool, without being in your face. Staff are equally discreet, drifting around in black uniforms. There's also a charming small hammam and massage area and a restaurant that serves Moroccan and Italian dishes. When it's time to leave, you're on the right side of town for a quick dash to the airport.

Dar Attajmil

23 rue Laksour, off rue Sidi El Yamami (024 42 69 66/www.darattajmil.com). $$. **Map** p55 D5 ❻

With just four bedrooms, Dar Attajmil is nothing if not cosy. It's run by the lovely (English-speaking) Italian Lucrezia Mutti and her small body of staff, which includes two slothful black cats. There's a tiny courtyard filled to bursting with banana trees and coconut palms that throw welcome shade on to a small recessed lounge and a library. Bedrooms overlook the courtyard from the first floor, and are beautifully decorated in warm, rusty tones with dark-wood ceilings and lovely *tadelakt* bathrooms. Best of all, though, is the astonishingly peaceful roof terrace, scattered with cushions, wicker chairs and sofas – guaranteed to get you in the holiday spirit. Dinner (trad Moroccan with Italian leanings) is available on request for 150dh per person. It's an easy six-minute walk from the house to the Jemaa El Fna, Mouassine and the main souks.

Dar Doukkala

83 Arset Aouzal, off rue Bab Doukkala (024 38 34 44/fax 024 38 34 44/www.dardoukkala.com). **$$**. **Map** p55 D2 ⑦

A bizarre mix of English country mansion and Moroccan townhouse, Dar Doukkala is like the home of some demented Victorian explorer-inventor with an obsession for the Orient. Its four bedrooms and two suites are filled with gorgeous period details and furnishings, including claw-foot tubs and pedestal basins in the bathrooms. Other wonderfully eccentric touches include Guimard-like glass canopies projecting into the central garden courtyard, and an artful array of lanterns patterning the wall behind the terrace-level pool. It's one of the most fun and delightful *maisons d'hôtes* in town. Both suites have two extra beds each for kids, while one of the doubles also comes with an extra bed. The location is good too, opposite the wonderland warehouse of Mustapha Blaoui and close to the taxis ranked outside the Dar Marjana restaurant.

Maison Arabe

1 Derb Assehbe, Bab Doukkala (024 38 70 10/fax 024 38 72 21/ www.lamaisonarabe.com). **$$$**. **Map** p54 C2 ⑧

Maison Arabe began life in the 1940s as a restaurant run by two raffish French ladies. It rapidly gained fame through its popularity with a series of well-known and illustrious patrons, including Winston Churchill. The last tagines were served here in 1983, and the premises lay dormant for over a decade before reopening under Italian ownership in January 1998 as Marrakech's first *maison d'hôte*. Today, there are nine rooms and eight suites set around two leafy, flower-filled courtyards. Inside, the prevailing style is Moroccan classic with French colonial overtones – plenty of orientalist paintings and antiques, high-backed armchairs and an elegant cedarwood library. The rooms and suites are supremely comfortable, most with their own private terraces and a couple with fireplaces. Our favourite is Sabah (all the rooms have names), which is ingeniously fitted around the curve of a dome. The hotel pool may be a 20-minute drive away on the outskirts of town (serviced by hourly shuttles), but it's set in a lovely garden planted with olive and fig trees; in their shade, lunch is served at Le Figuier snack bar. Back at the hotel, the smart restaurant (p78) is excellent, and there's also a fine bar, Le Club. Guests can also sign up for Moroccan cookery workshops.

Nejma Lounge

NEW *45 Derb Sidi M'hamed El Haj, Bab Doukkala (024 38 23 41/www. riad-nejmalounge.com).* No credit cards. **$**. **Map** p54 B1 ⑨

This notable new budget option, conveniently close to Bab Doukkala, shuns the traditional in favour of black and white floor tiles, playful accents in pinks and purples, and furniture by Laurence Corsin. It's the riad as pop art. The six rooms are named to reflect the colours that predominate – 'Rose' is pink, 'Rouge' is red and 'Chocolate' is, well, chocolate. They're not the biggest bedrooms in town but they're nice for the price. Young, anglophile French owners maintain a cool but animated atmosphere. There's a small bar off the courtyard, snacks and drinks are served all day long, and you can even imbibe from floating trays in the modest plunge pool. Naturally, there's also a roof terrace, but no TV anywhere on the premises. Closed for most of August.

ESSENTIALS

Riad Farnatchi p145

Riad Azzar

94 Derb Moulay Abdelkader, off Derb Debbachi (061 15 81 73/fax 024 38 90 91/www.riad azzar.com). No credit cards. **$$**. **Map** p56 B5 ⑲

Owned by a friendly, English-speaking Dutch couple, Azzar is a neat little six-room riad with the feel of a B&B. It's distinguished by a small, emerald green, heated plunge pool in the middle of the courtyard – nice enough, but if the riad is full it could be a bit like bathing in the main lobby. Walls are whitewashed and the decor is understated: it's a very tasteful place. Three of the rooms are suites and come with fireplaces and air-conditioning (as does one of the doubles); of these, the Taznarth suite also boasts a beautiful *mashrabiya* (wooden lattice) window overlooking the courtyard and a particularly lovely grey *tadelakt* bathroom. The owners admit with admirable honesty that the hammam is of a size suitable only for petite French ladies. Also admirable is Riad Azzar's support of a local orphanage; guests are encouraged to contribute by bringing children's toys and clothing or school materials for donation.

Riad El Fenn

2 Derb Moulay Abdallah Ben Hezzian, Bab El Ksour (024 44 12 10/www.riad elfenn.com). **$$$$**. **Map** p55 D5 ⑪

This riad has received plenty of media attention, partly because it's co-owned by Vanessa Branson (sister of Richard) and partly because it is such a fine place. Three historic houses have been joined to create nine spacious, sorbet-coloured bedrooms. Clutter-free, each room is dominated by an Egyptian cotton-swathed imperial-sized bed. There's also a split-level suite (the Douiria) that is arguably the most striking room for rent in the whole of Marrakech. Six new rooms have recently been added, including a huge garden suite with a sunken bath in the bedroom and a steam room in the bathroom. Another new suite has a private pool on the terrace above, accessed by a spiral staircase. Despite the grandeur of the architecture and some serious modern art on the walls, the mood is relaxed, with plenty of private spaces and two obligatory rooftop terraces. A garden in the foothills of the Atlas provides organic produce for the

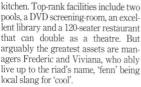

Riad Magi p147

kitchen. Top-rank facilities include two pools, a DVD screening-room, an excellent library and a 120-seater restaurant that can double as a theatre. But arguably the greatest assets are managers Frederic and Viviana, who ably live up to the riad's name, 'fenn' being local slang for 'cool'.

Riad Enija

9 Derb Mesfioui, off rue Rahba Lakdima (024 44 09 26/fax 024 44 27 00/www. riadenija.com). No credit cards. $$$. **Map** p56 B4 ⑫

Anyone lacking the pose and hauteur of a Karl Lagerfeld model risks being made to look shabby by comparison with the drop-dead gorgeousness of their surrounds at Riad Enija. Its 12 rooms and suites variously boast glorious old wooden ceilings, beds as works of art (wrought-iron Gothic in one, a green muslin-wrapped four-poster in another), some striking furniture (much of it designed by artist friends of Swedish/Swiss owners Björn Conerding and Ursula Haldimann) and grand bathrooms resembling subterranean throne chambers. Central to the

three adjoined houses (which originally belonged to a silk trader from Fes and 64 members of his family) is a Moorish courtyard garden gone wild, where maroon-uniformed staff flicker through the greenery. Distractions such as televisions and telephones are dispensed with (although there is a sweet little 'internet salon'), but alternative services include anything from a visiting aromatherapist and masseurs to cookery classes and heli-skiing excursions (in season). The service and food are both excellent, and the riad is just a few minutes' walk from Jemaa El Fna. The only downsides to this place are the lack of a swimming pool and the fact that taxis can't get you anywhere very near. Then there's the nuisance of having the latest fashion shoot going on outside your window – we warned you this place was a looker.

Riad Farnatchi

2 Derb Farnatchi, Kat Benahid (024 38 49 10/fax 024 38 49 13/ www.riadfarnatchi.com). $$$$. **Map** p56 C3 ⑬

ESSENTIALS

Farnatchi is the creation of Jonathan Wix (also responsible for 42 The Calls in Leeds, the Scotsman in Edinburgh and Hotel de la Tremoille in Paris). Originally intended as his private residence, it's now an intimate, top-class hotel. Eight suites, three of them recently added, are arrayed off three small courtyards, one of which has a modestly sized heated pool. The suites are vast and supremely luxurious, with large sunken baths, shower rooms, under-floor heating, desks and arm-chairs and private balconies. The design throughout is a striking update of the local aesthetic, with stark black and white as a neutral backdrop to intricate woodworked screens and finely carved stucco. All the furniture has been specially designed and man-ufactured in Marrakech, except for bathroom fittings by Philippe Starck. The hotel is superbly run (Canadian manager Lynn Perez is a walking directory of Marrakech) and right in the middle of the Medina, just north of the Ben Youssef Medersa; taxis can get to within 200m. Rates include com-plimentary hotel transfers. The hotel is closed during August.

Riad Kniza

34 Derb l'Hôtel, Bab Doukkala (024 37 69 42/www.riadkniza.com). **$$$**. **Map** p54 B1 ⑭
This grand and well-located 18th-century house has belonged to the family of current owner Mohammed Bouskri for two centuries, but only opened as a *maison d'hôte* in 2004. It's the most Moroccan of upmarket riads, decorated entirely in a conservative and traditional style. There are four suites and three rooms, and even the smallest is pretty spacious. The suites all have separate sitting rooms and there are working fireplaces through-out. The Bouskri family are antique dealers, which means a lot of old pieces in alcoves and cabinets. Mohammed Bouskri has also been a professional guide for over 30 years, so it's a good place for anyone who wants to 'do' Marrakech in an old-school kind of

way. They offer a free half-day tour for anyone staying for three nights. It deserves its reputation as a well-run establishment – the only downside is a slightly staid atmosphere. An exten-sion containing a hammam, a pool and four more suites should be completed by autumn 2007. No children under 12.

Riad Magi

79 Derb Moulay Abdelkader, off Derb Dabbachi (/024 42 66 88/UK phone 44 0208 834 4747/www.riad-magi.com). *No credit cards.* **$$**. **Map** p56 C5 ⑮
Petite, unpretentious and homely, Riad Magi has six carefully colour-coordi-nated rooms on two floors around its central orange-tree-shaded courtyard. The first-floor blue room is particularly lovely, with its step-down bathroom. Breakfast can be taken on the roof terrace or in the courtyard (which may or may not sport tree-clinging chameleons); other meals are available by arrangement. Guests can also take cooking lessons. When in town, English owner Maggie Perry holds court from her corner table, organising guests' affairs and spinning stories of local life – at such times Riad Magi becomes possibly the most entertain-ing hangout in Marrakech.

Riad Noir d'Ivoire

NEW *31 Derb Jdid, Bab Doukkala (024 38 09 75/fax 024 38 16 53/www.noir-d-ivoire.com).* **$$$**. **Map** p54 C1 ⑯
Opened in December 2006, Riad Noir d'Ivoire has that gratifying combina-tion of looking spectacular while feel-ing exceedingly comfortable. Interior designer and co-owner Jill Fechtmann has mixed specially commissioned Moroccan elements with assorted curiosities from sub-Saharan Africa (inspired by years in Swaziland), Europe (years more in Paris and the Dordogne) and India. Some of the more idiosyncratic details are the work of her husband, Jean-Michel Jobit. Three suites and one double room have huge beds imported from the USA, sheets of Egyptian cotton, big bathrooms and pleasingly eccentric furnishings that

ESSENTIALS

vaguely reflect an animal theme. Our favourite is the 'Chameau' suite, with its open fire, golden masks in alcoves, treacherously comfortable armchairs and sculpted wooden camel, as big as a mule. Off the chandeliered courtyard with plunge pool and baby grand there's a hammam in Tiznit marble, plus a lounge/library, small boutique, dining area and cosy bar. The vibe is essentially sociable – Jill is an able and amiable hostess who gets everyone talking – but that may make it the wrong place if you vant to be a-lone. There's also nowhere save the roof terrace to escape the Sting tunes and jazz standards played by the temperamental Georgian pianist some evenings. But these are quibbles.

Riad Samarkand

NEW *41 Derb Sidi Lahcen, Bab Doukkala (024 38 78 80/www.riadsamarkand.com).* **$$$**.
Map p54 C1 ⑰

Deep down a derb, but in one of the Medina's more convenient quarters, there are five 'suites' in this centuries-old house surrounding a leafier-than-usual courtyard with an 11-metre swimming pool. The decor is admirably uncluttered and restrained, incorporating much original detailing; the blue-green hammam truly deserves the description 'cosy', and the management is charm personified. Some rooms have private terraces.

Riad 72

72 Derb Arset Aouzal, off rue Bab Doukkala (024 38 76 29/fax 024 38 47 18/www.riad72.com). **$$**.
Map p55 D3 ⑱

Italian owned, this is one sleek and good-looking place – Marrakech has it away with Milan. The result is a trad townhouse given a black, white and grey *tadelakt* makeover. The structure, space and detailing are Moroccan, the furniture and fittings imported. There are just four guest bedrooms, all up on the first floor and arrayed around the central courtyard. Rooms include a master suite that's laugh-out-loud large; five metres or more in height and crowned by an ornate octagonal fanlight.

The roof terrace boasts one of the best views in town, with the green-tiled roofs of the Dar El-Bacha in the foreground and a cinemascopic jagged mountain horizon beyond. Being that much higher than the neighbouring houses means sunbathing is no problem (many riads are overlooked and modesty can be an issue). The Milanese owner and designer, Giovanna Cinel, has now also opened two other riads in the area, each with four more rooms and a similar aesthetic. The cosy Riad 12, off nearby rue Dar El-Bacha, includes a single room – a real rarity in Marrakech. Riad 2, just beyond the souks' northern tip, is more grand and spacious, with an enormous suite sporting a big copper bathtub in the huge main room. Both also have higher-than-usual roof terraces (Riad 12's is the better one) and all three houses have the same menu and portfolio of services. Riad 72, with its superior vehicle access, remains this small chain's main rendezvous point.

Riad Tizwa

NEW *26 Derb Gueraba, Dar El-Bacha (068 19 08 72/ UK +44 7973 238 444/www.riadtizwa.com).* **$$**.
Map p55 E2 ⑲

Small (five rooms), relaxed and comfortable, Riad Tizwa has a slightly rough-around-the-edges charm that is all its own. Laid out in the usual fashion on three open-fronted floors around a central tiled courtyard, this place is a great antidote to design excess. Rooms are white with splashes of colour, some with wood-beamed ceilings; bathroom *tadelakt* is in a limestone shade. Design solutions are simple but striking, like the thick, high azure *tadelakt* headboard that conceals clothing rails behind it in one of the rooms. There is a hammam, and each room is equipped with an iPod docking station. The roof terrace has a shaded area for al fresco dining (there's also an indoor dining area

ESSENTIALS

Riad El Fenn p144

downstairs) and offers privacy for sunbathing. The friendly owners encourage exclusive rentals of the whole riad as well as individual guests. One big advantage is that Tizwa is accessible to taxis, just a few yards down a narrow alley off rue Dar El-Bacha.

Riyad El Cadi

87 Derb Moulay Abdelkader, off Derb Debbachi (024 37 86 55/fax 024 37 84 78/www.riyadelcadi.com). **$$.** **Map** p56 C5 ⑳
Comprised of eight interconnected houses, El Cadi is a rambling maze of a residence in which getting lost is a pleasure – luckily, for it'll happen quite a lot in your first few days. The 12 well-appointed suites and bedrooms, as well as the various salons, corridors, staircases and landings, also double as gallery spaces for an outstanding collection of art and artefacts gathered by late former owner Herwig Bartels. The reception area alone boasts an ancient Berber textile with a Bauhaus chair and a Rothko-like abstract. Despite the rich details, the overall feel is uncluttered, cool and

contemporary. Bartels's daughter Julia now runs the riad, with the assistance of the dapper and charming general manager Ahmed El-Amrani, and standards remain high. Extensive roof terraces with tented lounging areas further add to the appeal of what, for the money, is some of the classiest accommodation in town. The only drawback is its distance from taxi dropping-off points, though cars can get quite near at the top end of the Jemaa El Fna, up to 1pm.

Talaa 12

12 Talaa Ben Youssef, El Moqf (024 42 90 45/ fax 024 44 26 07/www.talaa 12.com). **$$$.** **Map** p56 B3 ㉑
A serene, minimalist-style riad in the north-east of the Medina, Talaa 12 is owned by Belgian interior designer Marianne Lacroix. Three years of painstaking renovation have paid off well. Walls are white and shutters are grey, with judicious bolts of colour provided by rugs, furnishings and hangings. The courtyard is planted with lemon trees, and Arabic chill-out and gnawa-style music plays on the

ESSENTIALS

CD player. There are eight comfortable bedrooms, with limestone *tadelakt* bathrooms. Location is another plus factor: Talaa 12 is in the El-Moqf section of the Medina, close to the Musée de Marrakech, and just a ten-minute walk from Jemaa El Fna. The roof terrace has a 360-degree view of the rooftops of Marrakech and the peaks of the Atlas mountains.

Tchaikana

25 Derb El Ferrane, Kaat Benahid (tel/fax 024 38 51 50/www.tchaikana. com). No credit cards. **$$**.
Map p56 C3 ㉒

Run by a young and charming (and English-speaking) Belgian couple, Jean-François and Delphine, Tchaikana has just four rooms. However, most of them are enormous, particularly the two suites, each of which measures 11 metres by five metres (36ft by 16ft). The decor is beautiful, with a sort of *Vogue* goes Savannah look, and the central courtyard, laid out for dining, is gorgeously lit at night. Rates are per room, and given that all have banquettes in addition to double beds, each could sleep four or more impecunious souls – Jean-François has no objections (although no more than four breakfasts per room). Soft drinks and orange juice are free, and there's a library of comic books. Delphine is a buyer for several major UK high-street stores, and is the ideal person for advice on shopping the souk. In case you're wondering, a 'tchaikana' is a Central Asian teahouse.

South Medina

Casa Lalla

16 Derb Jamaa, off Riad Zitoun El Kedim (024 42 97 57/fax 024 42 97 59/www.casalalla.com). **$$**.
Map p82 B2 ㉓

Lalla is a beautiful little guesthouse, with eight rooms ranged on two floors around a grand central courtyard. It's elegant yet homely, with lots of attractive *tadelakt* surfaces in prevailing tones of off-white, mushroom and chocolate.

Two of the rooms have fireplaces, some of the bathrooms are wonderful and a couple of the suites have their own mezzanine areas. A lounge area off the courtyard has a fireplace, a small library and a couple of tables set up for chess; for more rest and relaxation, there's a plunge pool which you can set fizzing with bubbles and a nice green-tiled hammam. If you've heard of this place before, however, its probably because of its former connection with Michelin-starred British chef Richard Neat. He's now departed for Costa Rica, but word has it that French owner Pierre Olivier is no slouch in the kitchen either.

Dar les Cigognes

108 rue de Berima (024 38 27 40/ www.lescignognes.com). **$$$**.
Map p85 D2 ㉔

Across the street from the eastern ramparts of the Badii Palace, Dar les Cigognes (House of the Storks) comprises two 17th-century merchants' houses, converted into one elegant 11-room riad hotel. Indoor public spaces, including a library, restaurant and bar, feature arches and orientalist paintings. There is also an African-themed 'living room'. Courtyards are spectacular, with lots of comfortable nook seating. The guest rooms have a restrained kind of opulence, with deep, jewel colours and luxury furnishings. A European spa is on site, in addition to the usual hammam, and the location means there are great views from the roof terrace.

Dar Fakir

16 Derb Abou El Fadal, off Riad Zitoun El Jedid (024 44 11 00/fax 024 44 90 42/darfakir@yahoo.fr). **$$**. **Map** p82 B2 ㉕

The riad for the clubbing generation. Dar Fakir's central courtyard and surrounding salons are layered with casually strewn rugs and scattered with glittery throw cushions. The heady scent of incense hangs heavy in the air and tea candles serve for illumination. There's a bar counter, and every corner and recess is filled with exotic

Sultana p163

plunderings from South-east Asia and the Levant. A chilled soundtrack adds to the Buddha Bar vibe. Of the eight rooms, two are on the ground floor and six are upstairs; they're very simply done but attractive, including *tadelakt* bathrooms. Owner Noureddine Fakir, an ambitious young Casablancan, also runs the nearby Marrakchi (p49) restaurant. Residents can order from its menu and have the food delivered within around 20 minutes.

Dar Karma

51 Derb el Mennabha, Kasbah (024 38 58 78/fax 024 37 58 78/www.dar-karma.com). $$$. Map p84 B4

For much of its century-long existence, this big old house near the Royal Palace was the home of Mohammed V's French translator. An elegant *maison d'hôte* since 2003, it still retains something of a homely air, despite now being kitted out with such mod cons as a small swimming pool and a water-mist cooling system to alleviate searing summer temperatures on the roof

terrace. The five bedrooms are smart but unfussy, with fine bedlinen and spacious bathrooms finished with marble and *tadelakt*. Communal salons are comfortable, the hammam is very grand indeed, and the card supplied to guests bearing a map with the hotel's location and instructions for what to tell taxi drivers is an innovation that other Medina establishments would do well to imitate.

Hotel Gallia

30 rue de la Recette, off rue Bab Agnaou (024 44 59 13/fax 024 44 48 53/www.ilove-marrakesh.com/ hotelgallia). Map p82 A3

The lanes off rue Bab Agnaou – seconds from the Jemaa El Fna – are thick with budget options, but Gallia comes top of the class. This small, French-owned operation gets ticks in all the right boxes: it's smack-bang central, impeccably clean and aesthetically pleasing. Nineteen en-suite double rooms open on to two picture-pretty, flower-filled courtyards, where an excellent

ESSENTIALS

breakfast is served. Bathrooms are big, modern pink affairs with limitless hot water. The well-kept flowery roof terrace is an ideal spot for lounging. Unsurprisingly, Gallia is popular. Bookings should be made by fax and it is advisable to book at least one month in advance.

Les Jardins de la Medina

21 Derb Chtouka, Kasbah (024 38 18 51/fax 024 38 53 85/www.les jardinsdelamedina.com). **$$$.** **Map** p84 B4 ㉘

At the southern end of the kasbah, this former royal residence has been a luxurious 36-room hotel since 2001. You enter a beautiful reception area eccentrically decorated with a tree and wooden birds hanging upside down from a painted dome. From there, you emerge into a seriously big garden with rows of orange trees and a heated swimming pool actually large enough to swim in – which makes it a great place for families. Comfortable rooms, decorated in a sort of Moroccan-international style, come in three categories but most are in the middle 'superior' class – big enough to have sofas as well as beds, and all of them with DVD players and iPod docks. A big international restaurant, a splendid hammam, a decently equipped gym and a beauty salon round off the range of services. There is also a cookery school.

Jnane Mogador

116 Riad Zitoun El Kedim (024 42 63 24/fax 024 42 63 23/www.jnane mogador.com). **$.** **Map** p82 A2 ㉙

Arguably offering the best value accommodation in Marrakech, the Mogador is a small riad that has considerable charm and warmth. And it's clean. All this for an unbelievable 380dh per double with en suite bathroom – just don't expect a power shower. The 17 bedrooms are simple and predominantly pink with light pine and wrought-iron furniture and *tadelakt* bathrooms. Public areas are a lot more ornate, with fountain courtyards, stucco arches and a large roof

terrace where breakfast is served. Be prepared, however, to dress warmly in winter as the riad has no heating. Advance reservations are essential as the place is permanently full; prices are due to go up in autumn 2007 (rates still to be established at time of writing). English may or may not be spoken, but if the riad's website is anything to go by ('This supernatural riad opens to those that conjugate their dreams in the present'), you don't stand much chance of understanding anything even if it is.

Palais Calipau

NEW *14 Derb Ben Zina, Kasbah (024 37 55 83/www.palais-calipau. com).* **$$$$.** **Map** p84 A3 ㉚

A bright and stylish conversion of three houses, Palais Calipau opened in March 2006. It's French-owned, although the majority of guests are from the UK and USA. There are 12 suites – four on the ground floor and eight upstairs – though some are more suite-like than others. We liked the cedar ceiling and cosy fireplace area of 'Zagora', the stained-glass in 'Tanger' and the green-tiled bathroom in 'Marrakech', but all of the rooms are colourful, comfortable and well-furnished, with high-definition TVs complementing traditional touches. There are also two heated pools, a hammam in elegant grey *tadelakt*, a bar and restaurant, and a huge roof terrace for eating or sun-lounging. A great set of services, but somehow it could use a little personality.

Riad Alma

NEW *77 Derb Kbala, Kasbah (024 37 71 62/www.riad alma.com).* **$$$.** **Map** p84 A4 ㉛

Created out of two adjoining houses in the Kasbah, Riad Alma has adopted a design ethos mixing Moroccan features – judicious use of *tadelakt*, rugs, artefacts and so on – with pieces from India and the East. The style is restrained: comfortable but considered. Colour is used to dramatic effect against an overall white paint job. One of the seven

rooms has a pink theme, with fuchsia Indian fabrics; in another, dark grey *tadelakt* makes for a dramatic bathroom; in a third the *tadelakt* is chocolate brown. A comfortable suite features a fireplace and a bath, and some rooms have CD players. In the second courtyard is a plunge pool, and there's a hammam on the premises. The roof terrace is extensive, with great views.

Riad Hayati

27 Derb Bouderba, off Derb El Bahia, Riad Zitoun El-Jedid (UK 07770 431 194/www.riad hayati.com). **$$$**.
Map p82 C4 ③②
Could this be the most tasteful riad in town? It's a little piece of visual perfection, with three all-white bedrooms set around the galleried first floor of a white courtyard; intricately carved dark wooden doors complement the snowy expanses. If needed, the ground-floor study can serve as a fourth bedroom, with its own en suite bathroom. Complementing the classic Moorish architecture are subtle references to Ottoman Turkey, Persia and

Arabia (a mirror modelled on one seen in Istanbul's Dolmabahçe Palace, a fountain from Damascus), mementos of the British owner's many years in news broadcasting from the Middle East (*hayati* means 'my life'). The location – just beyond the north wall of the Bahia Palace – is extremely peaceful but only six or seven minutes' walk from the Jemaa El Fna. Evening aperitifs are included, ideally taken on the roof terrace with its lovely Atlas views. A separate garden suite was due to open as we went to press, with its own terrace, courtyard garden, fountain and plungepool.

Riad Ifoulki

11 Derb Moqqadem, Arset Loghzail (tel/fax 024 38 56 56/www.riadifoulki. com). **$$**. **Map** p83 D2 ③③
This may well be the only riad in Marrakech at which Latin is spoken; Latin and nine other languages, in fact – including Danish, which is the nationality of owner Peter Berg. The property is a former palace (or at least, four-fifths of one), with a total of 14

Renovated, owned and managed by architect Christian Ferré, who lives on the premises, the eight-room Kaiss is small but exquisite. Its Rubik's Cube layout has rooms linked by galleries, multi-level terraces and tightly twisting stairs, all around a central court filled with orange, lemon and pomegranate trees. The decor is traditional Moroccan: earthy ochre walls with chalky Majorelle-blue trim, stencilled paintwork (including some gorgeous ceilings), jade *zelije* tiling and frilly furniture (including four-poster beds). Guests are greeted by red rose petals sprinkled on their white linen pillows. It's the Merchant Ivory of riads. Modern tastes dictate a cool plunge pool on the roof and a well-equipped fitness room – it's worth a workout for the ache-relieving pleasures of the visit to the in-house hammam that comes afterwards.

Riad Mabrouka

56 Derb El Bahia, off Riad Zitoun El Jedid (tel/fax 024 37 75 79/ www.riad-mabrouka.com). **$$$**. **Map** p82 C3 ⑤
The Mabrouka is a vision of cool, understated elegance. Architect Christophe Siméon has gone for a Moroccan minimalist look, with whitewashed walls, billowing canvas in place of doors and some fabulous painted ceilings and shutters; kilims add selective splashes of colour. The result is stylish, but also very comfortable. The bathrooms are seductively sensuous; all soft corners and rounded edges, they look as if they've been moulded out of coloured clay. With just two suites, three doubles and a lone single room, it has a very intimate feel. There's a pleasant cactus-potted roof terrace with a canvas-shaded breakfast area, and a good kitchen turning out Moroccan, Mediterranean, French and Italian cuisine.

Riad Noga

78 Derb Jedid, Douar Graoua (024 38 52 46/ fax 024 38 90 46/www.riad noga.com). **$$$**. **Map** p82 C1 ⑥

rooms arranged on several levels around numerous whitewashed courtyards, large and small. For all its imperial origins and size, this is one of the least showy and 'designed' of riads; the rooms are simple and unpretentious, with big beds swathed in translucent shimmery fabrics. Parts of the residence are self-contained with their own doors, making them ideal for families, and have gates at the top of stairs for child safety. There's a small library with volumes on Morocco in various languages, some of which are signed by their authors with gratitude to the erudite Berg. More energetic guests can take lessons in the arts of *tadelakt* (traditional plastering), *zelije* (tiling) and calligraphy, and are welcome to accompany the kitchen staff on shopping expeditions and help with cooking. Airport transfers are free.

Riad Kaiss

65 Derb Jedid, off Riad Zitoun El Kedim (tel/fax 024 44 01 41/www. riadkaiss.com). **$$$**. **Map** p82 B4 ㉔

Dar Les Cigognes

Boutique Hotel Marrakech

an oasis of luxury and calm

For centuries, a discreet door opposite the gates to the Royal Palace led to a wealthy merchant's home. Today, behind that door, with the help of celebrity architect Charles Boccara, we have created an oasis of luxury and calm, a boutique hotel called Dar Les Cigognes. Built around two courtyards, with fruit trees, palm trees and fountains, you will find the beauty of a riad's private world.

Each of the bedrooms is unique, drawing on the rich cultural heritage of Moorish art and decor. The beds and bathrooms have been designed with the highest level of comfort in mind, and friendly and attentive service will make you feel at home.

Dar Les Cigognes is located in the heart of the old town of Marrakech. With many of the important sites only a few steps away, you will find Dar Les Cigognes an excellent base for exploring the city.

---

11 Rooms and Suites with en-suite bathrooms and air conditioning, most with fireplaces.

Library, salon, roof gardens, numerous living rooms.

Hammam, jacuzzi, and spa facilities.
Boutique, Restaurant, Chauffered 4 x 4, Excursions, Parking

To make a booking or for more information, please contact us via:
Dar Les Cigognes, 108 rue de Berima, Medina, Marrakech, Morocco
Tel : +212 (0) 24 38 27 40, Fax : +212 (0) 24 38 47 67
Website: www.lescigognes.com   Email: info@lescigognes.com

Riad Noir d'Ivoire

It may not have the peerless reputation of Riad Farnatchi (p145) or the art world credibility of Riad El Fenn (p144). But Riad Noir d'Ivoire has its own angle on the question of just what to do with a Medina mansion.

Anglo-French husband-and-wife team of Jill Fechtmann and Jean-Michel Jobit – she with a background in interiors, he a designer of luxury product packaging – came to Marrakech without any intention of opening a hotel. They wanted to produce some decorative objects, do a few interiors. The 19th-century house near Bab Doukkala was acquired to serve as their private home – until they realised it was way too big and thought, 'Why not?'

They renovated in record time and furnished with an eclectic selection from Africa, India and Europe, as well as Moroccan items made to measure and eccentricities of their own imagining. The result, named after Jean-Michel's favourite colour, is both quirkily grand and unashamedly comfortable. Six rooms and suites were given animal themes, expressed in engravings and sculpture. The courtyard has a baby grand, the library a grandfather clock. There's plenty to look at, but it never feels cluttered or pretentious.

The idea was a guesthouse in the classic sense: not only stylish, but sociable. Around the bar or over breakfast, everyone gets to know everyone else, but guests can also find their own nooks and corners. 'We still want it to be very much a home,' says Jill.

She and Jean-Michel have now bought the house next door. They're busily converting to add three huge suites with private terraces, an 11-metre swimming pool, a smoking room, a wine cellar and a hanging garden.

Olaf Galaburda, formerly of Dar les Cigognes (p151), has meanwhile arrived to manage the hotel. Among a hubbub of plans for new details and services, there is talk both of English breakfasts and afternoon teas, and of 'revisiting Moroccan cuisine'. Even in the kitchen, the homely shares space with the cutting edge in one of the best new riads in town.

ESSENTIALS

Jnane Mogador p153

One of the most homely of Marrakech's riads. Behind salmon-pink walls lies a bougainvillaea and orange tree-filled courtyard (complete with chatty grey parrot), serving as an antechamber to an inner, more private court centred on a shimmering, green-tiled, solar-heated swimming pool. Noga is very spacious (it's made up of three old houses knocked into one), and shared by just seven bedchambers. All of the rooms are bright, bold and cheery, displaying the hospitable touch (small libraries of holiday-lite literature, for instance) of the garrulous German owner, Gaby Noack-Späth. Expansive roof terraces filled with terracotta pots and lemon trees offer terrific views over the Medina and make for the perfect spot to enjoy aperitifs or fine cooking from the excellent in-house Moroccan chefs. The riad is closed during August.

Riad Omar

22 rue Bab Agnaou (024 44 56 60/ fax 024 38 75 22/www.riadomar.com). No credit cards. **$**. **Map** p84 A2 ③⑦

A brusque atmosphere and cramped rooms with no frills are the trade-off for budget prices and an excellent location on the pedestrianised rue Bab Agnaou, a short stroll south of the square. This is a hotel rather than a *maison d'hôte*, with 17 rooms and four suites set around a central courtyard with a small fountain. All are air-conditioned and en-suite, though only eight have bathtubs. The four suites have small sitting-rooms with fireplaces, but in the normal doubles you can either sit on the beds or lie on them, and that's pretty much it. The hammam is rather plain, but at least they have one. On the roof there's a tented restaurant that looks overpriced (menus at 150dh and 200dh) and bears no relation to the Snack Omar on the street downstairs.

Riad W

NEW *41 Derb Boutouil, Kennaria (065 36 79 36/www.riadw.com).* No credit cards. **$$**. **Map** p82 B2 ③⑧

Working on the premise that guests would get quite enough sensory input

from their forays into the Medina, Spanish owner Elsa Bauza designed her four-room riad with a philosophy of simplicity and 'quiet in the head'. The bedrooms – one huge, two big, and one small – have white walls, unadorned save for a few framed textiles. Downstairs, zen-like lines are matched by some quietly retro furnishings. This interior comes as a refreshing change in a town where there's often too much colour and clutter. Up top are two roof terraces, each shared by two rooms. Below is a spacious courtyard, a plunge pool, two sitting-rooms (one with a piano), and Bauza and her daughter's appartment. Breakfast is included, and dinner can be arranged on request.

Riyad Al Moussika

62 Derb Boutouil, Kennaria (024 38 90 67/fax 024 37 76 53/www.riyad-al-moussika.ma). **$$$. Map** p82 B2 ㉟
One reason laid-back Turinese owner Giovanni Robazza opened this former pasha's palace as a guesthouse was to showcase the Cordon Bleu cooking of his son Khalid. This is a riad for gourmands, dedicated, as their publicity puts it, 'to the art of good living', with a touch of pretension but a comfortable, worn-in feel. Both a big breakfast and two-course lunch are included in the rates, and it's not a place to lose weight. The palace has been restored in a relatively traditional style: fountains splash and birds sing in trees, while six bedrooms are complemented by a hammam, a formal dining-room, a music room with piano and a small library with some interesting volumes. There are three courtyards, one with a long, thin, 'Andalucian' pool for swimming, along with two flower-filled roof terraces for sunbathing, breakfasting or dining. Minimum stay of three nights.

Sherazade

3 Derb Djama, off Riad Zitoun El-Kedim (tel/fax 024 42 93 05/ www.hotelsherazade.com). **$. Map** p82 A2 ㊵
Probably the most popular budget accommodation in the Medina. Why

ESSENTIALS

Oasis of luxury

Come to the Palmeraie for Moroccan fantasy without Medina bustle.

Dar Zemora

An ever-growing number of resort hotels scattered around the **Palmeraie** (see box p109), a 20-minute drive from the Medina, offer the luxury of glorious isolation.

Set in lush rose and hibiscus gardens, the main house at **Dar Zemora** (72 rue El Aandalib, Ennakhil, 024 32 82 00, www.dar zemora.com, $$$$) contains just three beautiful and luxurious rooms and two huge suites. There's a large heated pool too.

The creation of designer Meryanne Loum-Martin and her ethnobotanist husband Dr Gary Martin, **Jnane Tamsna** (024 32 94 23, www.jnanetamsna.com, $$$$) is a 'Moorish hacienda' with seven opulent suites and 17 gorgeous rooms, scattered around gardens, each with its own pool. Surrounding fruit orchards, herb and vegetable gardens provide fresh produce for the kitchen.

Ksar Char-Bagh (024 32 92 44, www.ksarcharbagh.com, $$$$) has been built from scratch on a kasbah-sized scale. A handful of sumptuous suites (each with private terrace) share extensive grounds, flower gardens, an open-air spa and the deepest of pools. Lunch or dinner (the chef trained under Alain Ducasse and Joël Robuchon) can be served out on the terrace or by the pool.

Les Deux Tours (024 32 95 27, www.les-deuxtours.com, $$$) is the work of Marrakchi architect Charles Boccara. It's a walled enclave of earthen-red villas, in a lush blossom- and palm-filled garden. All rooms feature glowing tadelakt walls and zelije tiling with stunning sculpturally soft bathrooms. Guests share the attractive outdoor pools and a stunning subterranean hammam.

Run by French-Swedish couple Pierre Blanc and Pia Westh, **Villa Vanille** (024 31 01 23, www.villa vanille.com, $$) is a collection of unique villas set in gorgeous grounds with a heated swimming pool. There's a small playground for children, and a gym and massage room for grown-ups.

Riyad El Cadi p150

so? Perhaps because it's so much better run than most of its competitors at this end of the market. The desk staff speak a variety of languages, English included, rooms come with meal menus and services, trips out of town can be arranged, the place is cleaned regularly, and there's a general air of competency, which isn't always a given when it comes to budget accommodation. Some rooms are better than others; those on the roof share toilets and soon become overly hot in summer, while only a handful of the most expensive have air-conditioning. Breakfast is charged extra at 50dh per person. During high season an extra 50dh is added to room charges.

Sultana

Rue de la Kasbah, Kasbah (024 38 80 08/fax 024 38 77 77/la sultanamarrakech.com). **$$$$**.
Map p84 A3 ③
Opened in 2004, the Sultana is astonishing in that it's a completely new-build hotel of considerable size and scale slapped down in the middle of the Medina. And you'd never know it was there. It has no frontage to speak of, but beyond the arched street door are 11 guestrooms and ten suites, connected by seemingly acres of arcaded corridors, courtyards, landings and galleries and serviced by 62 staff. There's a good-sized swimming pool, a full spa complex, a row of boutiques and a vast roof terrace that overlooks the gardens of the Saadian Tombs. The hotel boasts all the facilities and amenities of a five-star but is packaged to look like a *maison d'hôte*. The architecture (Moorish-Gothic) and decoration is sumptuous going on camp (check out the life-size bronze camel beside the pool), piling Indian, African and Oriental on the Moroccan. Serving French and Moroccan cuisine, the restaurant is open to non-guests who reserve in advance, but the basement bar is for residents only. Kitted out to resemble a ship's cabin, the bar even has a window into the deep end of the swimming pool.

Villa El Arsa

18 Derb El-Arsa, off Riad Zitoun El-Jedid (tel/fax 024 42 63 26/www.villa elarsa.com). No credit cards. **$$**.
Map p82 B2 ④
Owned by a British couple, David and Susie Scott, this is a modest little house, but utterly charming with it. There's a rustic, vaguely Spanish air about the place, suggested by whitewashed walls, potted plants, and bare, weathered wooden doors and furniture. There are two attractive cushion-filled lounging salons off a central courtyard that comes with a tub-sized underlit plunge pool. The four bedrooms are ranged off the irregularly shaped upper gallery. Two of the rooms are on the small side, but the other pair are generous; all are rendered in calm neutral tones with splendid en-suite bathrooms. One of the larger rooms contains an additional single bed and is air-conditioned. Plus there's the ubiquitous roof terrace, in this case with an open fireplace for chill winter evenings. The Scotts have good connections with a pair of mountain guides, and can arrange one-day or overnight trekking in the Atlas.

Guéliz

Guéliz offers a continental-style café scene, boutique shopping, good eating and what passes locally for nightlife. It's a good antidote to the foreignness of the Medina, which is actually only five minutes from central Guéliz by taxi. Semlalia is the district just a few minutes' north of Guéliz on the route de Casablanca.

Hotel du Pacha

33 rue de la Liberté (024 43 13 27/fax 024 43 13 26). No credit cards. **$**.
Map p98 C4 ④
A standard two-star joint, nondescript and of a kind common to cities the world over. The only indication that this is Morocco is a handful of aged tourist office posters as decoration. The better rooms have small balconies

Beyond the riad

The Marrakech tourist phenomenon has, until now, been driven by the piecemeal conversion of Medina houses into boutique hotels. At the time of writing, 370 were registered as *maisons d'hôtes* (with more than five rooms but fewer than 30, each with private bathroom). A further 150 were awaiting classification. These are mostly idiosyncratic establishments, run according to the philosophies of individual owners.

But rising real estate prices are making things more difficult for the individual entrepreneur, the new hotel zone (see box p122) will have a capacity to dwarf even hundreds of riads, and a number of players in the international luxury hotel market are now arriving in Marrakech.

Flush with his recent success on the Champs Elysées, Lucien Barrière is to open a Fouquet's Barrière Marrakech in 2008. Located in the Medina, it will have 250 rooms plus spa and restaurant. Four Seasons also opens next year with 140 rooms, 40 villas and a golf course in the Menara. For 2009, Mandarin Oriental is planning a similarly sized complex in the Palmeraie, where a Murano Oriental Resort has also recently opened. Banyan Tree is another group set to arrive next year, with a 'sanctuary of the senses' complex in the Medina. And the latest news is that the W chain is also looking to move in. One way or another, Marrakech is moving beyond the riad.

overlooking a central courtyard. All are in need of a little investment, with worn furniture and fittings, but the beds are comfortable and the en-suite bathrooms are kept clean. For the price it's a reasonable deal – and one that has considerable appeal for independent tour groups, judging by the logo'd stickers on the door. The hotel business card announces that it has a 'restaurant gastronomique' but that's hardly the case – this is not a problem, though, as there are many good dining options in the neighbourhood. Note that there is an extra charge for breakfast (30dh).

Moroccan House Hotel

3 Rue Loubnane (024 42 03 05/ fax 024 42 02 97/moroccan househotels@menara.ma). **$.** **Map** p98 B4 ⑮

There are 52 rooms in this Moroccan-run hotel, open since 2004. Having struggled a little too hard to simulate a traditional atmosphere in a modern building, the result is a bit lurid and frilly. But on the positive side, there's a swimming pool and a hammam, the location is central for Guéliz, the atmosphere is friendly and it's not a bad option for the price. The table football by the pool is a pleasingly inauthentic touch, and there's a lift for people daunted by too many Medina staircases. A few doors away at No.12, Le Caspien (024 42 22 82/ fax 024 42 00 79/www.lecaspien-hotel.com) offers similar services at a similar price in surroundings that are are slightly less 'Moroccan'.

Hivernage

Aka the international enclave, Hivernage is home to the city's collection of big name chain hotels. The area is located between the airport and the walls of the Medina (five minutes from each), so the location is convenient, but the architectural neighbours are puffed-up villas and civic buildings and it's a taxi journey to reach anywhere of interest.

Hotel Es Saadi

Avenue El Qadissia (024 44 88 11/ fax 024 44 76 44/www.essaadi.com). **$$$. Map** p121 E4 ⓐ

The Saadi has been around forever. Cecil Beaton snapped the Rolling Stones beside its pool back in the late 1960s. Undoubtedly, then it looked like the chicest thing on the planet; now it looks more like a municipal hospital. Guests tend to be of the same era as the hotel (that is, a good few decades past their prime), but a lot of them are repeat customers, so folk are obviously well looked after here. Rooms (150 of them) are dated but comfortable, but be sure to get one facing south, overlooking the verdant gardens. We like the way the glass rear wall of the lobby slides up during the day so that the hotel blends seamlessly with the poolside terrace – and the irregularly shaped pool remains one of the biggest and best in town. Even if you aren't staying at the Es Saadi, the terrace is a good lunch option and the house club Théatro (p125) is currently one of the hippest nightspots in town.

Le Meridien N'Fis

Avenue Mohammed VI (024 44 87 72/www.lemeridien.com). **$$$. Map** p121 D5 ⓐ

For those in search of the comfortable familiarity of the chain hotel experience, Le Meridien N'Fis offers 278 rooms (including 12 suites), along with two restaurants, a bar, a tearoom, a pool and all the other amenities you'd expect at an international resort. The hotel is a five-minute taxi ride from the Medina.

Royal Mirage Marrakech

Avenue de la Menara (024 44 89 98/ www.royalmiragehotels.com). **$$. Map** p120 C5 ⓐ

Formerly the Sheraton, the Royal Mirage has 219 rooms, ten suites and a 'royal villa', plus five restaurants, a bar. Sports facilities include a pool, a putting green and tennis courts. It's a short taxi ride from the Medina.

Ryad Mogador Menara

Avenue Mohammed VI (024 33 93 30/ www.ryadmogador.com). **$$. Map** p120 B3 ⓐ

Opened in 2005, the Mogador Menara (directly opposite the Palais des Congrès) has all the comfort and facilities one would expect from a smart international hotel – the outdoor swimming pool and poolside area with snack bar are particularly impressive – as well as the common drawback of a slight lack of personality. On the plus side, with 244 rooms there's a good chance you'll find a bed for the night here, even during busy periods.

Sofitel Marrakech

Rue Harroun Errachid (024 42 56 00/www.sofitel.com). **$$$$. Map** p121 E4 ⓐ

We rate the Sofitel as the best chain hotel in Marrakech. It has a lovely garden with a big pool and it's also close to the Medina walls and within walking distance of Jemaa El Fna. There are 260 rooms and suites, each with private balcony or terrace (ask for south-facing, overlooking the garden with the mountains in the distance), as well as all the usual facilities.

Essaouira

There's no shortage of places to stay in Essaouira, but it's still wise to book in advance if you've got your heart set on a particular guesthouse, and essential if you want to secure anything at all over Christmas or Easter and during the gnawa festival in late June. Happily, there are rooms to suit all budgets and there's no such thing as a bad location – most places are a few minutes' walk from the central place Moulay Hassan and the fishing port.

As in the Marrakech Medina, small *maisons d'hôtes* have proliferated in the last few years.

Les Jardins d'Inès

*U*nder the discerning eye of Chef Jean Marie Gueraische, exquisite cuisine is magnificently choreographed to offer exclusive dining experience served in elegant minimalist surroundings.

The luxurious atmosphere extends to the terrace, which opens onto the gardens.

Circuit de la Palmeraie - BP 1488 - Marrakech
Tél.: +212 24 33 42 00 - Fax : +212 24 33 42 01 - Site web : www.lesjardinsdines.com

Old Essaouira houses are set around open courtyards and tend to be smaller and less fussy than their Marrakchi equivalents. Most rooms in such places overlook the inner patio, but Essaouira also boasts rooms with ocean glimpses and roof terraces affording cinematic vistas of sea and sky. On the other hand, terrace breakfasts can be prey to high winds, and some houses on the ocean side fight a running battle with damp. This is a town where you will be glad of a log fire or central heating in winter.

Self-contained apartments of one sort or another are available at Dar Beida/Dar Emma and also via Hotel Smara, Jack's Kiosk, Dar Al Bahar and Riad Gyvo.

Beau Rivage

14 place Moulay Hassan (024 47 59 25/ www.essaouiranet.com/beaurivage). $.
The pick of the inexpensive options, Beau Rivage has been operating above the Café Opera on the Medina's main square since 1939 – and was renovated in 2002. There are 15 bedrooms and six suites. All are clean, colourful and bright and have toilets and showers en suite. Rooms on the second floor also have balconies overlooking the square. The location can be noisy but is as central as it gets; though still offering big views from the roof terrace, it is cosier and more sheltered than those places overlooking the ramparts. Breakfast is extra, but it's just as easy to nip downstairs for croissants from Chez Driss and a coffee at one of the tables on the square.

Casa Lila

NEW *94 rue Med El-Qorry (024 47 55 45/www.riad-casalila.com).* $$.
Half-way between the souks and Bab Marrakech, this tasteful and unfussy *maison d'hote* has eight rooms and suites plus one two-bedroom apartment ranged around the usual central courtyard. Most of the rooms are equipped with baths (three just have showers)

and all except the apartment boast open fires. Common areas include a salon off the courtyard and a rambling roof terrace. The place is all nicely decorated in bold pinks and purples with lots of grey *tadelakt* in the bathrooms, complemented by a few well-chosen knicknacks.

Dar Adul

63 rue Touahen (tel/fax 024 47 3910/ mobile 071 52 02 21/www.dar-adul. com). No credit cards. $.
Houses on the ocean side of the Medina need a lot of maintenance if they're not to fall into decline and the five bedrooms of this unpretentious French-owned former notary's house were recently renovated to good effect. The owners also added – the first in Essaouira – a skylight to close off the atrium in inclement conditions. The shared sitting room with open fire is comfortable and there are excellent views from the roof terrace, where breakfast is served when it's not too windy.

Dar Al Bahar

1 rue Touahen (024 47 68 31/www.dar albahar.com). No credit cards. $.
The 'House by the Sea' is right on the northern ramparts, with waves crashing on the rocks below – there's no place in town quite as close to the ocean. The French-Dutch couple who own it have decorated their nine rooms in clean, bold colours, bright fabrics and local naïve art. Not all of them have sea views and they're not the biggest lodgings in town, but even the non-view ones are nice enough and more economically priced. The big roof terrace affords breakfast with a tang of sea spray. They also have an apartment (sleeps two) which is rented out for 1,000dh per night.

Dar Beida/Dar Emma

067 96 53 86 in Morocco/07768 352 190 in UK/www.castlesinthesand.com. $$$$.
Dar Beida, 'the White House' is worth considering if you're after something special. Deep in a corner of the Medina, a twist or two off the tourist trail, this

is a wonderful 200-year-old house owned by English partners Emma Wilson and Graham Carter. They've renovated and furnished with playful good taste, mixing Moroccan materials and flea-market finds with interesting imported antiques and a retro vibe. The result manages to be both idiosyncratically stylish and unpretentiously comfortable. It can sleep up to four couples, has two bathrooms, two roof terraces, lounge, a small library, open fires and a well-equipped kitchen plus two amiable cats for £300 per person per week (minimum booking of three persons).

In addition, Emma Wilson also runs the less pricey and slightly smaller Dar Emma. This compact 19th-century house in an alley off rue Derb Laâlouj has a kitchen, two double bedrooms and a roof terrace. The whole place can be rented at £600 a week for a couple, or £700 a week for more than two people.

Dar Loulema

2 rue Souss (024 47 53 46/mobile 061 24 76 61/www.riadloulema.com). $$.
A well-run and straight-faced sort of place at the Kasbah end of the Medina, just behind the Taros café, which the terrace overlooks. It's a nice old house, more generously proportioned than many of its competitors. There are eight rooms, mostly named, and vaguely themed, after Moroccan cities, so 'Essaouira' is blue and white and 'Marrakech' is pink. Breakfast can be served in your room, on the terrace, in the patio, by the central fountain, in one of the living rooms with open fires – just about anywhere, really. Staff will also make dinner (180dh).

Dar Mimosas

Km1 Route d'Agadir (024 47 59 34/ www.darmimosas.com). $$$$.
On the right-hand side of the Agadir road about a kilometre after it forks away from the route back to Marrakech, this is a walled compound of peace and luxury around the bay from Essaouira proper. Four suites and four villas are scattered in beautiful Italianate gardens. Two of the suites have their own gardens; the other two have terraces with views of the sea – 15 minutes' walk away across scrubby dunes. The villas have one or two bedrooms, sitting-rooms, well-equipped kitchens, two bathrooms each and walled gardens with fountains. All of the lodgings have log fires. You need never see another guest if you don't feel sociable, but it would be a shame to miss out on the gorgeous swimming pool, tiled in blue and white. The main house, coloured a brilliant terracotta, has dining rooms, TV room, a terrace, a well-stocked bar and the apartment of Morocco-born French owner Philippe Cachet. Service is nicely pitched between attentive and discreet and the food is excellent – staff bake their own bread for breakfast and serve honey from their own hives. Ridley Scott, Orlando Bloom, the Pet Shop Boys and King Mohammed VI have been among the guests since it opened in September 2000.

Dar L'Oussia

NEW *4 rue Mohammed ben Messaoud (024 78 37 56/fax 024 47 27 77/ www.darloussia.com). $$.*
More of a hotel than a *maison d'hôte*, this place near the Bab Sbâa nevertheless consists of a house with rooms ranged around a central courtyard. It's just a very big house with a very grand courtyard, and 24 rooms in its upper reaches. Well fitted and colourfully decorated, these come in three categories. Standard rooms are a decent 25 sq m, with king-size beds and big bathrooms. 'Deluxe' rooms are 35 sq m, with bigger beds and bigger bathrooms. And 'junior suites' are a whopping 50 sq m, with enormous beds and very big bathrooms. To top it all there's a vast roof terrace, but the architectural highlight is the spectacular carved archway in the courtyard by the entrance. Beyond it there's a vaulted dining-room.

L'Heure Bleue

*2 rue Ibn Batouta, Bab Marrakech
(024 78 34 34/ www.heure-bleue.com).*
$$$$.
This upmarket renovation of what was once a private mansion has 16 rooms and 19 suites around a spacious, leafy courtyard. It also has the Medina's only lift ascending to the Medina's only rooftop pool. The standard rooms (on the first floor) are spacious and African-themed – black marble, dark wood, zebra-patterned upholstery. Suites on the second floor, which get more light and seem better value, also come in Portuguese (blue and white), British colonial (19th-century engravings) and 'Eastern' (gold and burgundy) flavours. The British colonial theme – the 'clubroom' bar has big armchairs and mounted animal heads – seems pretentious and daft. There's also a DVD screening room, a beautiful hammam in black tadelakt, and a decent restaurant.

Hotel Smara

26 bis, rue de la Skala (024 47 56 55).
No credit cards. **$.**
Upstairs from Les Alizés Mogador (p130) are simple rooms with bed, sink and table, overlooking the ramparts and ocean or (at the cheaper rate) nothing. Bathrooms and toilets are shared. Breakfast is an extra 14dh, or 18dh with juice. It's all basic and the staff are a bit brusque, but you can't argue with the prices. They also have apartments in the Medina.

Hotel Souiri

*37 rue Lattarine (024 47 53 39/souiri
@menara.ma).* **$.**
This budget option has a central location but no sea views. There are 39 cool and colourful rooms, of which 24 have bathrooms en suite. An apartment is also available. There's nice stained glass throughout.

Madada

*5 rue Youssef El Fassi (024 47 55 12/
www.madada.com).* **$$.**
At the south-west corner of the Medina, this is a smart and stylish six-room affair that, refreshingly, doesn't work too hard at looking 'Moroccan'. Upstairs from, and owned by the same people as Le Cinq restaurant, the accents are mostly Parisian rather than Souiri. The four rooms on the first floor have their own crenellated terraces overlooking the town and the port, but these are separated from each other only by wrought-iron fences and lack a feeling of privacy. Two of the rooms are on the roof, where breakfast is also served, and there's a panoramic view of the whole bay from a small upper level.

La Maison des Artistes

*19 rue Derb Laâlouj (024 47 57 99/
mobile 062 60 54 38/www.lamaison
desartistes.com).* **$.**
A characterful French-run guesthouse making the most of its oceanfront location and the slightly eccentric taste of its original owners. It has six comfortable rooms, three overlooking the sea, three facing on to the patio, all furnished differently and some boasting intriguingly odd pieces. The suite is splendid, with the ocean on three sides and lording over it, the roof terrace like the bridge of a ship. It's pretty exposed, however, and can get a bit rattly in high winds. La Maison seems to be a home from home for an assortment of young and vaguely arty French folks, and whether you'll like it here depends greatly on whether you get on with the crowd. Manager Cyril is also proud of his 'Judeo-Berber' kitchen and lunch or dinner (150dh per person, non-residents 200dh, booking necessary) can be served on the terrace with the ocean view.

Ocean Vagabond Guest House

NEW *4 Boulevard Lalla Aicha (024 47 92 22/www.oceanvagabond.com).* **$$.**
In a modern villa on the seafront, just a short walk outside the old city walls, Ocean Vagabond boasts a few features alien to converted medina houses, such as a garden and a pool. Opened by the crew from the Ocean Vagabond café

ESSENTIALS

and surf station, it's a breath of fresh air in all senses. Common areas are cool, bright, stylish and simple. The 14 rooms are themed ('Bali' is vaguely Indonesian, 'Geisha' vaguely Japanese, and so on). Try to get one of the four ('Dogon', 'Felluca', 'Pondichéry' and 'Inca') that have balconies with an ocean view (two others have balconies with a view of the Medina – and the post office). A garden bungalow is the place for pampering: it houses a hammam and rooms for massage, beauty treatments and a hairdresser.

Riad Al Madina

9 rue Attarine (024 47 59 07/ www.riadalmadina. com). **$$**.
Once the location of the Hippy Café, this is now a rather lackadaisical mid-price hotel that trades on the myth that Jimi Hendrix once stayed here. The beautiful courtyard is one of the nicest breakfast spots in town, but the rooms that overlook it, though decorated with colourful materials, tend to be poky, dark and full of tour groups. The owners recently bought the house next door and added a hammam (70dh) and 30 new rooms to make a total of 54.

Riad Gyvo

3 rue Mohammed Ben Messaoud (024 47 51 02/ www.riadgyvo.com). **$$**.
This big 200-year-old house in the corner of town by Bab Sbaâ is handy for arrivals or departures, but it's the space rather than the location that is the real draw. Many Essaouira guesthouses can feel a bit poky, but the three studios, two apartments and one terrace room arranged around the big central courtyard are all truly spacious, and all but one have their own kitchenettes. The apartments (1,250dh) are particularly grand, and can sleep up to four, with a 200dh supplement per person beyond double occupancy (80dh for under-10s). The ground-floor rooms are a bit dark but there are sunbeds and genuinely panoramic views up on the roof terrace, where breakfast (60dh) can be served.

Ryad Watier

NEW *16 rue Ceuta (024 47 62 04/ www.ryad-watier-maroc.com).* **$$**.
Open as a hotel since April 2005, this building was formerly a school, which means a more rambling, less predictable arrangement than in the usual converted Medina house. There are seven double rooms and three suites with two bedrooms, all with small writing desks (a rarity in Essaouira) and all en suite, but none with baths, only showers. There's also a big dining-room, a terrace on what used to be the playground, a hammam and a massage room, a pair of roof terraces, and a pretty decent library by Moroccan riad standards. Rooms and common areas are decorated with paintings and old film posters from the idiosyncratic collection of French owner Jean Gabriel, for whom the whole thing is obviously a labour of love. Every picture tells a story, which he'll cheerfully relate.

Villa Maroc

10 rue Abdellah Ben Yassine (024 47 61 47/www.villa-maroc.com). **$$**.
The first boutique hotel in Morocco when it opened in 1990, Villa Maroc is now a mature, well-known establishment. It's conveniently located just inside the walls of the Kasbah quarter, its roof terraces overlooking the square and the fishing port. Twenty rooms and suites are nicely furnished and arranged around an intriguing warren of open terraces, narrow staircases and small, secluded spaces – the result of knocking together four old merchants' houses. No two rooms are alike; some are a bit cramped and gloomy, and the suites are built around a central patio, so you can hear what's happening on the next floor. The 'oriental spa' has a beautiful small hammam for individuals or pairs, and offers a variety of massage and beauty treatments – also open to non-residents. Dinner is 200dh and the food, served in one of several small salons, uses ingredients from the owners' own farm. Non-residents are welcome, but must book by 5pm.

Getting Around

Addresses

Streets in Marrakech are well signposted in both French and Arabic, except in the Medina where the majority of alleyways have signs in Arabic only, or none at all. Ask the locals; if the person questioned doesn't know, they'll often try to find someone who does.

Arriving & leaving

By air

Marrakech's international airport (Aéroport Marrakech Menara) is located six kilometres (four miles) west of the city. At press time a new terminal was in construction. There are banks offering currency exchange in the arrivals hall, open 8am-6pm daily, plus two ATMs. For flight information, call 024 44 78 65 or 024 44 79 10.

Taxis wait outside the arrivals building. In a *petit taxi* the official fare to anywhere in the Medina or Guéliz is 60dh (to the Palmeraie 120dh) but drivers usually demand more. Most will accept payment in dollars, euros or pounds at the equivalent dirham rate.

Airlines

Most airlines have their offices in Casablanca. An increasing number of budget carriers now fly to Morocco from across Europe.

British Airways
Avenue des FAR, Casablanca (022 47 30 23). **Open** 8.30am-12.30pm, 2.30-6.30pm Mon-Sat.
The main office is in Casablanca; you must call it to confirm all flights.

Royal Air Maroc (RAM)
197 avenue Mohammed V, Guéliz (024 42 55 00). **Open** 8.30am-12.15pm, 2.30-7pm Mon-Fri.

There is a 24-hour call centre (090 00 08 00) for flight reconfirmation, flight information and reservations.

Atlas-blue
www.atlas-blue.com
EasyJet
www.easyjet.com
Ryanair
www.ryanair.com
Thomsonfly
www.thomsonfly.com

By rail

Trains are operated by the national railway company **ONCF** (024 44 77 68, www.oncf.ma). The old train station is on avenue Hassan II (map pxxx xx); a new rail terminal facing on to avenue Mohammed VI is under construction and due to open at the beginning of 2008. Marrakech is the southernmost terminus of two lines, both of which pass through Casablanca and Rabat; some trains then continue north to Tangier, others north-east to Oujda on the Algerian border via Meknes and Fès. A swarm of taxis meets each incoming train; the *petit taxi* fare into central Guéliz is 5dh-6dh; to the Medina 10dh. Alternatively, you can wait for bus No.3 or 8, which pass by the station en route to the place de Foucault for Jemaa El Fna.

By bus

The *gare routière* is just beyond the Medina walls at Bab Doukkala. Most long-distance buses terminate here, including those operated by national carrier **CTM** (024 43 39 33). Both the central Medina and Guéliz are walkable from the station; a *petit taxi* will cost 5dh-6dh, or catch a local bus for place de Foucault (Jemaa El Fna). There is also a CTM office (which sells tickets) in Guéliz on boulevard Mohammed Zerktouni, a few doors along from the Cinema la Colisée, where buses also stop.

The superior **Supratours** (024 43 55 25) buses run to and from Essaouira, Agadir, Laayoune and Dakhla. They pull up at the forecourt of the company's own little terminus, next to the railway station.

Essaouira is a popular destination; the Supratour buses fill up fast so it's wise to purchase tickets in advance. Buses depart at 8.30am, 11am, 3.30pm and 7pm daily. It takes 3½ hours and costs 65dh one way. In Essaouira buses arrive and leave from outside Bab Marrakech (where there's a ticket kiosk; 024 47 53 17) at 6.10am, noon, 4pm and 6.45pm daily.

Public transport

Marrakech has a limited city bus network radiating from the Medina out to the suburbs. Few local bus services are of use to visitors. The exceptions are those services that run between the Medina and Guéliz, which is a fairly long walk, but it's less hassle to take a taxi.

Buses

City buses (024 43 39 33) are regular coaches with no air-conditioning. They charge a flat fee of 3dh payable to the driver – make sure you have the correct change. All the following buses leave from place de Foucault, opposite the Hotel de Foucault, 100m west of the Jemaa El Fna.

Local bus routes

No.1 to Guéliz along avenue Mohammed V.
No.2 to Bab Doukkala for the *gare routière*.
No.3 to Douar Laskar via avenue Mohammed V, avenue Hassan II and the train station.
No.4 to Daoudiate (a northern suburb) by avenue Mohammed V.
No.8 to Douar Laskar via avenue Mohammed V, avenue Moulay Hassan and the train station.
No.10 to boulevard de Safi via Bab Doukkala and the *gare routière*.
No.11 to the airport via avenue de la Menara and the Menara Gardens.
No.14 to the train station.

Taxis

A taxi can be handy simply for navigation – some hotels and eateries are so well hidden that only natives can find them.

Taxis are plentiful and easy to hail. They are also cheap enough that it makes little sense bothering with buses. The standard ride is known as a **petit taxi** (lettered on the side of the car as such). By law, they can carry a maximum of three passengers and cannot travel beyond the city limits.

Drivers are often reluctant to use the meter so it's often a question of knowing the right fare. From Jemaa El Fna to Guéliz costs around 6dh; from Jemaa El Fna to the Palmeraie around 40dh. Expect to pay about 50 per cent more after 8pm (9pm in summer). Taxis are also necessary for shuttling between the Medina and Guéliz, which is only a five-minute ride (roughly 20dh).

Grand taxis are bigger cars that can squeeze in six people and are more expensive. They loiter outside hotels and the railway station. Avoid them, unless you are a group of four or more or are travelling long distance; some *grand taxi*s operate like minibuses running fixed routes to outlying suburbs and towns. They are also the only way of getting to the Palmeraie, which is just beyond the range of *petit taxi*s. Shared *grand taxi*s to **Essaouira** leave from Bab Doukkala and cost around 80dh per person.

Note, it is mandatory for front-seat passengers to wear seat belts in a taxi.

Driving

A car is useful for venturing out of the city, but of limited use within Marrakech itself. For short-term visitors, taxis are cheap, plentiful and easily hired by the day for around 250dh; ask your hotel for help finding a reputable driver.

Vehicles drive on the right in Morocco. The French rule of giving priority to traffic from the right is observed at roundabouts and junctions. Speed limits are 40km/h (25mph) in urban areas, 100km/h (62mph) on main roads, 120km/h (74mph) on autoroutes. There are on-the-spot fines for speeding and other traffic offences. It is compulsory to wear seatbelts.

Be wary when driving at night as cyclists and moped riders often have no lights, and street lighting can also be poor. Report any accident to the nearest *gendarmerie* to obtain a written statement, otherwise insurance will be invalid.

Car hire

To hire a car, you must be over 21, have a full driving licence and carry a passport or national identity card. Rental isn't cheap; daily rates with a local agency start at about 400dh for a Fiat Palio, Citroen Saxo or Peugeot 205 with unlimited mileage. At the internationals like Avis, Budget or Hertz, expect to pay about 25 per cent more.

The drawback with many of the local hire firms is the back-up service – cars may be ancient and unreliable; breakdown and replacement vehicles may not always be forthcoming.

Payments made by credit card often incur an additional five per cent fee. This is one of several reasons why it works out cheaper

to arrange your car rental in advance via a travel agent or the internet.

Rental cars in Morocco are delivered empty of petrol and returned empty. Almost all agencies will deliver cars to your hotel and arrange pick-up at no extra charge but this service must be booked in advance.

If you are heading south over the mountains, remember that you are responsible for any damage caused off-road or along unsuitable tracks. Four-wheel drives, such as a Toyota Landcruisers, are available from most hire companies and start at around 1,200dh (£75/$147) per day.

Avis, Budget, Europcar and Hertz also have desks inside the terminal at Aéroport Marrakech Menara.

Always Car *15 rue Imam Chafi, Kawkab Centre, Guéliz (061 19 31 29)*. **Open** 8am-noon, 2.30-7pm daily. Can also arrange English-speaking drivers.

Avis *137 avenue Mohammed V, Guéliz (024 43 25 25/www.avis.com)*. **Open** 8am-7pm Mon-Sat; 8am-noon Sun.

Budget *68 boulevard Mohammed Zerktouni, Guéliz (024 43 11 80/ www.budget rentacar.com)*. **Open** 8am-noon, 2.30-7pm Mon-Fri; 9am-noon, 3-6pm Sat; 9am-noon Sun.

Concorde Cars *154 avenue Mohammed V, Guéliz (024 43 11 16/ concordecar@iam.ma)*. **Open** 8.30am-7.30pm Mon-Sat.

Europcar *63 boulevard Mohammed Zerktouni, Guéliz (024 43 12 28/ www.europcar.com)*. **Open** 8.30am-noon, 2.30-7pm Mon-Sat.

Fathi Cars *183 avenue Mohammed V, Guéliz (024 43 17 63)*. **Open** 8.30am-12.30pm, 2.30-7pm Mon-Sat.

Hertz *154 avenue Mohammed V, Guéliz (024 43 13 94/www.hertz.com)*. **Open** 8.30am-12.30pm, 2-6.30pm Mon-Sat.

Majestic Locations *21 rue Tarek Ibn Ziad, Guéliz (024 43 65 00/majesticloc @yahoo.fr)*. **Open** 8.30am-12.30pm, 2.30-7pm Mon-Sat.

ESSENTIALS

Parking

Wherever there's space to park you'll find a *gardien de voitures*. They're licensed by the local authority to look after parked vehicles and should be tipped about 10dh. You can park street-side where the kerb is painted orange; red and white kerbs mean no parking.

Repairs & services

Garage Ourika *66 avenue Mohammed V, Guéliz (024 44 82 66)*. **Open** 8.30am-noon, 2.30-6.30pm Mon-Sat. No credit cards.
BMW, Fiat, Honda and Toyota specialist.

Garage Renault *Route de Casablanca, Semlalia (024 30 10 08)*. **Open** 8am-noon, 2-6.30pm Mon-Sat. No credit cards.

Cycling

Bicycles, mopeds and motorbikes are a hugely popular mode of local transport.

In addition to the rental places listed below, there are a couple of hire outfits at the northern end of **rue Beni Marine**, the small street running parallel to and between rue Bab Agnaou and rue Moulay Ismail. Guys with bikes for hire can also be found on the central grassy verge outside **Hotel Imperial Borj** (5 avenue Echouhada) and across from the **Hotel El Andalous** on avenue de Paris, both in Hivernage, and at the **Hotel de Foucault** (off place de Foucault) in the Medina, though none are affiliated to the hotels mentioned. In Guéliz try the **Hotel Toulousain** on rue Tarek ibn Ziad behind the old Marché Central. Prices are roughly 20dh per hour with negotiable daily rates.

Most rental places do not offer helmets or locks (you'll have to leave the bike with a *gardien de voitures*). Before taking a bike, check the gears and brakes.

Action Sports Loisirs *1 boulevard Yacoub El Mansour, apartment No.4, Guéliz (tel/fax 024 43 09 31/mobile 061 240 145)*. **Open** 8am-7pm Tue-Sun.
Bicycle rental 150dh for 2hrs; 400dh per half-day. No credit cards.
The best bikes in town, owner Alain also organises excursions for 800dh.

Marrakech Motos *31 avenue Abdelkarim El Khattabi, Guéliz (024 44 83 59/mobile 061 31 64 13)*. **Open** 9am-10pm daily. **Scooter rental** 250dh-300dh per day, depending on model. No credit cards.
Also known as Chez Jamal Boucetta.

Salah Eddine *18 rue de la Recette, Medina (061 87 31 45)*. **Open** 9am-9pm daily. **Bicycle rental** 10dh per hr; 100dh per day. No credit cards.
Operates from a basement room just around the corner from the Hotel Galia.

Walking

Walking is the only way to get around the Medina. It's a compact area, perfect for exploring on foot. Many of the streets and alleys are too narrow for anything bigger than a motorcycle or donkey cart anyway.

Be sure to pack a pair of comfortable shoes – the streets in the Medina are rarely paved and full of ruts and potholes. Visitors coming any time from November to April should bring waterproof footwear because the slightest bit of rain turns the whole Medina into a mudbath.

Horse-drawn carriage

The green horse-drawn carriages you'll spot in the Medina are known as *calèches*. They seat four and can be hired for a circuit of the walls, or taken through the Palmeraie. The rate is 80dh an hour – per carriage not per person. Pick them up on the north side of place de Foucault, midway between the Koutoubia Mosque and Jemaa El Fna.

Resources A-Z

Accident & emergency

Police 19
Fire service 15 or 024 43 04 15
Ambulance service 024 44 37 24

Credit card loss

All lines of the companies listed below have English-speaking staff and are open 24hrs daily.
American Express 00 973 256 834
Barclaycard 00 44 1604 230 230
Diners Club 022 99 455/
00 44 1252 513 500
MasterCard 00 1636 722 7111
Switch 00 870 000459

Customs

The following allowances apply for bringing duty-free goods into Morocco: 400g of tobacco, 200 cigarettes or 50 cigars and 1 litre of spirits. The cap on foreign currency is set at €4,500 (£3,000), otherwise it must be declared upon entering the country.

If you are bringing a significant amount of camera or other electrical equipment – even sometimes just a laptop – into Morocco, you may have it written into your passport. Anything that cannot be presented on leaving will be assumed to have been 'sold' and liable to a heavy duty tax. If the property has been stolen, you need police documentation to prove it.

Disabled

Marrakech is tough on anyone with a mobility problem. Roads and pavements are uneven and pitted and routes through the Medina are narrow. Aside from the bigger hotels (the Royal Mirage Marrakech and the Sofitel lay claim to disabled facilities), few buildings make concessions. In smaller hotels and riads stairs are pretty much unavoidable and banisters do not exist in traditional Moroccan homes.

Drugs

Morocco is the world's largest cannabis producer; most of it is exported. Although discreet use by locals is tolerated, Moroccan law maintains stiff penalties for sale or consumption.

Electricity

Morocco operates on 220V AC. Plugs are of the European two-pin variety. Visitors from the USA will need to bring a transformer if they intend to use appliances from home.

Embassies & consulates

There's just one diplomatic office in Marrakech: the French Consulate is next to the Koutoubia Mosque. Other embassies and consulates are in Rabat and Casablanca.

British Consulate

17 boulevard de la Tour Hassan, Rabat (037 72 96 96/www.britain. org.ma/consular/services.html).
Also handles Irish and New Zealand consular affairs. In the event of an emergency in Marrakech, contact Residence Jaib (55 boulevard Mohammed Zerktouni, 024 43 60 78, mobile 061 14 84 44). Britain also has consulates in Casablanca and Tangier.

Canadian Consulate

13 rue Jaafar Es Sadiq, Agdal, Rabat (037 68 74 00).
The Canadians also handle Australian consular affairs.

French Consulate

Rue Ibn Khaldun, Medina, Marrakech (024 38 82 00).

US Consulate

2 avenue de Marrakech, Rabat (037 76 22 65/ www.usembassy.ma).
The US also has a consulate in Casablanca (8 Boulevard Moulay Youssef, 022 26 45 50).

Health

Morocco has no reciprocal health care agreements with other countries, so taking out your own medical insurance is essential. Should you become ill, be warned: the Moroccan healthcare system is ropey. While good doctors can be found and pharmacies are well stocked and knowledgeably staffed, for anyone afflicted with a serious illness the best route to take is the route home.

The most common ailment affecting tourists is an upset stomach; bring anti-diarrhoeal capsules, such as Imodium, and avoid tap water: bottled water is inexpensive and available at all restaurants and cafés.

Dentists

Dental care in Marrakech is generally offices and equipment may not be state of the art. It may be hard to get an appointment with the best practitioners.

Docteur Youssef Dassouli

Résidence Asmae, apartment No.6, 1st floor, above Pâtisserie Yum Yum, route de Targa (024 43 53 03, emergency contact 064 90 65 14).
No credit cards.
English spoken.

Doctors

We can recommend the following:

Doctor Samir Bellmezouar

Polyclinique du Sud, rue Yougoslavie, Guéliz (061 24 32 27). **No credit cards.**
Doesn't speak English but does make house calls.

Doctor Béatrice Peiffer Lahrichi

Résidence Lafrasouk, 1st floor, 10 rue Oued El-Makhazine, Guéliz (024 43 53 29). **No credit cards.**
French doctor (speaks no English) working out of a very modern surgery with full lab facilities.

Doctor Frederic Reitzer

Above Café Zohra, Immeuble Moulay Youssef, 4th floor, rue de la Liberté, Guéliz (024 43 95 62/emergency contact 061 17 38 03). **No credit cards.**
Speaks English.

Doctor El-Oufir (gynaecologist)

125 avenue Mohammed V, Guéliz (024 43 18 28). **No credit cards.**
Speaks English.

Hospitals

The only place to go is the Polyclinique du Sud. Avoid public hospitals, where the severe lack of personnel, equipment and funding is shocking.

Polyclinique du Sud

Rue Yougoslavie, Guéliz (024 44 79 99). **Open** 24hr emergency service.

Pharmacies

Pharmacies are clearly marked with a green cross and/or green crescent. Many of the brands will be familiar, but some drugs may have strange names; staff can usually translate. When closed, each pharmacy should display a list of alternative pharmacies open after hours.

Internet

In the Medina internet cafés are concentrated along rue Bab Agnaou. In Guéliz the best are up around place Abdel-Moumen. Prices are about 10dh an hour. The cheapest internet access is at the **Arset Abdelsalam**, Marrakech's 'internet park', opposite the Centre Artisanal (map p84 A3), which has several public-access terminals in a glass building at the park entrance charged at 5dh per hour. Wi-Fi is available for customers at **Le Café du Livre** (p103).

Askmy

6 boulevard Mohammed Zerktouni, Guéliz (024 43 06 02). **Open** 8am-2am daily. No credit cards.

Cyber Club

Avenue Mohammed V (next to Café Koutoubia), Medina (no phone). **Open** 9.30am-1pm, 3-10.30pm daily. No credit cards.

Mohammed Yasin Cyber Café

38 rue Bab Agnaou, Medina. **Open** 7am-midnight daily. No credit cards.

Éspace Internet

5 avenue de l'Istiqlal, Essaouira (024 47 50 65). **Open** 24 hrs daily.

Money

Local currency is the Moroccan dirham, abbreviated dh (in this book) and sometimes MDH, or MAD. At the time of writing, conversion between currencies was 10dh = 60p or US$1.20. Hoard small change; you'll need it for tips and taxi fares.

Excess dirhams can be exchanged for euros or US dollars (pounds sterling are often not available) at a bank. You may be asked to show the exchange receipts from when you converted your hard currency into dirhams – this is because banks will only allow you to change back up to half the amount of Moroccan currency that you originally purchased.

ATMs

Cashpoints, or *guichets automatiques*, are common in most Moroccan towns and cities, and it's perfectly possible to travel on plastic – although most banks set a daily withdrawal limit of 2,000dh (currently around £120) per day on ATM withdrawals. If you need more, go to an exchange bureau with your card and passport and get a cash advance. Wafa Bank (213 avenue Mohammed V, Guéliz), allows withdrawals of up to 8,000dh (£490), if your home bank permits it. Beware of attempting to withdraw money on Monday mornings; machines are often empty.

Credit cards

MasterCard and Visa are widely accepted at shops, restaurants and hotels; American Express less so.

Credit-card fraud is also a problem in Morocco, so keep all receipts to check against your statement. Chip and PIN has yet to reach Morocco.

Opening hours

The working week is Monday to Friday, with a half-day on Saturday. Hours vary in summer (from around 15 June to the end of September) and during Ramadan (see box p25), and will generally be erratic in the Medina, where many shop-owners take siestas or prayer breaks.

Banks 8.30-11.30am, 2.30-3.30pm Mon-Fri.

Shops 9am-1pm, 3-7pm Mon-Sat.

Museums & tourist sights Usually closed Tue.

ESSENTIALS

Police

Crime against visitors is rare but watch your pockets and bags, particularly around Jemaa El Fna. If you are robbed go to the tourist police office of the **Brigade Touristique** (north side of Jemaa El Fna, 024 38 46 01).

Note, if you are the victim of crime outside Marrakech, then you must make a report to the local police wherever the incident occurred – do not wait until your return to the city.

Hôtel de Police
Rue Oued El-Makhazine, Guéliz.

Essaouira Police
Avenue du Caire, Essaouira.

Post

Stamps are sold at a dedicated *timbres* counter, but can also be bought at a *tabac* or at the reception desks of big hotels. Parcels should be taken unwrapped for examination.

Mail delivery is painfully slow. Post offices provide an express mail service (EMS), also known as *poste rapide*. For really urgent mail, use an international courier.

PTT Centrale
Place du 16 Novembre (opposite McDonald's), Guéliz. **Open** 8am-2pm Mon-Sat.
Other locations Rue Moulay Ismail, between Jemaa El Fna and Koutoubia Mosque.

Essaouira; PTT Centrale
Avenue El-Moqaoumah,Essaouira. **Open** 8am-6pm Mon-Fri; 8am-noon Sat.

Poste restante
Send letters to 'Poste Restante, PTT Centrale, Marrakech'; make sure the surname is clear. Pick up is from the PTT Centrale; you'll need your passport.

Smoking

Morocco is firmly in thrall to nicotine. Non-smokers are outcasts and few cafés and restaurants recognise the concept of a clean-air environment. Foreign cigarette brands cost 32dh, or about £2, for 20, while the best of the domestic product goes for even less.

Telephones

To call abroad from Marrakech it's best to use either use the cardphones (cards are bought from post offices, *tabacs* or news vendors) or one of the numerous *téléboutiques*. The latter are identified by a blue and white sign depicting a telephone receiver. They are small premises with anything from two to a dozen coin-operated phones in booths.

Dialling & codes
To call abroad from Morocco, first dial 00, then the country code followed by the telephone number.

When calling within Morocco you need to dial the three-digit area code even if you are calling from the same area. Note that codes changed fairly recently; the area code for Marrakech and Essaouira is 024, but some business cards may still bear the now-defunct 044. The international dialling code for Morocco is 212; follow this with the area code, minus the initial zero.

Operator services
The international operator can be accessed by dialling 120. To make a reverse charge call say '*Je voudrais téléphoner en PCV*' but you will wait. To get the domestic operator dial 10. For directory enquiries dial 16. Operators don't speak English.

Time

Morocco follows Greenwich Mean Time (GMT) all year round. This means that it's on the same time as Britain and Ireland in winter but an hour behind during British Summer Time, from late March to late October.

Tipping

Tipping is expected in cafés and restaurants (round up the bill or add 10-15 per cent), by guides, porters and toilet attendants, or by anyone else who renders you any sort of small service. Five or ten dirhams is sufficient.

It is not necessary to tip taxi drivers, who can just be content with overcharging.

Toilets

Public toilets are a rarity in Morocco– use the facilities when in bars, hotels and restaurants – they're usually decent enough. It's a good idea to carry toilet paper; the wastebasket beside the toilet is for used tissue. Tip attendants a few dirhams.

Tourist information

The ONMT (Office National Marocain du Tourisme) has a fairly useless presence in Marrakech and Essaouira. Basic tourist information can be found at its website, www.visitmorocco.com.

ONMT Marrakech

ONMT, place Abdel-Moumen, Guéliz (024 43 61 31). **Open** 8.30am-noon, 2.30-6.30pm Mon-Fri; 9am-noon, 3-6pm Sat.

ONMT Essaouira

10 rue du Caire, BP 261, Essaouira (024 78 35 32/www.tourisme.gov.ma). **Open** 9am-noon, 2-4.30pm Mon-Fri.

Visas

No visas are required for nationals of Australia, Britain, Canada, Ireland, New Zealand, the US and most EU countries. If in doubt check with your local Moroccan embassy.

Travellers can stay in Morocco for three months from the time of entry. Extensions require applying for an official residence permit – a tedious procedure. First you must open a bank account in Morocco, which requires a minimum of 20,000dh (£1,250) in your account and an *attestation de résidence* from your hotel or landlord. Then you need to go to the Bureau des Etrangers equipped with your passport, seven passport photos, two copies of the *attestation*, two copies of your bank statement, and a 60dh stamp (available from any *tabac*). Once the forms have been filled out twice you should receive a residence permit a few weeks later.

For a simpler option, leave the country for a few days and re-enter, gaining a new three-month stamp.

Bureau des Etrangers

Comissariat Central, Guéliz. **Open** 8am-noon, 2-6pm Mon-Thur; 8am-noon Fri.

What's on

The monthly French-language listings freebie, *Couleurs Marrakech* (www.marrakech pocket.com), is about as good as it gets for what's on infomation. It's also worth looking at www. madeinmarrakech.com. The recently launched quarterly newpaper *La Tribune de Marrakech* is a professional product with news and reviews. The only English periodical, *Last Exit Marrakech*, is laughably poor. You can pick up all these for free in hotels, shops and restuarants.

ESSENTIALS

French

In French, as in other Latin languages, the second person singular (you) has two forms. Phrases here are given in the more polite *vous* form. The *tu* form is used with family, friends, children and pets. You will also find that courtesies such as *monsieur*, *madame* and *mademoiselle* are used more often than their English equivalents.

General expressions

good morning/hello *bonjour*
good evening *bonsoir*
goodbye *au revoir*
hi (familiar) *salut*
OK *d'accord*; yes *oui*; no *non*
How are you? *Comment allez vous?/vous allez bien?*
How's it going? *Comment ça va?/ça va?* (familiar)
Sir/Mr *monsieur* (M)
Madam/Mrs *madame* (Mme)
Miss *mademoiselle* (Mlle)
please *s'il vous plaît*; thank you *merci*; thank you very much *merci beaucoup*
sorry *pardon*; excuse me *excusez-moi*
Do you speak English? *Parlez-vous anglais?*
I don't speak French *Je ne parle pas français*
I don't understand *Je ne comprends pas*
Speak more slowly, please *Parlez plus lentement, s'il vous plaît*
how much?/how many? *combien?*
Have you got change? *Avez-vous de la monnaie?*
I would like… *Je voudrais…*
it is *c'est*; it isn't *ce n'est pas*
good *bon* (m)/*bonne* (f); bad *mauvais* (m)/*mauvaise* (f)
small *petit* (m)/*petite* (f); big *grand* (m)/*grande* (f)
beautiful *beau* (m)/*belle* (f); well *bien*; badly *mal*
expensive *cher*; cheap *pas cher*

a bit *un peu*; a lot *beaucoup*; very *très*; with *avec*; without *sans*; and *et*; or *ou*; because *parce que* who? *qui?*; when? *quand?*; which? *quel?*; where? *où?*; why? *pourquoi?*; how? *comment?* at what time/when? *à quelle heure?* forbidden *interdit/défendu* out of order *hors service/en panne* daily *tous les jours (tlj)*

Getting around

When is the next train for…? *C'est quand le prochain train pour…?*
ticket *un billet*; station *la gare*; platform *le quai*
bus/coach station *gare routière*
entrance *entrée*; exit *sortie*
left *gauche*; right *droite*; interchange *correspondence*
straight on *tout droit*; far *loin*; near *pas loin/près d'ici*
street *la rue*; street map *le plan*; road map *la carte*
bank *la banque*; is there a bank near here? *est-ce qu'il y a une banque près d'ici?*
post office *La Poste*; a stamp *un timbre*

Sightseeing

museum *un musée*
church *une église*
exhibition *une exposition*; ticket (for museum) *un billet*; (for theatre, concert) *une place*
open *ouvert*; closed *fermé*
free *gratuit*; reduced price *un tarif réduit*

Accommodation

Do you have a room (for this evening/for two people)? *Avez-vous une chambre (pour ce soir/pour deux personnes)?*
full *complet*; room *une chambre*
bed *un lit*; double bed *un grand lit*; (a room with) twin beds *(une chambre) à deux lits*

ESSENTIALS

with bath(room)/shower
avec (salle de) bain/douche
breakfast *le petit déjeuner*
included *compris*
lift *un ascenseur*
air-conditioned *climatisé*

At the café or restaurant

**I'd like to book a table (for three/
at 8pm)** *Je voudrais réserver une table
(pour trois personnes/à vingt heures)*
lunch *le déjeuner*; **dinner** *le dîner*
coffee (espresso) *un café*; **white
coffee** *un café au lait/café crème*;
tea *le thé* **wine** *le vin*; **beer** *la bière*
mineral water *eau minérale*;
fizzy *gazeuse*; **still** *plate*
tap water *eau du robinet/une
carafe d'eau*
the bill *l'addition*

Behind the wheel

no parking *stationnement interdit/
stationnement gênant*;
speed limit 40 *rappel 40*
petrol *essence*; **unleaded** *sans plomb*

Numbers

0 *zéro*; 1 *un* (m), *une* (f); 2 *deux*; 3 *trois*;
4 *quatre*; 5 *cinq*; 6 *six*; 7 *sept*; 8 *huit*; 9
neuf; 10 *dix*; 11 *onze*; 12 *douze*; 13
treize; 14 *quatorze*; 15 *quinze*; 16 *seize*;
17 *dix-sept*; 18 *dix-huit*; 19 *dix-neuf*;
20 *vingt*; 21 *vingt-et-un*; 22 *vingt-deux*;
30 *trente*; 40 *quarante*; 50 *cinquante*;
60 *soixante*; 70 *soixante-dix*; 80
quatre-vingts; 90 *quatre-vingt-dix*; 100
cent; 1,000 *mille*; 1,000,000 *un million*.

Days, months & seasons

Monday *lundi*; **Tuesday** *mardi*;
Wednesday *mercredi*; **Thursday**
jeudi; **Friday** *vendredi*; **Saturday**
samedi; **Sunday** *dimanche*.

January *janvier*; **February** *février*;
March *mars*; **April** *avril*; **May** *mai*;
June *juin*; **July** *juillet*; **August** *août*;
September *septembre*; **October**
octobre; **November** *novembre*;
December *décembre*.

Spring *printemps*; **summer** *été*;
autumn *automne*; **winter** *hiver*.

Arabic

Within Marrakech (and other
main towns and cities) you
can get by in French, which is
widely spoken by all educated
Moroccans. However, a little effort
with Arabic goes a long way, even
if it is just a few stock phrases like
'hello' and 'goodbye'. Moroccan
Arabic is a dialect of the standard
Arabic language and is not the
same as that spoken elsewhere in
North Africa and the Middle East,
although there are some words and
phrases in common. Transliteration
from Arabic into English is a highly
inexact science and a wide variety of
spellings are possible for any given
word (for example Koran vs Quran).
You are also likely to encounter

Berber, which comes in three
dialects. Most Berber speakers
will also be fluent in Arabic.

Arabic pronunciation

Arabic has numerous sounds
that non-speakers have trouble
in pronouncing.
gh - like the French 'r', slightly rolled
kh - like the 'ch' in loch

Emergencies

leave me alone *esmahli la*
help! *tekni!*
help me, please *awenni afak*
call the police *ayyet el bolice*
thief *sheffar*
I'm lost *tweddert*

General expressions

good evening *masr el kheir*
good morning/hello *sabah el kheir/salaam aleikum*
goodbye *masalaama*
please *min fadlak* (to a male); *min fadlik* (to a female)
yes *aywa/anam*; no *la*
How are you? *labas/kifhalak* (to a male)/*kifhalik* (to a female)
thank you *shukran*
no thanks *la shukran*
sorry/excuse me *esmahli*
Do you speak English? *Itkelim Ingleezi?*
I don't speak Arabic *Metkelimsh Arabi*
I don't understand *Mafayimtish*
who? *shkun?*; why? *lash?*; which? *ashmen?*; where? *feyn?*
today *el youm*; tomorrow *ghedda*; yesterday *imbara*
tips *baksheesh*
let's go *yalla*
passport *basseport*

Shopping

how much?/how many? *bekam?*
Do you have...? *Wahesh andakum...?*
Have you got change? *Maak sarf?*
credit card *kart kredi*
good *mleah*; bad *mish imleah*
small *seghir*; big *kebir*
that's expensive *ghali bezzaf*
enough *kafi*

Getting around

Where is...? *Feyn keyn...?*
Where is the hotel? *Feyn keyn el otel?*
airport *el mattar*
station *el mahatta*
bus/coach station *mahatta d'el ottobisat*
ticket office *maktab el werka*; ticket *werka*
train station *el gar*
bus stop *plasa d'el ottobisat*
museum *el mathaf*
embassy *el sifara*
pharmacy *farmasyan*
bank *el banka*
post office *el busta*; stamp *etnaber*

restaurant *el mattam*
mosque *jamaa*
left *yassar*; right *yemeen*
stop here *haten hinayer*
here *hina*; there *hinak*

Accommodation

Do you have a room? *Andak beit?*
key *srout*
room *beit*
shower *doush*
toilet *vaysay*
breakfast *iftar*

At the café or restaurant

table for... *tabla dyal...*
I'm a vegetarian *makanakulsh el lahm*
I don't eat... *makanakulsh...*
meat *el lahm*
chicken *dzhazh*
fish *elhut*
bread *elkhobz*
coffee *qahwa*; tea *atay*
beer *birra*; wine *shshrab*
mineral water *sidi ali*
the bill, please *lahsab afak*

Numbers

0 *sifer*; 1 *wahid*; 2 *itnehn*; 3 *telata*; 4 *arbaa*; 5 *khamsa*; 6 *setta*; 7 *seba*; 8 *tamanya*; 9 *tesa*; 10 *ashra*; 11 *hadasha*; 12 *itnasha*; 13 *teltash*; 14 *arbatash*; 15 *khamstash*; 16 *settash*; 17 *sebatash*; 18 *tamantash*; 19 *tesatash*; 20 *eshreen*; 21 *wahid w'eshreen*; 22 *itnehn w'eshreen*; 30 *telateen*; 40 *arba'een*; 50 *khamseen*; 60 *setteen*; 70 *seba'een*; 80 *tamaneen*; 90 *tesa'een*; 100 *mea*; 1,000 *alef*.

Days & months

Monday *el itnehn*; Tuesday *el teleta*; Wednesday *el arbaar*; Thursday *el khemis*; Friday *el jomaa*; Saturday *el sebt*; Sunday *el ahad*.

January *yanayir*; February *fibraiyir*; March *maris*; April *abril*; May *mayu*; June *yunyu*; July *yulyu*; August *aghustus*; September *sibtimber*; October *oktobir*; November *nufimbir*; December *disimbir*.

ESSENTIALS

Index

ESSENTIALS

ESSENTIALS

ESSENTIALS

Notes

Marrakech Riads

Riads, Bed & Breakfast

Marrakech Riads 8, Derb chorfa Lakbir Mouassine 40 000
MARRAKECH Maroc.
Tél: +212 24 39 16 09/+212 24 42 64 63 Fax: +212 24 42 65 11
Email: reservation@marrakech-riads.net   www.marrakech-riads.net

Association Al Kawtar

Day Care Centre for Disabled Women

Officially registered non-profit association to give their members a safe place to spend their days and earn a living.

Providing

Medical & Technical Assistance, Education & Empowerment and a place to work together

Producing

Table & Dining cloths, Bed & Bath linen, Children's wear

Day Care & Embroidery Workshop:
Rue Jbel Lakhdar 35
Ramila, Marrakech-Medina

Boutique:
Rue Laksour 57
Ksour, Marrakech-Medina

For more information visit www.alkawtar.org